Problems in Microeconomics

Problems in Microeconomics

MARCIA L. STIGUM, Ph.D.

Associate Professor
Loyola University, Chicago

1975

RICHARD D. IRWIN, INC. *Homewood, Illinois 60430*
Irwin-Dorsey International London, England WC2H 9NJ
Irwin-Dorsey Limited Georgetown, Ontario L7G 4B3

First Printing, May 1975

ISBN 0-256-01734-3
Library of Congress Catalog Card No. 74–24446

Printed in the United States of America

Preface

In teaching microeconomics, the instructor's major goal is not to get across facts about the real world but to give the student a set of theoretical tools that he can use to analyze and understand various real life situations as he encounters them. In this sense a course in microeconomics resembles a course in mathematics; the primary goal is not to teach facts but to equip the student to solve problems. No one would think of teaching mathematics without giving students the opportunity to practice using the tools presented, and the same should be true in microeconomics. To grasp and use the tools of microeconomic theory, the student needs to practice applying them, to solve one problem after another. The objective of this book is to give the intermediate student a body of problems on which he can hone his skills in using microeconomic theory.

To this end the problems in this book have been designed to provoke thought on the part of the student. Rote-type exercises have been avoided. Also, so that the student can focus all his attention and time on the theory, the problems require minimal mathematical manipulations; and labeled, scaled graphs are provided wherever needed.

Most of the problems in the book are well within the grasp of the ordinary intermediate student but a few are more challenging. These problems are marked with an asterisk. The book does not generally assume calculus but a few problems requiring the use of calculus have been included for students who have the background to solve them. Such questions are also marked with an asterisk.

The problems in the book are grouped in chapters, each of which deals with a standard area of microeconomic theory: derivation of demand curves, production functions, supply and demand, and so forth.

The general order of topics is that found in *Microeconomic Theory,* 4th ed (1975) by C. E. Ferguson and J. P. Gould, and in *Economic Analysis,* rev. ed. (1974) by C. E. Ferguson and S. C. Maurice. But since the problems all cover standard topics, the book can easily be used with any intermediate microeconomics text. To help the instructor match problems with chapters in other texts, a Cross Reference Table linking chapters in this book with chapters in other widely used intermediate texts has been provided.

To facilitate independent study on the part of the student, answers to half of the problems are included in the book. Answers to all of the Review and Definitions and Multiple Choice sections which begin each chapter are also included in the book.

Most of the problems in this book have been tried out on Loyola students and their reception was enthusiastic. It is the author's hope that others using this book will meet equal success.

April 1975   MARCIA L. STIGUM

Contents

Topics of Problems

Note: Some chapters contain one or two problems that deal with more difficult points of theory or require the use of calculus. Such problems generally appear at the end of a chapter and are denoted in this list, as in the text, with an asterisk. All un-starred problems are at the level of a normal intermediate micro theory course.

	Chapters															
	1	*2*	*3*	*4*	*5*	*6*	*7*	*8*	*9*	*10*	*11*	*12*	*13*	*14*	*15*	*16*
Ferguson, C. E., and J. P. Gould, *Microeconomic Theory,* 4th ed. (Homewood, Ill.: Richard D. Irwin, 1975).	1	2	3	4	5	6	7	8	9	10	11	12	13	14	15	16
Ferguson, C. E., and S. C. Maurice, *Economic Analysis,* Rev. ed. (Homewood, Ill.: Richard D. Irwin, 1974).	3	3,4	4	2	6	6	7	8	9	8,9	10	10	11	11	12	12
Mansfield, Edwin, *Microeconomics* (N.Y.: W. W. Norton, 1974).	2	3	3	4	5	5	7	8	9	8,9	10	11	12	13	14,15	15
Leftwich, Richard, *The Price System and Resource Allocation* (Hinsdale, Ill.: The Dryden Press, 1973).	5,6	5,6	3,5	3,6	8	8	9	3,4, 7,10	7,11	4,10, 11	7,13	7,12	5,14	15	16,18	17,18
Thompson, Arthur A., Jr., *Economics of the Firm* (Englewood Cliffs, N.J.: Prentice-Hall, 1973).	3,4	4	2,4,5	5	7	7	8	10	11	10,11	10	2,11	14	14	—	—
Scott, Robert H., *The Pricing System* (San Francisco: Holden-Day, 1973).	2	2	2	3	3	7,8	8	7,8	8,9	7,9	10	10	5	—	4,6	5,6,9
Nicholson, Walter, *Microeconomic Theory* (N.Y.: Holt, Rinehart and Winston, 1972).	3	3,4,5	5,9	6,10	11	11	12	14	15	14,15	16	9,16	7,17	18	20, 21, 22	20–22, 25
Lancaster, Kelvin, *Introduction to Modern Microeconomics,* 2d ed. (Chicago: Rand McNally, 1974).	7	7	7	6	4	4	5	1	6	1	6	6	6,7,8	6,8	9,10	10
Watson, Donald, *Price Theory in Action* (Boston: Houghton Mifflin Co., 1973).	4	5	5,7	3,5	9	9	10,11	2,13, 14	16	13,14, 16,17	18	19,20	5,10 21,22	21,22	15	15

	Chapters															
	1	*2*	*3*	*4*	*5*	*6*	*7*	*8*	*9*	*10*	*11*	*12*	*13*	*14*	*15*	*16*
Hibdon, James, *Price and Welfare Theory* (N.Y.: McGraw-Hill Book Co., 1969).	2	2,3,4	2,3,4	2,3,4	5	5	6	8	11	8,11	12	12,13	14,15	11,14,15	17,18	17,18
Clower, Robert, and John Due, *Microeconomics* (Homewood, Ill.: Richard D. Irwin, 1972).	4	4	4	—	6	6	6	3,7,8	9	8,9	10	11	7,12,15	12	—	—
Shows, E. Warren, and Robert Burton, *Microeconomics* (Lexington, Mass.: D. C. Heath, 1972).	3	3	3	4	5	5,6	5,6	2,7	8	7,8	9	9	10,11	10	13	13
Brigham, Eugene, and James Pappas, *Managerial Economics* (N.Y.: Holt, Rinehart and Winston, 1972).	—	—	3	4	6	6	8,8	10	10,11	10	10	10	—	—	—	12
Cole, Charles L., *Microeconomics* (N.Y.: Harcourt Brace Jovanovich, 1973).	3	4	4,5	2,9	6	6,7	7	8	9,10	8,9	11	12,13	14	15	16,17	10,16,17
Grossack, Irwin, and David Martin, *Managerial Economics* (Boston: Little, Brown and Co., 1973).	8	8	8	5,8	4	4,11	4,11	5,7,9	9	5,7,9	9	9,13	7,10	10	—	—
Bilas, Richard, *Microeconomic Theory*, 2d ed. (N.Y.: McGraw-Hill Book Co., 1971).	3	3,4,5	3,4,5	2	6	6	7	2,8	9	8,9	10	10	11	11	12,13	12,13
Trescott, Paul, *The Logic of the Price System* (N.Y.: McGraw-Hill Book Co., 1970).	3	3	3	4	6,7	6,7,8	8,9	7,10,12	20	10,20	21	11–14,21	11	22	16	16,19,23
Levenson, Albert, and Babette Solon, *Essential Price Theory*, 2d ed. (N.Y.: Holt, Rinehart and Winston, 1971).	4	4,5	4,5	3	6	6	7	2,8	9	8,9	10	10	11,12	11	13,15	13,15

Theory of Utility and Preference

A. DEFINITIONS AND REVIEW

1. Consumer X is confronted with two commodity bundles, A and B, made up of two goods q_1 and q_2. Bundle A contains more q_1 and the same amount of q_2 as bundle B does. If consumer X has "normal" preferences, we know that he will

prefer bundle _____ to bundle _____ unless _____.
Also, if consumer X tells us that he is indifferent between bundle B and some other bundle C, the assumption of transitivity implies that his ordering of A and

C will be that he prefers _____ to _____.

2. An indifference curve in consumer X's (q_1, q_2)-preference map is defined

as _____

_____.

Consumer X's (q_1, q_2)-preference map is composed of many different indiffer-

ence curves, one corresponding to each _____

_____.

In the preference map higher indifference curves correspond to _____.

3. A consumer's utility function gives a (cardinal/ordinal) measure of the utility he derives from consuming different commodity bundles; his preference or in-difference curve map gives a (cardinal/ordinal) ranking of different commodity

bundles. For the purposes of consumer theory, all that is required is a _____ ranking.

4. If consumer X derives utility from both q_1 and q_2 and if he always prefers larger commodity bundles to smaller ones, his indifference curves through any (q_1, q_2)-point must have a _____ slope. If a consumer's (q_1, q_2)-indifference curves are horizontal or vertical, this tells you that _____

_____ .

If the consumer's indifference curves intersect, his preferences cannot be _____ .

5. The consumer's marginal rate of substitution (or rate of commodity substitution) between two goods, q_1 and q_2, equals at any consumption point (i.e., point in commodity space) _____

_____ .

If we plot q_2 on the vertical axis and q_1 on the horizontal axis, the assumption that the consumer's indifference curves are convex to the origin is equivalent to assuming that his marginal rate of substitution of q_1 for q_2 _____ as q_1 is substituted for q_2.

B. MULTIPLE CHOICE

1. Figure A below shows four commodity bundles that a consumer, call him Smith, might purchase. If Smith's preferences satisfy the assumptions normally made in consumer analysis, we can be sure that:

FIGURE A

a. Smith prefers C to A.
b. he's indifferent between C and B.
c. he prefers B to A.
d. he prefers B to C.

2. If Smith tells you that he's indifferent between bundles C and D in Figure A, then—assuming his preferences are transitive—you know that:

a. he probably prefers C to A.   *c.* he probably prefers C to B.
b. he could not prefer B to C.   *d.* he might be indifferent between C and B.

3. Brown tells you that he derives utility from consuming both q_1 and q_2. Which of the following relationships could not represent his utility function:

a. $U = 2q_1 + 3q_2$ *c.* $U = q_1 - q_2$
b. $U = q_1 q_2$ *d.* $U = q_1^2 + 2q_1 q_2$

4. The assumptions, (*a*) that the consumer will prefer larger commodity bundles to smaller ones and (*b*) that his preferences are consistent, imply all of the following except:

    a. his indifference curves will be convex to the origin.
    b. his indifference curves will be nonintersecting.
    c. his indifference curves will be negatively sloped.
    d. in his preference map, higher indifference curves will correspond to higher levels of utility.

C. PROBLEMS

1. *a.* John Jones, who lives in a rather spartan economy, finds that there are only two goods available to him for consumption, soybeans and sardines. Jones, like the typical consumer, always *prefers more consumption to less;* that is, relative to a particular consumption bundle such as *A* in Figure 1–1, he will always prefer any other bundle offering more soybeans but no less sardines, more sardines but no less soybeans, or more of both. Using this information, show that Jones' indifference curve through point *A* in Figure 1–1 must have a *negative* slope. [Hint: First locate in Figure 1–1 the areas containing (*a*) all points that are *certain* to be more preferred than *A* and (*b*) all points that are *certain* to be less preferred than *A*.]

FIGURE 1–1
Jones' Indifference Curve through *A*

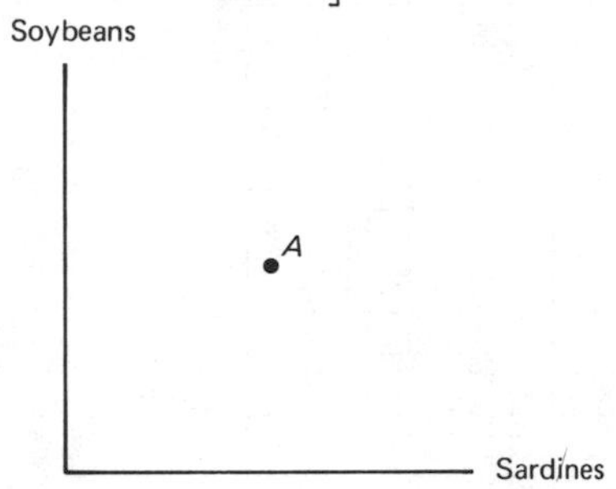

b. Also prove that "higher" (that is, upward and rightward) indifference curves must correspond to higher levels of utility.

Name

2. Various bundles of apples and avocados are listed in Table 1–1. Adams, a health addict who lives on these two goods, is indifferent between bundles 1 and 3 and between bundles 4 and 6. On the basis of this information, what if anything, can you say about which of each of the following pairs of bundles is more preferred by him: Bundles 1 and 2? _____ Bundles 3 and 6? _____ Bundles 4 and 5? _____ Bundles 5 and 7? _____ Bundles 6 and 7? _____ Bundles 6 and 8? _____ [Hint: Plot bundles 1–8 in Figure 1–2 and sketch in the indifference curves through points 1 and 3 and through points 4 and 6.]

TABLE 1–1
Apple and Avocado
Bundles

	Bundles							
	1	2	3	4	5	6	7	8
Apples	2	1	1	3	1	2	1	1
Avocados	1	1	2	2	3	3	5	4

FIGURE 1–2
Adams' Preferences

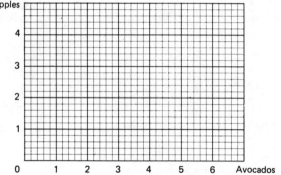

3. If Constant Cassius prefers alternative A to B and B to C, then he's sure to prefer A to C; in a word his preferences, like those of most consumers, are *transitive*. Show that this fact implies that no pair of Cassius' indifference curves can cross. [Hint: Consider points A_1, A_2, and A_3 in Figure 1–3.]

FIGURE 1–3
Intersecting Indifference
Curves

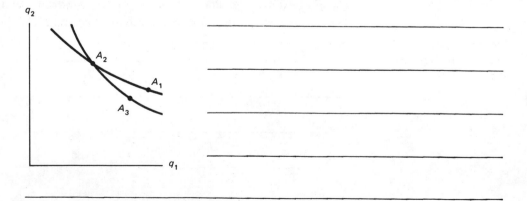

4. Sarah Smith is a very particular martini drinker. She insists that the only way to make a martini is to mix four parts gin to one part vermouth. Also the only use Sarah ever makes of gin and vermouth is in making martinis (she never, for example, slips a little vermouth into the crab grantinée). Graph Sarah's preference map for gin and vermouth in Figure 1–4.

FIGURE 1–4
Sarah's Preference Map

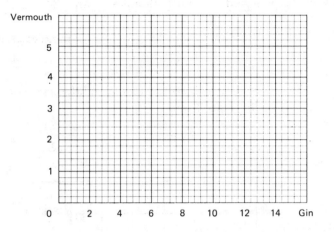

5. Ester Jones' preference map for goods q_1 and q_2 takes the rather odd form pictured in Figure 1–5. What does this map tell you about how Ester views goods q_1 and q_2, as complements, substitutes, or what? Give a practical example of two goods a rational consumer might view this way.

FIGURE 1–5
Ester's Preference Map

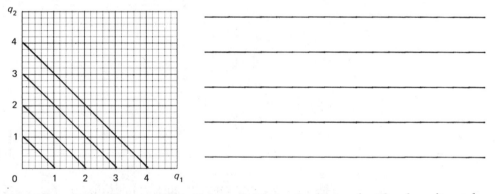

_____

_____

_____

_____

_____

6. James Jones likes to drink Cokes, the more the better, but he doesn't smoke (i.e., Jones derives utility from Coke but not from cigarettes). Plot Jones' Coke-cigarette preference map in Figure 1–6. On your map number indifference curves so that higher numbers correspond to higher levels of utility.

FIGURE 1–6
Jones' Coke-Cigarette
Preference Map

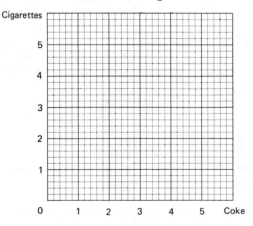

7.* The marginal rate of substitution MRS (or the rate of commodity substitution RCS depending on your jargon) is defined as the negative of the slope of an indifference curve; i.e.,

$$MRS = -\frac{\Delta q_2}{\Delta q_1} = -\frac{dq_2}{dq_1}$$

A "normal" (i.e., convex to the origin) indifference curve displays a *diminishing MRS.*

A set of points is said to be *convex* if any two points in the set can be connected by a straight line that lies everywhere within the set. To say that an indifference curve is characterized by a diminishing marginal rate of substitution (MRS) is equivalent to saying that all points preferred to or equally preferred to any point on the indifference curve form a convex set.

Show that the indifference curves plotted in parts (a) and (b) of Figure 1–7 illustrate this equivalence. [Hint: Calculate the slopes of each indifference curve at points A, B, and C. Also determine for each curve whether the points preferred to and equally preferred to the point (2,2) form a convex set.]

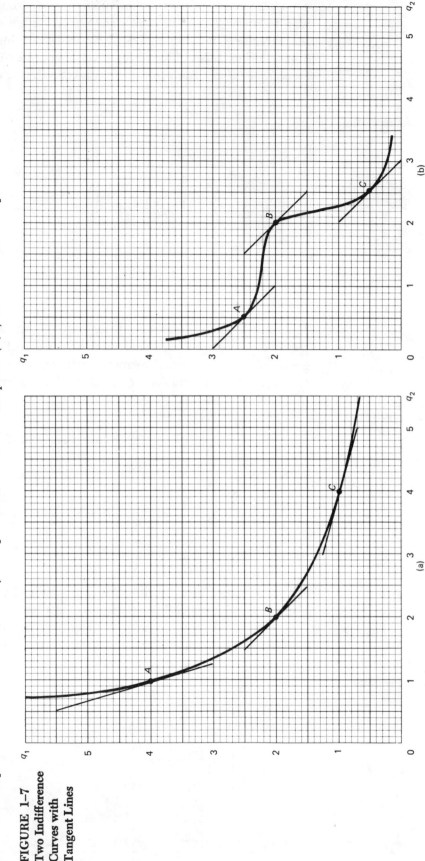

FIGURE 1–7
Two Indifference Curves with Tangent Lines

*Asterisks denote the more difficult problems.

8.* Consumer X has the utility function $U = 10q_1q_2$. (*a*) Derive the formula for this consumer's *MRS*. (*b*) Does his *MRS* diminish along any isoquant? (*c*) Show that for consumer X, *MRS* equals the ratio of the marginal utility of q_1 to that of q_2; i.e.,

$$MRS = \frac{\partial U/\partial q_1}{\partial U/\partial q_2}$$

Chapter 2

Theory of Consumer Behavior

A. DEFINITIONS AND REVIEW

1. *a.* A consumer's budget line or budget constraint is defined as _____

    _____

    _____.

    Consumer X uses a fixed amount of money M to purchase two goods q_1 and q_2 at prices p_1 and p_2; his budget line can be expressed with the following equation:

    _____

    b. If we plot this equation with q_2 on the vertical axis and q_1 on the horizontal axis, the vertical intercept of the budget line will be _____, the horizontal intercept will be _____, and the slope of the line $(\triangle q_2/$ __ $)$ will be (positive/negative).

    c. The fact that the slope of our consumer's budget line is negative makes intuitive sense for the following reason: the consumer has only M dollars to spend; consequently, if he purchases more of one good, he must purchase _____ of the other good; e.g., if $\triangle q_2$ is positive, $\triangle q_1$ must be _____ for the consumer to stay on his budget line.

d. The fact that the slope of our consumer's budget line depends on p_1 and p_2 also makes intuitive sense because the relative sizes of p_1 and p_2 determine the _____

_____.

e. A rise in the amount of money consumer X budgets for spending on q_1

and q_2 will shift his budget line _____, but

have _____ effect on its slope.

f. In contrast, a rise in the price of q_1 (recall q_1 is measured along the

horizontal axis) will _____ the slope of consumer X's budget

line, move the q_1-intercept _____,

and have _____ effect on the q_2-intercept.

2. Consumer X will attain equilibrium on the point on his budget line where

this line is _____ to one of his indifference curves; i.e., at a point where the

slope of his budget lines equals _____. In symbols we can express this condition as follows:

_____

The reason consumer X attains equilibrium at this point on his budget line is

that no other point on this line would yield him more _____.

3. *a.* For consumer X the marginal utility of good q_1 is defined as _____

_____.

We can restate this definition in symbols as follows:

_____

b. Consumer X's marginal rate of substitution of q_1 for q_2 equals the

of the ratio of the marginal utility of q_1 to _____.

In symbols $MRS = $ _____

c. From this it follows that an alternative statement of the condition for consumer equilibrium, one using marginal utilities, is

_____ / _____ = _____ / _____

4. *a.* Consumer X's income-consumption curve shows _____

_____

_____.

b. In contrast his Engle curve for either q_1 or q_2 shows _____

_____

_____.

5. *a.* How much consumer X demands of q_1 depends not only on p_1, but also on a number of other factors, including the amount of money M he has to spend on consumption. The *income elasticity* (η_M) of consumer X's demand for q_1 measures the responsiveness of his purchases of q_1 to the size of his consumption budget. In words we define this elasticity as

_____

_____. In symbols we can express it as follows:

$$\eta_M = \underline{\hspace{1cm}} / \underline{\hspace{1cm}}$$

b. The *price elasticity* of consumer X's demand for q_1 (η) measures the responsiveness of his purchases of q_1 to the p_1. Specifically we define the

price elasticity of our consumer's demand for q_1 as _____

_____

_____.

In symbols $\eta = \underline{\hspace{2cm}} / \underline{\hspace{2cm}}$

c. We define price elasticity as the *absolute value* of a ratio because price elasticity is, for any negatively-sloped demand curve, always a (positive/ negative) number. In contrast the ratio that defines income elasticity of demand is a (positive/negative) number except in the case of an inferior good. A good is said to be an inferior good if a consumer responds to a rise in income by buying (more/less) of it.

6. *a.* To derive consumer X's price-consumption curve for q_1, we have to

take the values of three variables, _____, _____, and _____

as givens and vary _____. The price-consumption curve for q_1

shows _____

_____.

b. Using information in the price-consumption curve for q_1, we can construct and plot consumer X's demand for q_1. In contrast to his price-consumption curve, his demand curve shows _____

_____. In symbols we can

express the consumer's demand curve for any good q selling at price p as

$$q_d = f(\quad)$$

7. The price elasticity (η) of consumer X's demand for q_1 is important because it tells us how his spending on q_1 will vary in response to a change in p_1.

If for example p_1 falls, consumer X will: (*a*) spend *more* dollars on q_1 if η_____;

(*b*) spend the *same* number of dollars on q_1 if η _____; and (*c*) spend

fewer dollars on q_1 if η_____.

B. MULTIPLE CHOICE

1. Brown has budgeted M dollars to purchase goods q_1 and q_2, which sell at prices p_1 and p_2 respectively. Brown's budget line can be expressed by any of the following equations except:

a. $q_2 = - (p_1/p_2)q_1 + M/p_2$ c. $q_1 = - (p_2/p_1)q_2 + M/p_1$
b. $M - p_1q_1 = p_2q_2$ d. $M/p_1 = - (p_2/p_1)q_1 + q_2$

2. Brown's (q_1,q_2)-budget line depends on all of the following except:

a. the amount he budgets for purchasing q_1 and q_2.
b. the price of q_1.
c. his preferences with respect to q_1 and q_2.
d. the price of q_2.

3. The consumer's budget line would shift upward, but remain parallel to his initial budget line if:

a. the price of q_1 fell.
b. the price of q_1 fell by 5% and the price of q_2 fell by 10%.
c. the prices of q_1 and q_2 both fell by 10%.
d. the amount he had budgeted to spend on p_1 and p_2 were decreased by 10%.

4. If a consumer respects his budget constraint (i.e., spends the amount he planned to on consumption), he can purchase any commodity bundle:

a. above his budget line.
b. on his budget line.
c. below his budget line.
d. on or below his budget line.

5. Smith, who consumes many goods, currently drives a VW although he'd prefer to drive a Cadillac. Consumer theory suggests that the explanation is that:

a. the amount Smith has budgeted for consumption is less than the price of a Cadillac.
b. Smith doesn't pay any attention to his preferences when he decides what to buy.
c. Smith's preferences are influenced by car prices.
d. Smith maximizes his satisfaction relative to a budget constraint.

6. A consumer purchasing two goods, q_1 and q_2, attains equilibrium by operating at the point on his budget line where that line is tangent to one of his indifference curves. The reason is that at that point:

    a. the consumer attains more utility than he could from any other commodity bundle on, below, or above the budget line.

    b. the consumer is sort of in the middle of commodity space and gets a diversified bundle of consumption goods.

    c. the consumer gets more utility than he could at any other point on his budget line.

    d. the condition, $-p_1/p_2 = MRS$, holds.

7. The income elasticity of demand for an inferior good is:

  a. less than zero.   *c.* equal to one.
  b. less than one.   *d.* greater than one.

8. Adams consumes two goods, q_1 and q_2. To generate his demand curve for q_1, we need to know all of the following but:

    a. the price of q_1.

    b. the price of q_2.

    c. Adams' preference map.

    d. the amount Adams has to spend on q_1 and q_2.

9. If the price of q_2 falls, this will alter Adams' equilibrium consumption of q_1 by:

    a. shifting his demand curve for q_2.

    b. shifting his demand curve for q_1.

    c. altering his preferences for q_1 and q_2.

    d. causing his budget line to shift upward and rightward with *no* change in slope.

10. Adams' price elasticity of demand for q_1 (denote it by η) is given by the following formula:

  a. $\eta = \dfrac{\%\Delta q_1}{\%\Delta p_1}$ *c.* $\eta = \dfrac{\%\Delta q_1}{\%\Delta M}$

  b. $\eta = \left|\dfrac{\%\Delta q_1}{\%\Delta p_1}\right|$ *d.* $\eta = \left|\dfrac{\%\Delta q_1}{\%\Delta p_2}\right|$

11. When the price of q_1 falls, Adams will respond by spending less money on q_1 if his price elasticity of demand for q_1:

  a. is zero.   *c.* equals one.
  b. is less than one.   *d.* exceeds one.

C. PROBLEMS

1. Sam Thrifty budgets $4 each week to buy lunches. Currently at the cafeteria there are only two choices, chili and tuna salad. The price of a bowl of chili is $1.00, that of a tuna salad $0.50.

a. Write out the budget constraint that Sam faces when he decides how many tuna salads (T) and bowls of chili (C) to consume during the week:

_____

FIGURE 2–1
Sam's Budget Lines

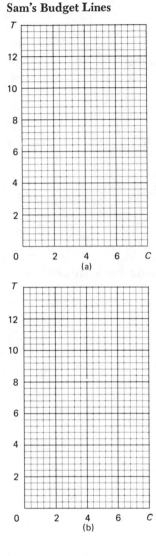

Plot this budget line in Figure 2–1(a), and label it $b = \$4$.

b. Suppose Sam gets richer and and decides to budget $6 a week for lunches. Write out his new budget constraint:

_____

Plot this line in Figure 2–1(a) and label it $b = \$6$.

c. Sam of course might get poorer and budget only $2 a week for lunches. If he did, what would his budget constraint be then?

_____

Plot this third budget line in Figure 2–1(a) and label it $b = \$2$.

d. From Figure 2–1(a), it's clear that the more funds Sam budgets for lunches the (higher/lower) his budget line will be. Also how much Sam decides to spend on lunches (does/does not) affect the slope of his budget line.

e. Assume again that Sam has $4 to spend on lunches and that the price of chili and tuna salads are $1.00 and $0.50 respectively. Plot Sam's budget constraint in Figure 2–1(b) and label it $p_T = 50¢$. Suppose now that an old friend, inflation, appears on the scene. The price of tuna salads shoots to $1.00. Write out Sam's new budget constraint:

_____

Plot this line in Figure 2–1(b) and label it $p_T = \$1.00$.

f. Finally suppose the unexpected occurs—tuna salads drop in price to say 40¢. Write out the budget line corresponding to this new low price of tuna salads:

_____

Plot this third budget line in Figure 2–1(b) and label it $p_T = 40¢$.

g. A comparison of the budget lines in Figure 2–1(b) shows that the price of

tuna salads affect both the _____ and the _____ of Sam's luncheon budget constraint. Specifically, the lower the price of tuna salads, the (steeper/flatter) the budget line and the (higher/lower) the point where this line intercepts the tuna salad (T) axis. The price of tuna salads (does/does not) affect the chili (C) intercept of Sam's budget line.

2. Ernest Edwards, who consumes apples (A) and bananas (B), has a "regular" (i.e., convex-to-the-origin) preference map. It's pictured in Figure 2–2 along with his budget line, *bb*.

a. Assuming that the price of apples (A) equals $1, write out the equation of Ernest's budget line:

_____

b. What quantities of apples and bananas will Ernest, who's a utility-maximiz-

ing consumer, buy when he attains equilibrium? _____

c. Suppose the price of apples falls to 75¢. How will this affect Ernest's equilibrium? [Hint: Write out Ernest's new budget line. Then plot it in Figure 2–2.]

_____

d. Suppose that the price of apples is again $1, but now Ernest reduces to $4 the amount he has to spend on apples and bananas. How will this affect his

equilibrium consumption of them? _____

_____

FIGURE 2–2
Ernest Edward's
Equilibrium

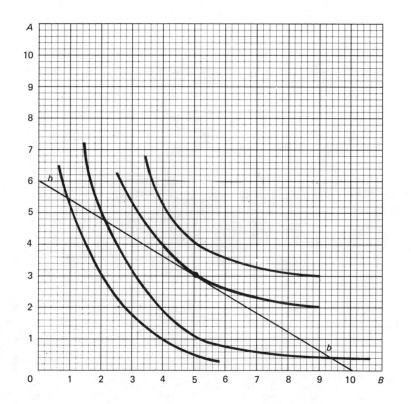

Name

3. a. Arrow Smith uses the money, *M*, he has available for current consumption to buy two goods, q_1 and q_2, both of which happen to sell for $5 apiece. *Smith's Engle curve for q_2* shows the relationship between the quantity of q_2 he demands and the quantity of money *M* he has to spend, given the prices of q_1 and q_2. This curve is plotted in Figure 2–3(a). Draw, in Figure 2–3(b), a preference map that would yield this Engle curve. [Hint: Start by using your information on prices and on *M* to plot appropriate budget lines.]

   b. Is q_2 an inferior good for Smith? _____
   c. Draw Smith's Engle curve for q_1 in Figure 2–3(c).
   d. For Smith, could q_1 and q_2 ever *both* be inferior goods simultaneously

   (i.e., both be inferior goods over a given range of *M* values)? _____

FIGURE 2–3

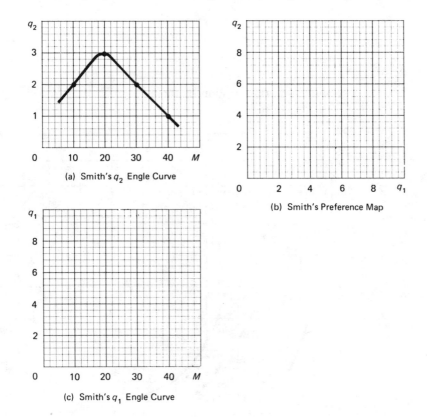

(a) Smith's q_2 Engle Curve

(b) Smith's Preference Map

(c) Smith's q_1 Engle Curve

4. *a.* For Sally Odd, as for other consumers, higher indifference curves correspond to higher levels of utility. However, Sally has a different sort of preference map—all her indifference curves are *concave* to the origin. Sally's preference map is plotted in Figure 2–4. If Sally's budget line is *bb,* at what point will she attain equilibrium? (THINK)

*b.** In Figure 2–4 is the point labeled T for tangency a point of maximum

or minimum satisfaction? _____ A comparison of Figures 2–2 and 2–4 indicates that the consumer will maximize his satisfaction at a point of tangency between his budget constraint and one of his indifference curves (i.e., where the *first-order* condition, $MRS = p_1/p_2$, holds) only if a second-order condition holds. What is the appropriate second-order condition?

_____

_____

_____

_____

_____

_____

FIGURE 2–4
Sally Odd's Equilibrium

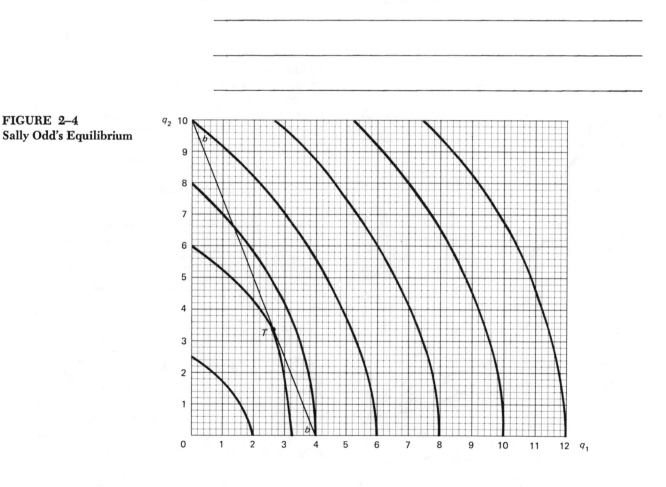

Name

_____
*Asterisks denote the more difficult problems.

5. *a.* Tom Thumb has $4.80 to spend on beans and beef. Figure 2–5(a) pictures his preferences with respect to these two goods. Assuming that the price of beef is 60¢, derive Thumb's demand curve for beans. Note that each budget line shown in Figure 2–5(a) corresponds to a different price for beans. Determine these prices and fill in Table 2–1. Then plot in Figure 2–5(b) the number-pairs in Table 2–1.

b. What items are included in the assumption of all else constant (i.e., the assumption of *ceteris paribus*) underlying the demand curve you plotted in Figure 2–5(b)? [Hint: Look at Figure 2–5(a) and determine what information you needed to determine Thumb's demand curve for beans.]

_____

c. A change in any item included in the *ceteris paribus* assumption under-

lying Thumb's demand curve will cause this curve to _____.

d. Would a change in the price of beans also cause Thumb's demand curve

for beans to shift? _____ How would it affect his demand for beans?

_____

FIGURE 2–5
Deriving Thumb's Demand Curve

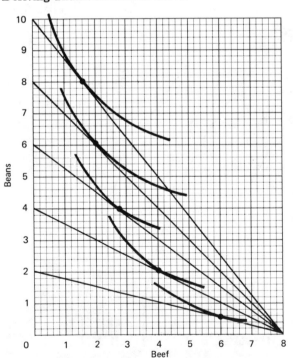

(a) Thumb's Preference Map and Budget Lines

TABLE 2–1
Thumb's Demand Curve for Beans

p_{beans}	$q_{beans\ demanded}$

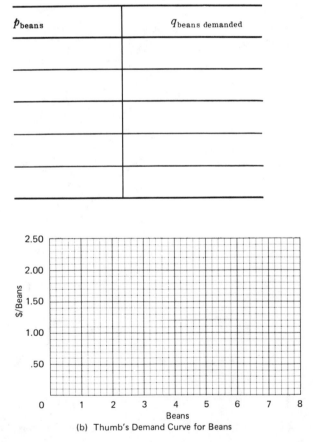

(b) Thumb's Demand Curve for Beans

6. In Oz right and left shoes are sold separately. Alice, who has two feet and always wears two shoes, has the preference map pictured in Figure 2–6. Alice has $6 to spend and the prices of right and left shoes are each $1. How many left shoes and how many right shoes will she purchase in equilibrium? [Hint: Sketch in an appropriate budget line in Figure 2–6.]

FIGURE 2–6
Alice's Preference Map

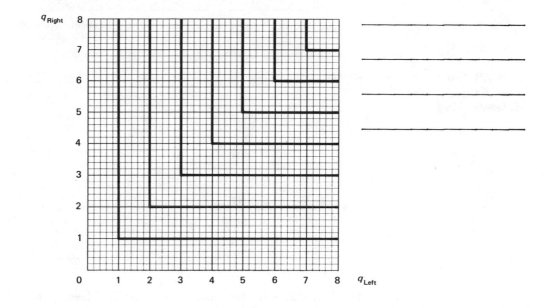

7. Recall Ester Jones of problem 5, Chapter 1. If she had $2 to spend and the prices of q_1 and q_2 were $1 and 50¢ respectively, what quantities of q_1 and q_2 would she purchase in equilibrium? [Hint: Sketch in an appropriate budget line in Figure 1–5, which is repeated here.]

FIGURE 1–5
Ester's Preference Map

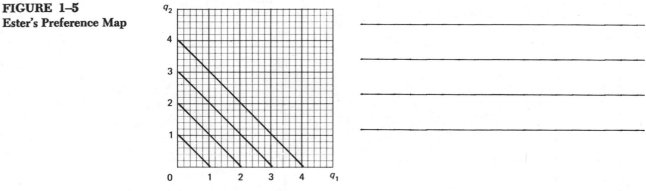

Name

8. *a.* If Jones of problem 6, Chapter 1, has $3 to spend and the prices of cigarettes and Coke are 60¢ and $1 respectively, what quantities of Coke and cigarettes will he purchase in equilibrium? [Hint: Begin by adding Jones' budget line to Figure 1–6, which is repeated here.]

_____

b. Could you have answered the question without knowing the price of cigarettes? Explain your answer.

FIGURE 1–6
Jones' Coke-Cigarette
Preference Map

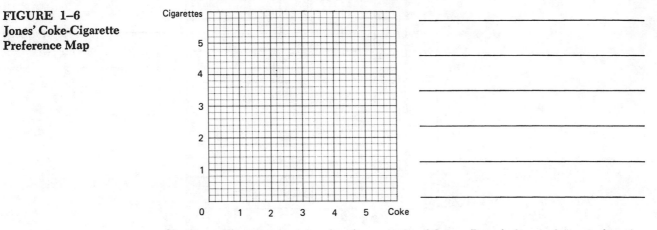

9. Jones lives on two goods, cigarettes and beer. Jones' demand curve for cigarettes has, as shown in Figure 2–7, zero elasticity for prices from zero to $1.50. In Figure 2–8 sketch a preference map that would yield this sort of demand curve for cigarettes. Adding appropriate budget lines, show how you could drive a zero-elasticity demand curve for cigarettes from your preference map.

FIGURE 2–7
Jones' Demand Curve for Cigarettes

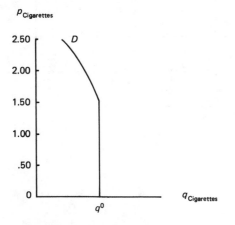

FIGURE 2–8
Jones' Preference Map

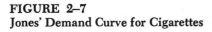

10.* *a.* If a consumer purchases a particular bundle of goods, A_1, in a price-income situation in which he could have purchased some other bundle, A_2, then bundle A_1 is revealed preferred to A_2. The axioms of revealed preference state that if bundle A_1 is revealed preferred to A_2, then A_2 must never be revealed preferred to A_1. Rustler Jones an old cow hand, lives on tobacco T and beans B. He has been observed to purchase the following bundles:

(1) $T = 3$ and $B = 2$ when $p_T = \$4$ and $p_B = 2$, and

(2) $T = 2$ and $B = 3$ when $p_T = \$1$ and $p_B = 2$

Is Rustler's behavior consistent with the axioms of revealed preference? [Hint: Compare the costs of both bundles at both sets of prices.]

Name ---------------------------------

b. In Figure 2–9 plot two points A_1 and A_2 that represent Rustler's equilibrium purchases 1 and 2 as described above. Next sketch appropriate budget lines through these points. Can you draw an indifference curve through A_1 and another through A_2 in such a way that each indifference curve is tangent to the appropriate budget line but does not intersect the other indifference curve? Rechoose A_2 so Rustler's behavior is consistent with the axioms of revealed preference. Now can you draw indifference curves as described above that do not intersect? What does your answer imply about the relationship between the assumption that the consumer's preferences are transitive and the axioms of revealed preference?

FIGURE 2–9
Rustler Jones

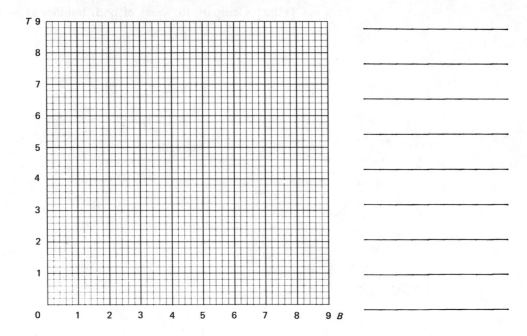

11.* *a.* Problem 8 in Chapter 1 introduced consumer X who has the utility function, $U = 10q_1q_2$. Using M to denote the money this consumer has to spend and p_1 and p_2 the prices of q_1 and q_2, derive consumer X's demand curve for q_1.

Name

b. If $M = \$50$ and $p_1 = \$5$, what quantity of q_1 will consumer X purchase?

Chapter 3

Topics in Consumer Demand

**A. DEFINITIONS
AND REVIEW**

1. *a.* A consumer's *money* income equals _____

   _____.

   b. In contrast his *real* income equals _____

   _____.

2. *a.* Consumer X can buy with his money income M two goods, q_1 and q_2, which sell at prices, p_1 and p_2. The effect of a change in p_1 on the quantity of q_1 consumer X demands can be viewed as consisting of two parts, the substitution effect and the income effect. The substitution effect is

   consumer X's response to _____

   _____.

   b. The income effect is consumer X's response to _____

   _____

   _____

   c. The substitution effect will always make consumer X respond to a fall

   in p_1 by buying _____ q_1. The income effect will lead consumer X to respond to a fall in p_1 by buying more q_1 only if for him q_1 is not a/an

   _____ good.

Name

3. *a.* To say that a good is an inferior good for consumer X means that _____

_____

_____ .

b. To say that a good is a Giffen good for consumer X means that _____

_____

_____ .

c. For a good to be a Giffen good, the following two conditions must be

met: (1) _____

_____

and (2) _____

_____

d. Giffen goods are unusual because _____

_____

_____ .

4. *a.* The "own" price elasticity of demand, which measures the responsive-ness of consumer X's demand for q_1 to changes in p_1 is given by the formula:

$$\eta_{11} = \underline{\hspace{3cm}}$$

The cross elasticity of demand, which measures the responsiveness of con-sumer X's demand for q_1 to changes in p_2 is given by the formula:

$$\eta_{12} = \underline{\hspace{3cm}}$$

b. According to the cross elasticity approach, if η_{12} is positive, q_1 and q_2 are

said to be _____ goods; if η_{12} is negative, q_1 and q_2 are said to

be _____ goods; and if η_{12} equals zero, q_1 and q_2 are said to

be _____ goods.

B. MULTIPLE CHOICE

1. Consumer X can buy two consumption goods, q_1 and q_2, which sell at prices p_1 and p_2. His *real* income will be changed by any of the following but:

a. a change in his money income.　　*c.* a change in p_1.
b. a change in his preferences.　　*d.* a change in p_2.

2. When p_1 rises or falls, consumer X will respond by changing his demand for q_1. The part of this change that is referred to as the *substitution effect* represents consumer X's response to:

    a. the change in his money income.
    b. the change in relative goods prices.
    c. the change in his real income.
    d. an induced change in his preferences.

3. The part of the demand change (described in question 2 above) that we call the *income effect* represents consumer X's response to:

    a. the change in his money income.
    b. the change in relative goods prices.
    c. the induced change in his real income.
    d. a change in his preferences.

4. When p_1 falls, the substitution effect per se is certain to lead consumer X to:

    a. increase his demand for both q_2 and q_1.
    b. increase his demand for q_1 but decrease his demand for q_2.
    c. decrease his demand for both q_1 and q_2.
    d. do the opposite of what the income effect leads him to do.

5. Last week Jones got a big raise, decided to budget more money for current consumption, and, as a result, ended up eating fewer hot dogs. This tells us that for Jones:

    a. hot dogs are a Giffen good.
    b. preferences are a function of income.
    c. hot dogs are an inferior good.
    d. hot dogs are overpriced.

6. A necessary but not sufficient condition for hot dogs to be a Giffen good for Jones is that:

    a. the substitution effect generated by a fall in the price of hot dogs must be negative.
    b. hot dogs must be cheaper than other goods.
    c. Jones' money income must fall.
    d. hot dogs must be an inferior good.

7. The cross elasticity of demand between hamburger and catsup is negative. This tells us that:

    a. catsup and hamburger are substitutes.
    b. catsup and hamburger are complements.
    c. catsup and hamburger are independent goods.
    d. the person calculating the elasticity forgot to include an absolute value sign.

Name ......

8. It would be extremely unusual for an individual's demand curve for a consumption good to be positively sloped. But it would not be unusual for a consumer's supply curve of labor to be backward bending. The reason is that in the case of the supply curve of labor:

    a. the income and substitution effects work in opposite directions.
    b. the income effect always outweighs the substitution effect.
    c. the substitution effect switches signs as the wage rate is increased.
    d. consumers are more rational about spending income than about earning it.

9.* The axioms of von Neuman and Morgenstern imply that an individual who chooses under uncertainty among various alternatives will:

    a. seek to maximize the utility of the expected outcome of his choice.
    b. be risk averse.
    c. seek to maximize the expected utility of his choice.
    d. try to avoid uncertainty.

10.* An individual is risk averse implies if:

    a. he only makes decisions under certainty.
    b. he is willing to make large fair bets.
    c. his utility function is convex.
    d. he seeks to maximize expected utility and his utility function is concave.

---

*Asterisks denote the more difficult problems.

C. PROBLEMS

1. *a.* Ms. King, a tennis player with a large appetite, consumes just two goods, steak and Gucci clothes. For King, steak is an inferior good. Using an appropriate diagram (preference map plus budget lines), illustrate what this means.

FIGURE 3–1
Steak as an Inferior Good

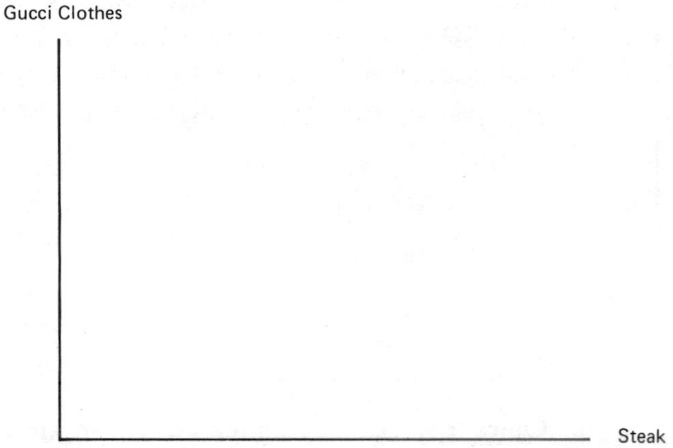

Gucci Clothes

Steak

b. If steak is an inferior good for Ms. King, what can you say *for sure* about the slope of her demand curve for steak? Explain your answer.

_____

_____

_____

_____

_____

c. In Figure 3–2, show, using appropriate budget lines, how Ms. King's preference map would have to look in order for steak to be a Giffen good for her.

FIGURE 3–2
Steak as a Giffen Good

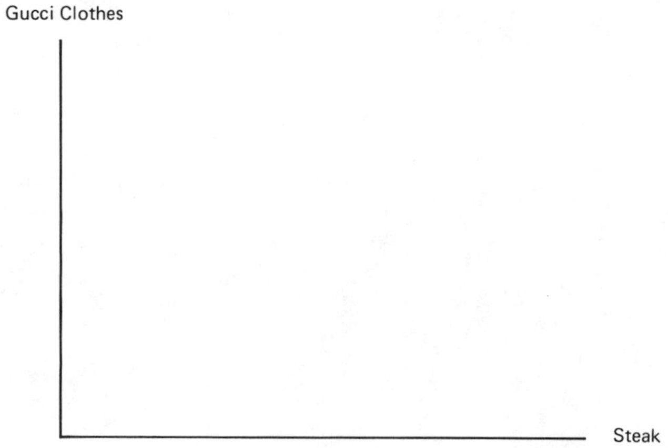

Gucci Clothes

Steak

Name

d. In Figure 3–3 show what Ms. King's demand curve for steak would look like if steak were a Giffen good for her.

FIGURE 3–3
King's Demand Curve for the Giffen Good, Steak

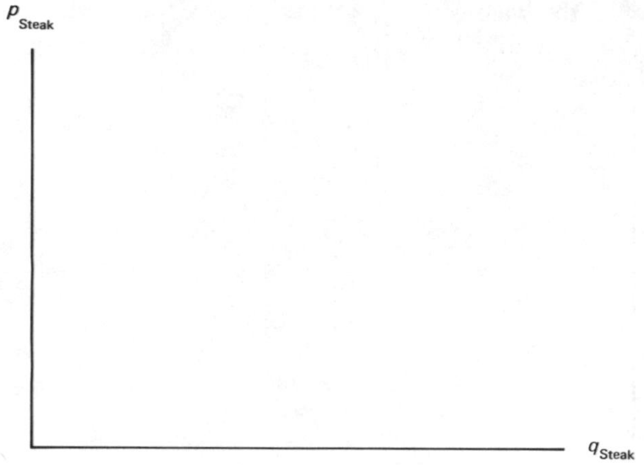

p_{Steak}

q_{Steak}

2. Susie Quirk enjoys being different. For example, she asserts that, while the typical woman has a negatively-sloped demand curve for shoes, her demand curve slopes upward; i.e., the higher price of shoes, the more of them she buys. Yet when questioned, she also admits that, when her income rises, she responds the way most women do—by buying more shoes. Are Susie's assertion and admission *consistent?* Explain.

_____

_____

_____

_____

_____

_____

3. *a.* Sally Odd of Chapter 2 has $100 to spend on q_1 and q_1. The price of q_2 is $10. Table 3–1 lists various prices that might be charged for q_1; to Figure 2–4, repeated below, add budget lines corresponding to each of the listed values of p_1. Then derive Sally's demand curve for q_1 and plot it in Figure 3–4. [Hint: After you draw the budget lines, fill in Table 3–1.]

FIGURE 2–4
Sally Odd's
Preference
Map

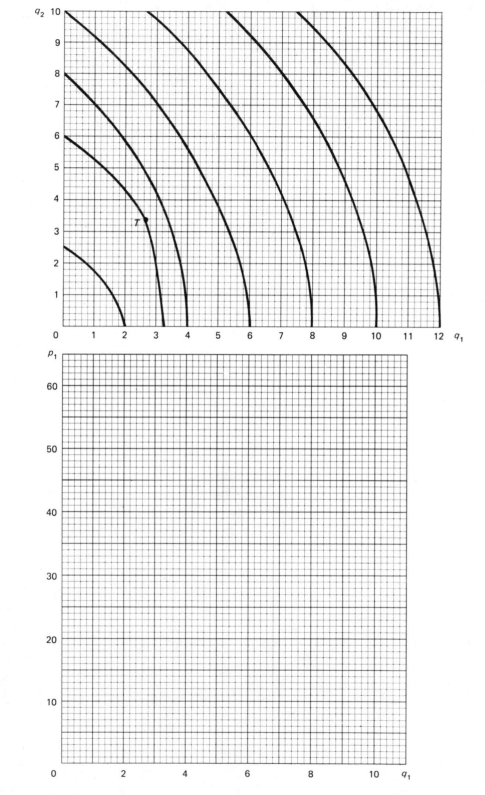

FIGURE 3–4
Sally's Demand Curve
for q_1

TABLE 3–1
Sally's Demand for q_1

p_1	q_1
$50.00	
$25.00	
$16.66	
$12.50	
$10.00	

Name

b. What role do the income and the substitution effects play in determining the slope and shape of Sally's demand curve? Be specific.

_____

_____

_____

_____

_____

_____

_____

_____

4. *a.* Alice, of problem 6, Chapter 2, has $6 to spend and the price of a right shoe is $1. Derive her demand curve for left shoes. [Hint: Using the prices in Table 3–2, add appropriate budget lines to Figure 2–6, which is repeated below. Then fill in the missing values in Table 3–2 and plot Alice's demand curve in Figure 3–5.]

FIGURE 2–6
Alice's Preference Map

FIGURE 3–5
Alice's Demand Curve for Left Shoes

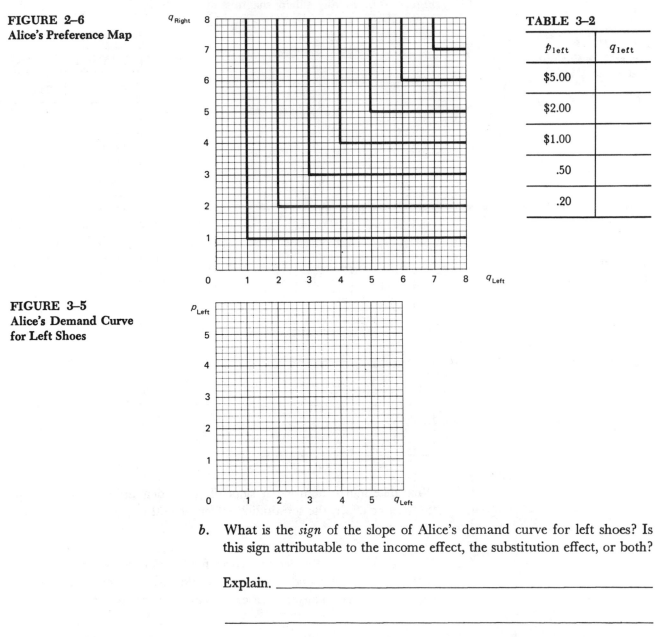

TABLE 3–2

p_{left}	q_{left}
$5.00	
$2.00	
$1.00	
.50	
.20	

b. What is the *sign* of the slope of Alice's demand curve for left shoes? Is this sign attributable to the income effect, the substitution effect, or both?

Explain. _____

_____

_____

_____

_____

Name ----------------------------

5. *a.* Jones of problem 6, Chapter 1, has $10 to spend on Coke and cigarettes. Jones derives utility from Coke, but not from cigarettes. The price of a pack of cigarettes is $1. Derive Jones' demand curve for Coke. [Hint: Add Jones' preference curves to Figure 1–6 which is repeated here. Then using the prices in Table 3–3, add appropriate budget lines to Figure 1–6. Finally fill in the missing values in Table 3–3, and plot Jones' demand curve in Figure 3–6.]

FIGURE 1–6
Jones' Coke-Cigarette Preference Map

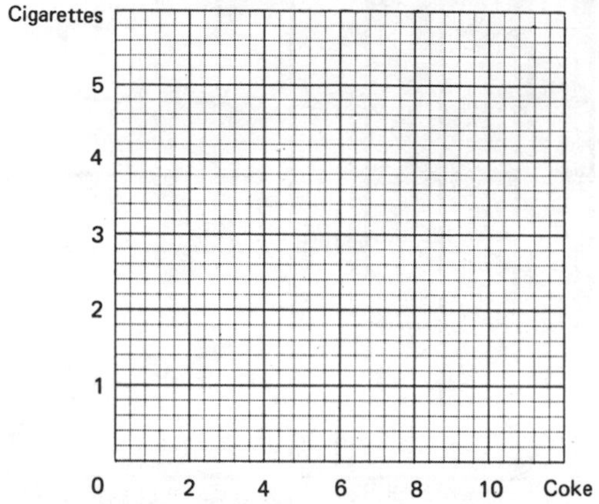

TABLE 3–3
Jones' Demand for Coke

p_{Coke}	q_{Coke}
$5.00	
$4.00	
$3.00	
$2.00	
$1.00	

FIGURE 3–6
Jones' Demand Curve for Coke

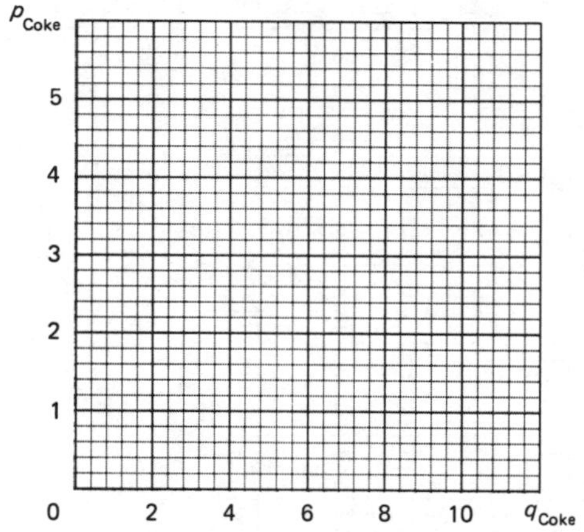

b. What determines the negative slope of Jones' demand curve for Coke—the income effect, the substitution effect, or both?

_____

c. Normally to derive the demand curve for Cokes of a consumer who can buy both cigarettes and Coke, you would have to know the price of cigarettes. Is that so in Jones' case? Explain why or why not.

_____

d. The income elasticity of a consumer's demand for a commodity q is the following:

$$\frac{\% \ \Delta \ \text{in} \ q}{\% \ \Delta \ \text{in income}}$$

What is the income elasticity of Jones' demand for Coke? _____

For cigarettes? _____

6. a. Figure 1–5 in Chapter 1 pictures Ester Jones' preferences with respect to q_1 and q_2. Ester has $8 to spend on q_1 and q_2 and the price of q_2 equals $4. By adding appropriate budget lines to Figure 1–5, which is repeated here, derive Ester's demand curve for q_1. [Hint: Start by filling in Table 3–4; then plot the resulting figures in Figure 3–7.]

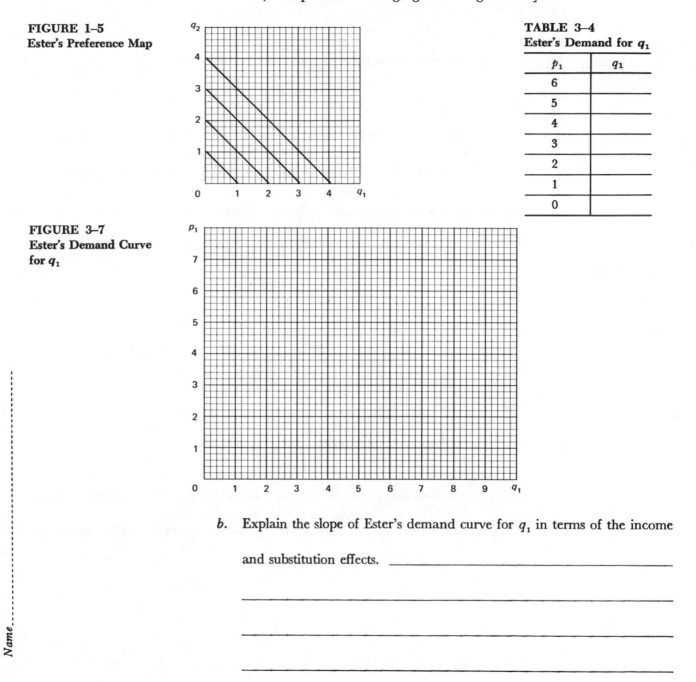

FIGURE 1–5
Ester's Preference Map

FIGURE 3–7
Ester's Demand Curve for q_1

TABLE 3–4
Ester's Demand for q_1

p_1	q_1
6	
5	
4	
3	
2	
1	
0	

b. Explain the slope of Ester's demand curve for q_1 in terms of the income and substitution effects. _____

_____

_____

_____

Name -----------------------

7. *a.* Smith's demand for good one, q_1^d, is given by

$$q_1^d = 10 - p_1 + p_2$$

In symbols, the "own" price elasticity of Smith's demand for q_1 is given by

$$\eta_{11} = \left| \frac{\% \, \Delta \, q_1}{\% \, \Delta \, p_1} \right|$$

while the cross elasticity is given by

$$\eta_{12} = \frac{\% \, \Delta \, q_1}{\% \, \Delta \, p_2}$$

Determine the sign of the cross elasticity of Smith's demand for q_1.

_____ For Smith are q_1 and q_2 substitutes or complements?

_____

b. Brown's demand for good one, q_1^d, is given by

$$q_1^d = 10 - p_1 - p_2$$

Calculate the sign of the cross elasticity of Brown's demand for q_1.

_____ For Brown are q_1 and q_2 substitutes or complements?

_____

8.* Suppose an individual buys in period one goods q_1^0 and q_2^0 at prices p_1^0 and p_2^0, and that in period two he buys goods q_1' and q_2' at prices p_1' and p_2'. Then his index of income (or expenditure) change between the two periods is given by:

$$E = \frac{\Sigma p_i' \, q_i'}{\Sigma p_i^0 \, q_i^0}$$

We can also calculate for the individual a price (change) index weighted by period-one quantities called the Laspeyre index. In symbols:

$$L = \frac{\Sigma p_i' \, q_i^0}{\Sigma p_i^0 \, q_i^0}$$

An alternative price index weighted by period-two quantities is the Passche index. In symbols:

$$P = \frac{\Sigma p_i' \, q_i'}{\Sigma p_i^0 \, q_i'}$$

    a. Prove that if $E > L$ the consumer was better off in period two than in period one. Prove also that if $E < P$ the consumer was better off in period one than in period two. [Hint: Note and verify that if

$$\Sigma p_i' \, q_i' > \Sigma p_i' \, q_i^0$$

the consumer is better off in period two, while if

$$\Sigma p_i' \, q_i^0 > \Sigma p_i^0 \, q_i'$$

the opposite is true.]

b. Applying the above results, what, if anything, can you say about whether Rustler Jones (problem 10, Chapter 2) was better off in period one when he purchased bundle (1) than in period two when he purchased bundle

(2)? _____

_____

c. How would your answer be modified if in period two Rustler Jones had purchased at the then prevailing prices $T = 6$ and $B = 1$? _____

_____

d. How would your answers to (b) and (c) have been modified if in period one Rustler had purchased $T = 1$ and $B = 6$? _____

_____

e. The results that you proved in (*a*) assume that the consumer behaves according to the axioms of revealed preference described in problem 10 of Chapter 2. To confirm your results for (*b*), (*c*), and (*d*) above, plot all four goods bundles Rustler purchased and the relevant budget lines (there are two of them) in Figure 3–8. Then check to see whether your results in (*b*) through (*d*) are consistent with what the axioms of revealed preference imply about how Rustler's welfare changed between the two periods in the situation described.

FIGURE 3–8
Rustler Jones

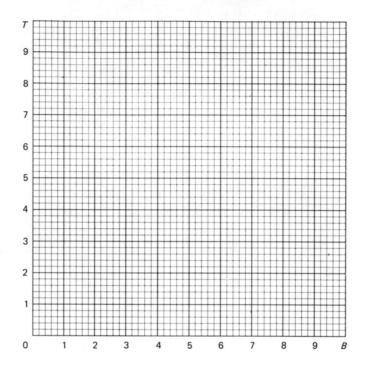

9. Hustler Harris finds that each day has 24 hours, which he divides between free time (F) and labor (L). He makes his decision about how many hours to work on the basis of his income-leisure preference map and an appropriate budget constraint.

   a. Write out Hustler's budget constraint. [Hint: Hustler's income Y equals the wage rate w he receives times the number of hours L he labors.]

   _____

   b. From Figure 3–9 derive Hustler's supply curve of labor; i.e., a schedule showing how many hours he would choose to work at each of the wage rates incorporated in the four budget lines shown in the figure. [Hint: Start by filling in the missing numbers in Table 3–5. Then plot Hustler's supply schedule in Figure 3–10.]

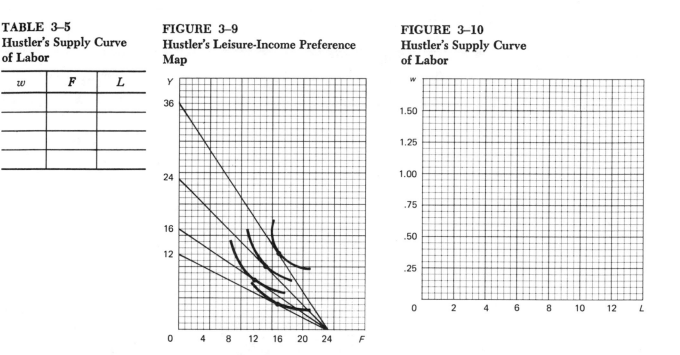

TABLE 3–5
Hustler's Supply Curve of Labor

w	F	L

FIGURE 3–9
Hustler's Leisure-Income Preference Map

FIGURE 3–10
Hustler's Supply Curve of Labor

   c. Using the income and the substitution effects, explain why it is reasonable for Hustler's supply curve of labor to have first a positive and then a negative slope. _____

   _____

   _____

   _____

   _____

   _____

Name --------------------------------

10.* Russ Ryan always seeks to maximize expected value when he invests. How would you expect Russ to rank the four assets for which probability distributions of possible returns are shown in Table 3–6? [Hint: Calculate the expected value of $1 invested in each asset.]

TABLE 3–6
Russ' Expectations

	Possible Rates of Return, %	Probability that the Rate Will Occur
	−10	2/5
Asset I	0	1/5
	10	2/5
	−10	1/5
Asset II	0	2/5
	10	2/5
	−20	2/5
Asset III	0	1/5
	20	2/5
	−10	2/5
Asset IV	0	2/5
	10	1/5

11. *a.* Risktaker Riley has $10,000 to invest and he's planning to put his money into the stock of two companies, PDQ Delivery and Astro Jet. As Table 3–7 shows, the two stocks offer identical distributions of possible returns. Because of this, Smith figures that it doesn't matter which stock he puts his money in, but his secretary argues that he'd decrease his risk by *diversifying*, putting some of his money in one stock and some in the other. Assuming that the returns yielded by PDQ and Astro Jet are independent (i.e., the one doesn't influence the other), could Riley in any sense cut his risk by putting $5,000 in one stock and $5,000

in the other? To answer, fill in Table 3–8. _____

_____

_____

TABLE 3–7
Riley's Expectations

	Possible Rates of Return, %	Probability that the Rate Will Occur
PDQ	−10	1/3
	10	2/3
Astro Jet	−10	1/3
	10	2/3

TABLE 3–8
Distribution of Possible Returns on Riley's Diversified (50–50) Portfolio

Possible Rates of Return, %	Probability that the Rate Will Occur
−10	
0	
	4/9

b. Is diversification a strategy you'd expect every rational investor to

follow (i.e., does the cut in risk it promises involve some price)? _____

_____

_____

_____

Name --

12.* A fair bet is one whose expected value equals zero. For example a coin is flipped: heads you win $1, tails you lose $1. Most individuals are unwilling to enter into fair bets for any sizable amount. Show that if a consumer seeks to maximize expected utility, such unwillingness implies that he is risk averse (i.e., that his utility function of wealth is concave). Hint: An unwillingness to engage in a fair bet for an amount h on the part of a consumer with initial wealth X implies that:

$$U(X) > \tfrac{1}{2} U(X + h) + \tfrac{1}{2} U(X - h)$$

Chapter 4

Characteristics of Market Demand

A. DEFINITIONS AND REVIEW

1. Consumer X, who is still buying two goods (q_1 and q_2) at prices p_1 and p_2, has a demand curve for q_1, which shows the relationship between the price charged for q_1 and the amount of q_1 he demands. If we plot this demand relationship, $q_1 = f(p_1)$, we will get a negatively-sloped curve unless, for consumer X,

q_1 is a _____ good. Any change in _____ will cause consumer X to *move along* his demand curve for q_1. In contrast, a change in

_____, _____, or _____ will would cause a *shift* in consumer X's demand curve for q_1.

2. The market demand curve for a commodity shows the relationship between

_____

_____ .

It is obtained by summing _____

_____ .

3. *a.* The price elasticity of the market demand curve is given by the expression

$$\eta = \underline{\hspace{3cm}}$$

This elasticity measures _____

_____ .

b. Market demand for q_1 is said to be elastic if η has a value _____.
When demand for q_1 is elastic, a fall in p_1 will cause consumers to

_____ their spending on q_1.

4. *a.* Marginal revenue is defined as _____

_____

In symbols

$$MR = \rule{4cm}{0.4pt}$$

b. The relationship between MR and the TR curve is that at any quantity

level, MR equals the _____ of the TR curve.

5. At any point along the market demand curve, a close relationship exists among the elasticity of demand at that point, marginal revenue, and the shape of the TR curve.

a. If $\eta > 1$, then MR is _____, and the TR curve is _____.

b. If $\eta = 1$, then MR equals _____, and the TR curve _____.

c. If $\eta < 1$, then MR is _____, and the TR curve is _____.

6. *a.* In a perfectly competitive market, the market demand curve will normally

have a _____ slope, and its price elasticity may be _____,

_____, or _____.

b. In contrast, the demand curve facing an individual seller in a perfectly

competitive market will normally have an _____ slope and an

_____ elasticity. Explain this contrast: _____

_____

_____

_____

B. MULTIPLE CHOICE

1. Consumer X buys q_1 at the price p_1. If p_1 rises, this will:

   a. change consumer X's preferences for q_1.
   b. shift consumer X's demand curve for q_1.
   c. lower consumer X's money income.
   d. cause consumer X to move upward along his existing demand curve for q_1.

2. If q_1 is a superior (or "normal") good, a fall in p_2 will induce a downward shift in consumer X's demand for q_1:

   a. if the substitution effect on demand for q_1 caused by the fall in p_2 is zero.
   b. only if q_2 is an inferior good.
   c. only if the substitution effect on demand for q_1 caused by the fall in p_2 outweighs the income effect on demand for q_1 caused by the fall in p_2.
   d. only if the fall in p_2 causes a fall in p_1.

3. The fundamental reason we draw the market demand curve for any commodity q_1 with a negative slope is that:

  a. economists have made, for analytic convenience, the assumption that market demand curves have a negative slope.

  b. even if some individuals' demand curves for q_1 may be subject to Giffen's paradox, the demand curves of most consumers won't be.

  c. whether Giffen's paradox is prevalent or not among consumers of q_1, summing across individual demand curves will *always* produce a positively-sloped market demand curve.

  d. consumers' indifference curves are assumed to be convex to the origin.

4. If the market demand curve is linear and negatively sloped, we can be sure that:

  a. it will have unitary elasticity everywhere.

  b. the slope of the market demand curve will be everywhere the same but elasticity will fall as quantity sold is increased.

  c. price elasticity will be everywhere greater than one.

  d. price elasticity will be everywhere less than one but greater than zero.

5. The imposition of a minimum wage high enough to decrease employment will cause the total wage bill paid by employers to rise:

  a. if the demand for unskilled labor has an elasticity less than one.

  b. if the demand for unskilled labor has unitary elasticity.

  c. if the demand for unskilled labor is elastic.

  d. always.

6. Statistical studies indicate that the income elasticity of demand for food is typically:

a. less than one.   *c.* negative.

b. greater than one.   *d.* zero.

7. If the market demand curve is inelastic at any point, we can be sure that, at the quantity level corresponding to this point, marginal revenue:

a. will be positive.   *c.* will be negative.

b. will be zero.   *d.* will exceed average revenue.

8. It has been suggested by statistical studies that in the U.S. demand for automobiles is price inelastic. If this is so, then to raise their total revenue from sales, U.S. auto manufacturers should:

  a. raise price.

  b. cut price.

  c. increase quantity sold.

  d. take measures to increase the elasticity of the demand for autos.

9. The demand curve facing an individual seller in a perfectly competitive market:

    a. has a negative slope like any other demand curve.
    b. has elasticity less than one.
    c. is horizontal.
    d. has zero elasticity.

10. A perfectly competitive firm faces a horizontal demand curve because:

    a. demand for goods sold in perfectly competitive markets is highly elastic.
    b. each seller in such a market services only a negligible fraction of total market demand.
    c. there are many buyers in such markets.
    d. the product sold in a perfectly competitive market is usually homogeneous.

11. If an individual selling in a perfectly competitive market wants to double the amount he sells in this market, he:

    a. should lower price.
    b. should advertise his product.
    c. should take steps to increase the elasticity of demand for his output.
    d. need only double his output and the amount he offers for sale.

C. PROBLEMS

1. *a.* Smith, Green, and Jones are all consumers of commodity X. Figure 4–1 shows their individual demand curves for this commodity. Construct their joint demand curve for commodity X and plot it in Figure 4–1(d). [Hint: Begin by filling in Table 4–1.]

TABLE 4–1
Deriving a Joint Demand Curve

Price	Smith's Demand (1)	Jones' Demand (2)	Green's Demand (3)	Joint Demand (1) + (2) + (3)
10				
9				
8				
7				
6				
5				
4				
3				
2				
1				
0				

Name ----------

b. The market demand curve for any commodity is the joint demand curve of all consumers in the market for that commodity. Your construction of the joint demand curve in Figure 4–1(d) shows that the market demand for any commodity will slope downward for two reasons. List them:

(1) _____

_____

_____

(2) _____

_____

_____

FIGURE 4–1
Constructing a Joint Demand Curve

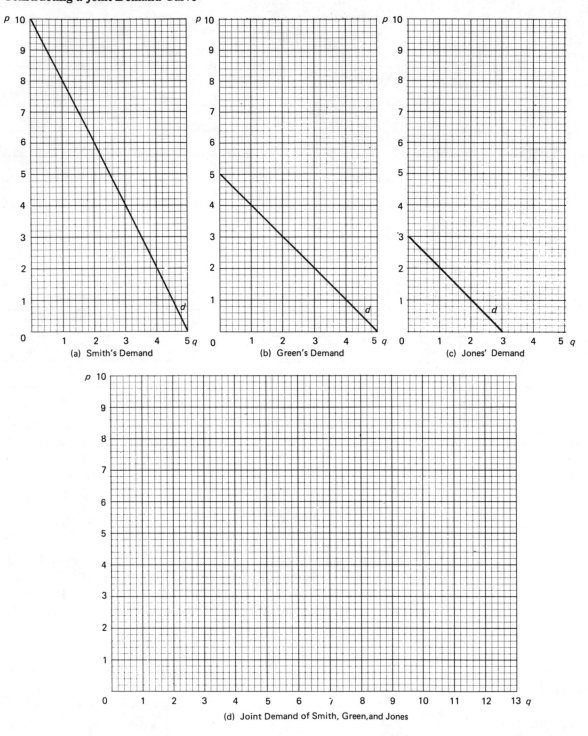

(a) Smith's Demand

(b) Green's Demand

(c) Jones' Demand

(d) Joint Demand of Smith, Green, and Jones

2. The market demand curve for gismos is given by $q_d = 10 - p$.

  a. Plot this demand curve in Figure 4–2.

FIGURE 4–2
The Market Demand for
Gismos

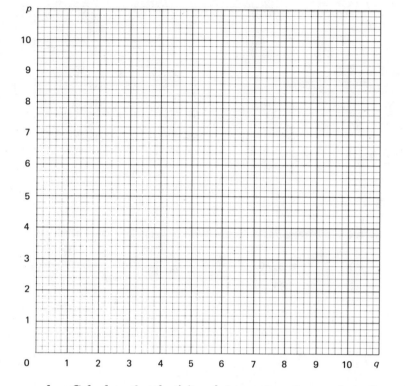

  b. Calculate the elasticity of demand at three points along this curve, those corresponding to (1) $p = 9$, (2) $p = 5$, and (3) $p = 1$. [Hint: Recall

$$\eta = \left| \frac{\% \, \triangle \, \text{in} \, q}{\% \, \triangle \, \text{in} \, p} \right| = \left| \frac{\triangle q/q}{\triangle p/p} \right| = \left| \frac{\triangle q}{\triangle p} \cdot \frac{p}{q} \right|$$

Note also that $\triangle q / \triangle p$ equals the inverse of the slope of the demand curve which for the demand curve in question is *constant* at all points along the curve. Thus step one is to calculate the numerical value of $\triangle p / \triangle q$.]

  (1) _____ (2) _____ (3) _____

c. Using the hint in (b), show that the elasticity of demand falls steadily for movements downward along the demand curve you plotted in Figure 4–2.

_____

_____

_____

3.* How does elasticity vary along the demand curve $pq = 10$? Note solving for

q, this can be written $q_d = 10/p$. _____

4. *a.* When the Georgia Transit Authority raised its basic fare in 1972 from
30¢ to 40¢, the number of riders declined from 20,000 per week to
18,000. How elastic, in the price range in question, is demand for transit
rides? In answering, use the formula for arc elasticity.

$$\eta = \left| \frac{\Delta q}{\Delta p} \cdot \frac{\left(\dfrac{p_1 + p_2}{2}\right)}{\left(\dfrac{q_1 + q_2}{2}\right)} \right| = \left| \frac{\Delta q}{\Delta p} \cdot \frac{p_1 + p_2}{q_1 + q_2} \right|$$

where (p_1, q_1) are the initial values of p and q, and (p_2, q_2) are the post-
fare-hike values.

Name --

b. Is increasing fares a good way for this transit authority to increase its

total revenue? _____

_____

_____

―――――――――
*Asterisks denote the more difficult problems.

5. When interviewed about how much they spend on beer, students responded in various ways. Graph a demand curve consistent with each answer and determine what its price elasticity is.

a. "I never drink beer except on Saturday night and then it's always one six-pack, no more, no less."

η:_____

FIGURE 4–3(a)

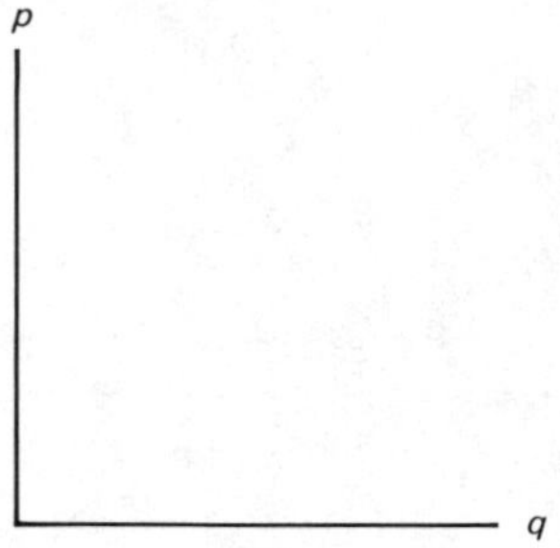

p

q

b. "When beer gets above $1.25 a six-pack, I never drink it; and at $1.25 I get only one six-pack for Saturday night; but when the price falls to 89 cents I buy four or five six-packs a week for myself and to entertain my friends."

η:_____

FIGURE 4–3(b)

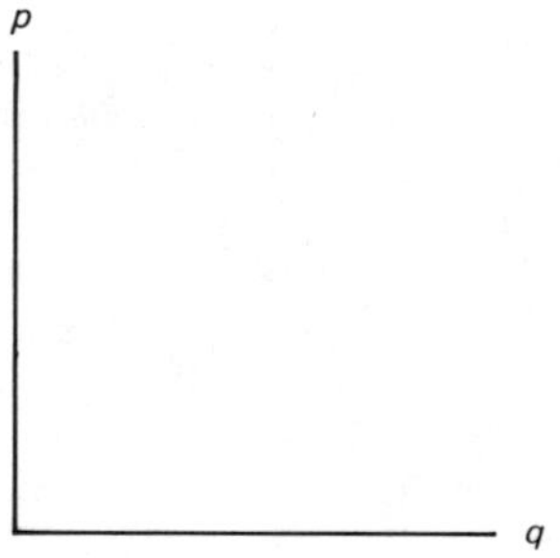

p

q

c. "I haven't got much money so I have to live on a close budget. Every week I spend $4 on beer, no more no less."

η:_____

FIGURE 4–3(c)

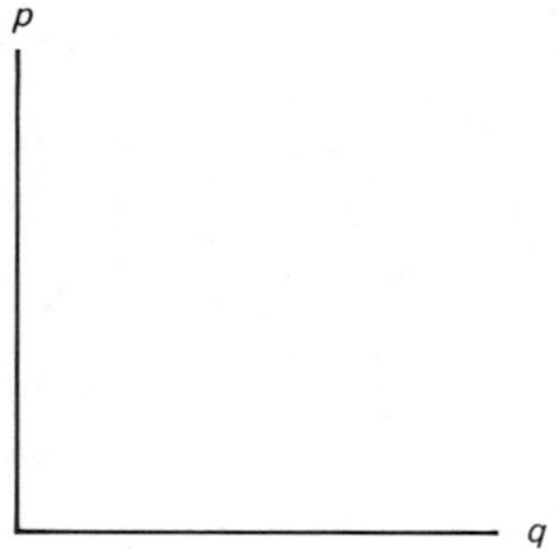

p

q

d. "I quit drinking last New Year's Eve."

η:_____

FIGURE 4–3(d)

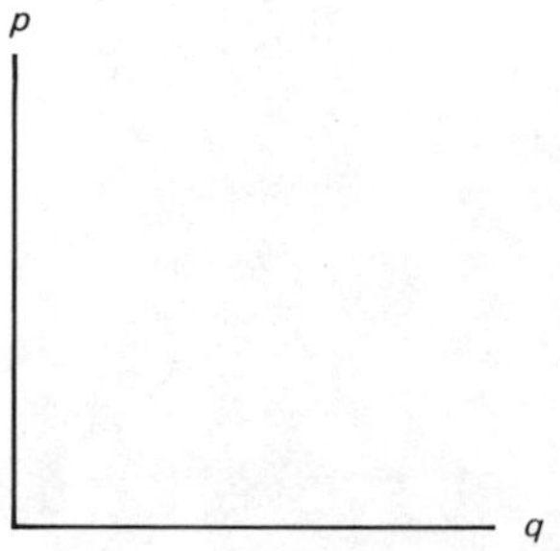

p

q

6. Harry Aldrich, President of XYZ Corporation, thought that the more output he sold, the more total revenue he would receive. His sales manager did a study that showed demand for XYZ's output was downward sloping (see Figure 4–4).

a. Write the equation for demand for XYZ's output as a function of price

$$q_a = \underline{\hspace{8cm}}$$

b. Fill in Table 4–2, and plot XYZ's *AR, MR,* and *TR* curves in Figure 4–4. [Hint: Since the marginal revenue XYZ gets from the first unit sold equals the change in its total revenue as sales rise from 0 to 1, plot *MR* on the first unit sold halfway between 0 and 1; i.e., over the quantity level 0.5. Also do likewise in plotting all other *MR* figures.]

TABLE 4–2
Revenue Data of the XYZ Corporation

Quantity Sold (1)	Price (2)	Total Revenue (3)	Marginal Revenue (4)
0			
1			
2			
3			
4			
5			
6			
7			

FIGURE 4–4
Revenue Curves of the XYZ Corporation

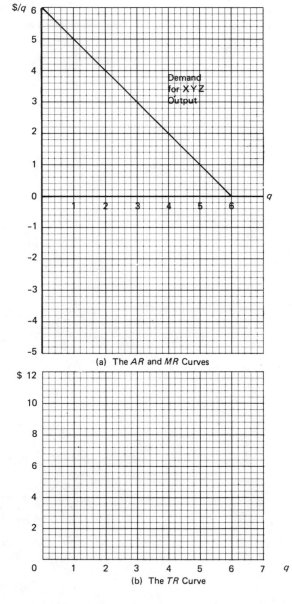

(a) The *AR* and *MR* Curves

(b) The *TR* Curve

Name _____

c. At any level of output, marginal revenue equals the slope of the total revenue curve. Therefore, as the curves you plotted in Figure 4–4 should show: whenever MR is positive, the TR curve is (rising/falling/at a maximum); at the point where MR is zero, the TR curve is (rising/falling/at a maximum); and whenever MR is negative, the TR curve is (rising/falling/at a maximum).

d. Over what range of prices is demand for XYZ's output elastic?

_____ Over what range of prices is it inelastic? _____ At what price-output combination does it display unitary elasticity?

_____ Over what range of prices is demand for XYZ's output

inelastic? _____ [Hint: Look at the MR curve or at what is happening to TR. If demand is elastic, MR will be positive and a decrease in price (which raises quantity sold) will increase TR, etc.]

7.* *a.* Prove, using calculus, that if the demand curve facing a producer is given by $q = a - bp$, then marginal revenue is given by

$$MR = \frac{a - 2q}{b}$$

[Hint: $TR = p(q) \cdot q$, where $p(q)$ denotes p as a function of q.]

b. Prove more generally that if $p = p(q)$, then

$$MR = p + q \frac{dp}{dq}$$

c. Interpret your result in (b). Is that result consistent with what you got in (a)?

8. Jack Jones is a wheat farmer. The market for wheat is perfectly competitive, and at the moment Jack can sell all the wheat he wants to at the going market price of $5.00 a bushel. Plot Jack's demand, *AR, MR,* and *TR* curves in Figure 4–5.

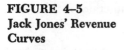

FIGURE 4–5
Jack Jones' Revenue Curves

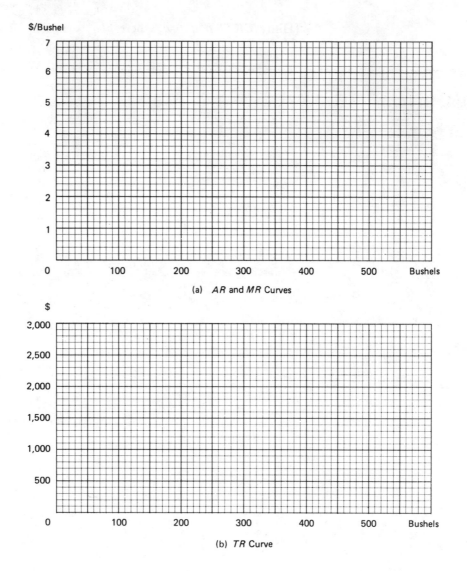

(a)   *AR* and *MR* Curves

(b) *TR* Curve

Chapter 5

Production with One Variable Input

A. DEFINITIONS AND REVIEW

1. During any short-run period a firm typically combines both fixed and variable inputs to produce output. A fixed input is one _____ _____. In contrast a variable input is one _____. A good example of a fixed input would be _____, while an example of a variable input would be _____.

2. *a.* A production function can be defined as _____ _____ _____.

   b. If a production function is characterized by fixed factor proportions, this means that _____ _____. In contrast a production function characterized by variable factor proportions is one in which _____ _____.

3. *a.* The average product of an input is defined as _____

_____. The mar-

ginal product of an input is defined as _____

_____.

b. Suppose that product q is made by combining a fixed capital input $\overline{K}$ with a variable labor input L. Then the short-run production function for q can be written as

$$q = f(\underline{\quad}, \underline{\quad})$$

and we can express the average product of labor and the marginal product of labor in symbols as follows:

$$AP_L = \underline{\quad\quad} / \underline{\quad\quad}$$

$$MP_L = \underline{\quad\quad} / \underline{\quad\quad}$$

c. As labor is added to a production process employing a fixed input, the

marginal product of labor MP_L typically first rises, then _____,

then _____, and eventually may turn _____.

d. AP_L rises as more labor is added to the production process so long as

MP_L _____ AP_L. AP_L reaches a maximum when MP_L

_____ AP_L. AP_L falls when MP_L _____ AP_L.

4. *a.* According to the *law of diminishing returns,* as the amount of the vari-

able input is increased, other inputs being held constant, _____

_____

_____.

b. The law of diminishing returns comes into play because, as the variable

input is increased, _____

_____

_____.

5. In any production process the marginal product of labor gives, at any level

of labor inputs, the _____ of the total product of labor curve. Thus,

when MP_L is rising, the TP_L curve rises at a _____ rate; and when

MP_L is negative, the TP_L curve is _____.

6.* A production function is said to be linearly homogeneous if _____

_____

_____

Another term synonymous with linear homogeneity is _____ returns to scale. When a production function is linearly homogeneous, the average and

marginal products of any input depend on the _____ in which inputs are combined, but not on the absolute magnitudes of the input quantities used (i.e., not on the scale of production).

B. MULTIPLE CHOICE

1. During the short run, a production process that uses plant and equipment is sure:

    a. to be characterized by fixed factor proportions.
    b. to require greater expenditures on fixed inputs than on variable inputs.
    c. to use no variable inputs.
    d. to use some fixed inputs.

2. To say that a production process is characterized by fixed factor proportions implies that:

    a. the production process uses only fixed inputs.
    b. the level of output cannot be changed.
    c. the firm's fixed capital stock cannot be expanded.
    d. input use will be efficient (i.e., all inputs can be fully employed) only if inputs are combined in some fixed ratio.

3. The production function facing a firm will change whenever:

    a. input prices change.
    c. relevant technology changes.
    b. the firm employs more of any variable input.
    d. the firm increases its level of output.

4. In any production process, the marginal product of labor equals:

    a. the value of total output minus the cost of the fixed capital stock.
    b. the change in total output that occurs when a one-unit change is made in labor inputs.
    c. total output divided by total labor inputs.
    d. total output produced with the given labor inputs.

5. In a production process the marginal product of labor:

    a. may, depending on the process, turn negative if many workers are employed.
    b. will, no matter how much or how little labor is used, always exceed the average product of labor.
    c. will rise as the amount of labor used is increased.
    d. will fall as the number of workers employed is increased only if the total product of labor also falls.

_____
* Asterisks denote the more difficult problems.

Name ----------

6. According to the law of diminishing returns, the *marginal product* of labor employed in a production process that also uses fixed inputs:

    a. must rise initially as labor inputs are increased.
    b. must fall eventually as labor inputs are increased.
    c. must exceed AP_L over some range of labor inputs.
    d. must exceed AP_L over all ranges of labor inputs.

7. If, as labor inputs are increased, the total product of labor curve eventually turns down, we can be sure of all of the following but:

    a. MP_L at that point is negative.
    b. AP_L at that point is negative.
    c. the law of diminishing returns has come into play.
    d. MP_L is less than AP_L.

1. *a.* The Speedy Taxi Service ("Save your gas, use ours") produces a single output, taxi rides with one fixed input (seven taxis) and one variable input (drivers). Fred Flat, owner of Speedy Taxi, notices that initially, as he hires more full-time drivers, total output goes up; but when he gets to the point where his drivers are not always fully occupied (some hours there are more drivers than taxis around), his drivers start playing poker and neglecting calls and total output falls. Fred wants to know what the marginal productivity (MP) of his drivers is. Calculate this for him and record your figures in Table 5–1. Also while you are at it, fill in the average productivity of drivers (AP) column in Table 5–1.

TABLE 5–1
Driver Productivity at Speedy Taxi

Drivers (1)	$TP_{drivers}$ (2)	$MP_{drivers}$ (3)	$AP_{drivers}$ (4)
0	0		—
1	5		
2	14		
3	27		
4	40		
5	55		
6	66		
7	70		
8	72		
9	72		
10	70		
11	60		

Name ----------

b. For Fred the total productivity of drivers equals total rides produced. Plot the *TP*, *MP*, and *AP* curves of drivers at Fred's establishment in Figure 5–1.

c. By inspecting the relationship between the curves you have drawn in Figure 5–1, it's obvious that:

(1) So long as *MP* is rising, *TP* is rising at an _____ rate.

(2) When *MP* is falling but positive, *TP* is rising at a _____ rate.

(3) When *MP* is zero, *TP* is _____.

(4) When *MP* is negative, *TP* is _____.

(5) So long as *MP* is greater than *AP*, *AP* is (rising/falling).

(6) When *MP* equals *AP*, *AP* is _____.

FIGURE 5–1
Productivity Curves
for Drivers

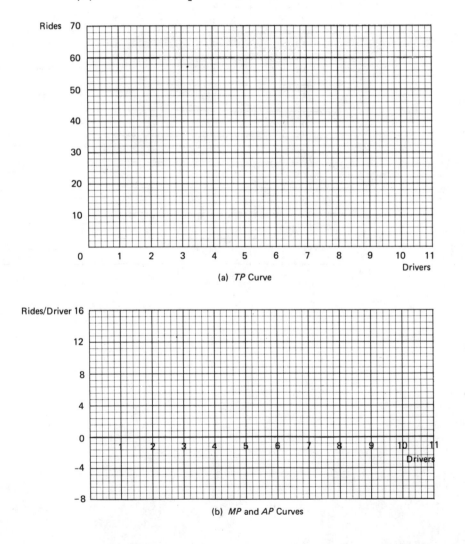

(a) *TP* Curve

(b) *MP* and *AP* Curves

2. *a.* How do you think that the *TP, MP,* and *AP* curves for drivers, which you plotted in Figure 5–1, would be affected by a doubling of Fred's taxi fleet from 7 to 14? Explain your reasoning.

_____

_____

_____

_____

_____

b. From your answer in (*a*), it's obvious that the position and shape

of the productivity curves for the *variable* input depend both on _____

_____ and on _____.

3. Figure 5–(a) shows the TP_L curve for the production of Whatnots, a new adult toy. Using this curve, sketch in Figure 5–2(b) the general shapes of the AP_L and MP_L curves for Whatnot production. [Hint: Start with the AP_L curve. At

what level of labor inputs does AP_L achieve a maximum? _____ What

is the maximum? _____ What is AP_L at $L = 16$? _____ Now add

the MP_L curve. Where does MP_L achieve a maximum? _____

Where does MP_L equal zero? _____]

Name----------------

FIGURE 5–2
Deriving the MP_L and AP_L Curves from the TP_L Curve

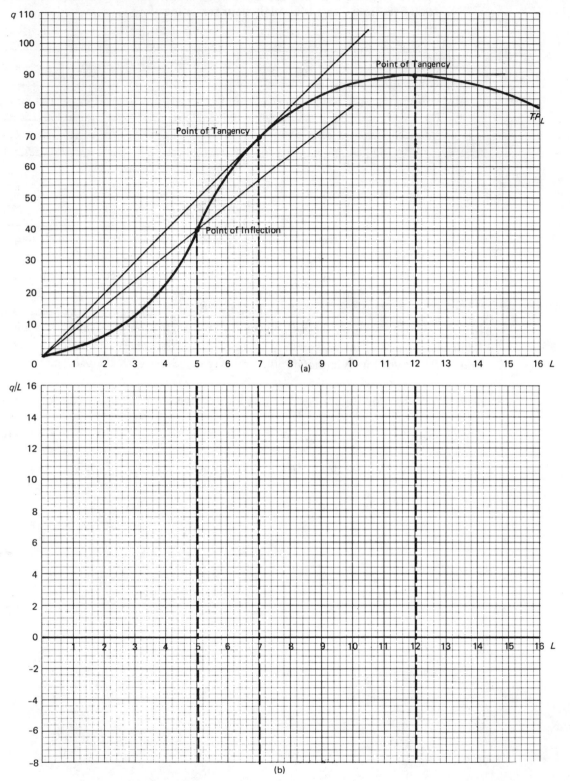

4. a. The XYZ Corp. produces output q by combining one variable input, labor L, with a fixed capital stock. Its rather unusual total product of labor curve is pictured in Figure 5–3. Using this curve sketch out in Figure 5–4 the rough shapes of the firm's marginal and average product of labor curves. [Hint: Begin by filling in Table 5–2. Also, plot MP_L figures at the midpoint of each labor interval; i.e., MP_L of the fifth worker over the point 4.5 on the labor axis.]

   b. The AP_L and MP_L curves you have plotted in Figure 5–3 do not have the usual smooth inverted-bowl shapes. Do they nevertheless conform to the general rules you have learned concerning the relationship between the shapes of the productivity curves? Specifically, is AP_L falling

   when MP_L is less than AP_L? _____ Is AP_L rising when MP_L exceeds AP_L? _____ Does MP_L equal AP_L when AP_L attains either

   a maximum or a minimum? _____ Does MP_L equal zero at the

   labor input value at which TP_L is maximized? _____

TABLE 5–2
Labor Productivity Figures for the XYZ Corporation

L (1)	$q = TP_L$ (2)	AP_L (3)	MP_L (4)
0			
1			
2			
3			
4			
5			
6			
7			
8			
9			
10			
11			
12			

Name --------------------------------

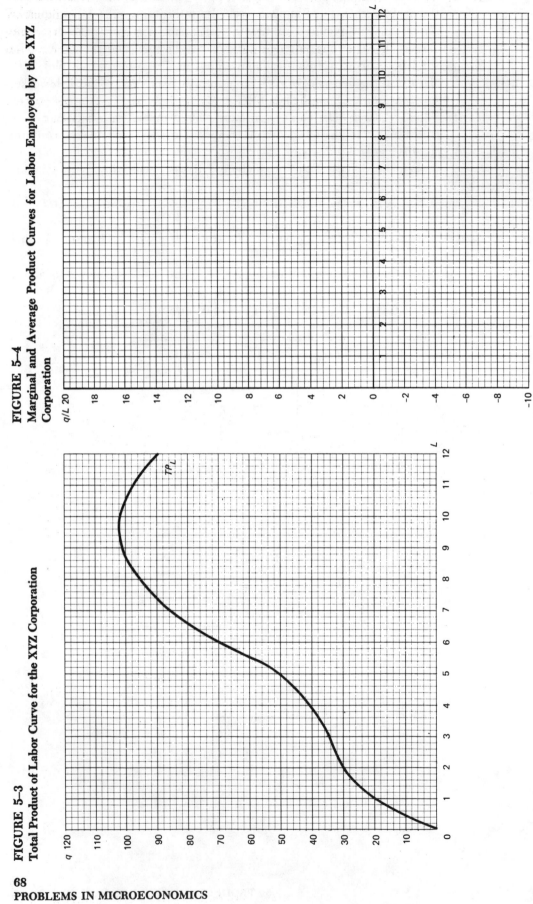

FIGURE 5-4
Marginal and Average Product Curves for Labor Employed by the XYZ Corporation

FIGURE 5-3
Total Product of Labor Curve for the XYZ Corporation

5. If doubling all inputs doubles output, a production function is said to display *constant returns to scale*; i.e., to be homogeneous of degree one. If doubling inputs more than doubles output, a production function is said to display *increasing returns to scale*. Finally, if doubling inputs less than doubles output, a production function is said to display *decreasing returns to scale*.

What sort of returns to scale are displayed by each of the production functions listed below? Note in the equations for these functions, q denotes output; L, R, and K denote respectively labor, capital, and raw material inputs.

(1) $q = 5L$ _____

(2) $q = 5\sqrt{L}$ _____

(3) $q = L^2$ _____

(4) $q = 10 L^{1/2} K^{1/2}$ _____

(5) $q = 10 L^2 K^{1/2}$ _____

(6) $q = 5 L^{1/3} K^{2/3}$ _____

(7) $q = 5 L^{1/3} K^{1/3} R^{1/3}$ _____

(8) $q = LKR$ _____

6.* The ABC Corporation has the following production function

$$q = f(L, K) = 9 L^2 K^2 - L^3 K$$

a. Assume that in the short run, ABC holds capital inputs constant at one unit; i.e., $\overline{K} = 1$. Then their *short-run* production function can be written

$$q = f(L, \overline{K}) = \underline{\hspace{3cm}}$$

b. Using calculus and the short-run production function in (a),
   (1) Derive expressions for the MP_L and AP_L curves

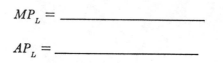

$$MP_L = \underline{\hspace{4cm}}$$

$$AP_L = \underline{\hspace{4cm}}$$

   (2) At what level of labor inputs is MP_L maximized? $\underline{\hspace{3cm}}$

   At what level of L does $MP_L = 0$? $\underline{\hspace{3cm}}$

   (3) At what level of labor inputs does AP_L reach a miximum? $\underline{\hspace{2cm}}$

   (4) Show that $MP_L = AP_L$ when AP_L achieves a maximum.

c. Repeat (a) and (b) for $\bar{K} = 2$.

a.' $q = f(L, \bar{K}) =$ _____

b.' (1) $MP_L =$ _____ (3) _____ _____

$AP_L =$ _____ (4) _____ _____

(2) _____ _____

7.* Using the general production function, $q = f(L)$, prove with calculus that, if labor is subject to diminishing returns, $MP_L = AP_L$ at the point where AP_L attains a maximum.

Chapter 6

Production and Optimal Input Proportions: Two Variable Inputs

A. DEFINITIONS AND REVIEW

1. *a.* Consider a production process in which a single output q is produced using two inputs, labor L and capital K. Each isoquant representing the relationship between output produced and inputs used in this production

   process shows _____

   _____

   _____.

   b. Plotting a number of (L, K)-isoquants yields what is called an isoquant

   map. In such a map "higher" isoquants correspond to _____
   levels of output. If a firm, by increasing inputs, moves along a ray
   from the origin outward across its isoquant map, the level of output it

   produces will _____, but the _____ in which it combines inputs will remain constant.

2. *a.* If a production process calling for capital and labor inputs is characterized by *fixed factor proportions*, every isoquant in the corresponding

   isoquant map will turn a right angle along _____.
   A firm that utilizes such a production process will employ its inputs
   efficiently (i.e., fully) only if it operates at a point on an isoquant where

   _____.

   b. If a firm operating at such a point decided to hire one more worker,

   its total output would _____ and the marginal pro-

   ductivity of the extra worker would be _____.

3. a. The *marginal rate of technical substitution* (or *rate of factor substitution*) equals at any point along an isoquant the _____ of the isoquant at that point. For the production function, $q = f(L, K)$, the marginal rate of technical substitution equals the negative of the ratio of the marginal product of labor to the _____

_____ and consequently can be written in symbols as

$$MRTS = \underline{\hspace{3cm}}$$

b. The interpretation of the marginal rate of technical substitution is that it tells us the rate at which _____

_____,

while output is held constant. Along a "normal" (i.e., convex to the origin) isoquant, $MRTS$ _____ as the firm moves rightward along the isoquant.

c. A firm would never operate at a point along an isoquant where the slope of that curve was positive because at such a point _____

_____

_____.

4. a. An isocost line is defined as _____

_____.

For a firm that spends some fixed amount $\bar{c}$ on capital and labor inputs, costing r and w respectively, we can write out the isocost line in symbols as follows:

$$\bar{c} = \underline{\hspace{3cm}}$$

b. In this expression _____, _____, and _____ are constants, while _____ and _____ are variables.

c. If we plot the above isocost line with K on the vertical axis and L on the horizontal axis, the vertical intercept of the line will be _____. This makes intuitive sense because the value of this intercept tells us

_____

_____.

Similarly, the horizontal intercept will be _____, which makes

intuitive sense because this intercept tells us _____

_____.

d. The slope of our isocost line equals _____. The fact that this

slope is negative makes sense because _____

_____.

Also the fact that the slope depends on the prices of K and L makes

sense because _____

_____

_____.

e. One can plot a family of isocost lines for a given set of input prices. As one moves from lower to higher isocost lines within this family, $\bar{c}$

_____, but the slope of the isocost lines (does/does not) change.

5. a. To minimize the cost of producing a given level of output $\bar{q}$, a firm should operate on the $\bar{q}$-isoquant at a point where this isoquant is

tangent to _____. The reason is that

_____

_____.

b. To maximize the amount of output it gets from spending a fixed amount $\bar{c}$ on inputs, a firm should operate on the $\bar{c}$-isocost line at a point

where this line is tangent to _____. The reason is that

_____

_____

_____.

Name _____

c. From these observations it is obvious that the condition for cost minimization can be derived either by thinking of the firm as maximizing output for a given level of input expenditures *or* as minimizing input expenditures for a given level of output. In symbols the condition for cost minimization can be written:

_____

6. A rise in the price of labor (no change in the price of capital), will (assuming labor inputs are measured on the horizontal axis), tend to make the firm's isocost

lines _____ in slope. In response to this change in slope, a cost-

minimizing firm would tend to substitute _____ for _____.

7. A firm's expansion path is the locus of all points of tangency between

_____.

The expansion path shows what input combinations a cost-minimizing firm would

use to produce _____. A firm's expansion path will be a

straight line if its production function is _____.

8. Ridge lines through the production function define the economic region of production. At any point along a ridge line the marginal product of the input

with the lowest marginal product must equal _____. At points beyond

the ridge line, the marginal product of this input will be _____. A cost-minimizing firm would never operate at a point beyond one of its ridge lines

because _____.

B. MULTIPLE CHOICE

1. An isoquant is:

a. an equal input contour.
b. an equal output contour.
c. a constant MP_L contour.
d. a constant AP_L contour.

2. If a firm moves from one point on an isoquant to another point on the same isoquant, all of the following will occur except:

    a. the level of output will change.
    b. the ratio in which inputs are combined will change.
    c. the marginal productivities of inputs used will change.
    d. the rate of technical substitution between inputs used will change.

3. Firm X combines capital and labor to produce output according to a fixed-factor-proportions production function. Currently Firm X is operating at a point where the marginal productivity of labor is zero; therefore the marginal productivity of capital:

a. must also be zero.
b. must be positive.
c. must be negative
d. may be any of the above.

4. If a firm moves rightward along an isoquant by substituting labor for capital, its rate of technical substitution will:

a. increase.   c. remained unchanged.
b. decrease.   d. turn negative.

5. If a firm, by substituting labor for capital, moves from a point on an isoquant where the isoquant is negatively sloped to a point where the isoquant is positively sloped, we can be sure that at the latter point:

a. the marginal productivity of both inputs is negative.
b. the marginal productivity of labor is zero.
c. the marginal productivity of labor is negative.
d. the marginal productivity of capital is negative.

6. Firm X buys two inputs, labor and capital. A rise in the price of labor will:

a. alter the firm's production function.
b. change the intercept on the capital axis of the firm's isocost lines.
c. alter the slope of the firm's isocost lines.
d. cause an equal percentage change in the price of capital.

7. Firm X wants to produce the output level $\bar{q}$ with the least costly bundle of capital and labor inputs possible. To determine which bundle this is, we need to know all of the following but:

a. the marginal rate of technical transformation at all points along the $\bar{q}$-isoquant.
b. the current price of labor.
c. the current price at which the firm sells output.
d. the current price of capital.

8. To minimize the cost of producing a fixed level of output, a firm should operate at a point:

a. along one of its ridge lines.
b. where the marginal product of labor is maximized.
c. where the marginal product of both labor and capital are maximized.
d. along its expansion path.

Name

C. PROBLEMS

1. *a.* The Jazzy Gem Company produces artificial rubies by combining labor and raw materials. Table 6–1 gives data from their production function. Use this data to plot in Figure 6–1 the isoquant map corresponding to Jazzy Gem's production function.

TABLE 6–1
Selected Data from Jazzy Gem's Production Function

Labor L	Raw Materials R	Output q	Labor L	Raw Materials R	Output q
1	6	10	3	6	40
1.5	5	10	3.5	5	40
2.5	3.5	10	4	4	40
4	2	10	5	3	40
1.5	7	20	3	7	50
2.5	5	20	4	5	50
4	3	20	5	4	50
5	2	20	4	7	60
2	7	30	5.5	5	60
3	5	30	7	5	66
4	3.5	30	5	7	66
6	2	30	6	7	70

FIGURE 6–1
Jazzy Gem's Isoquant Map

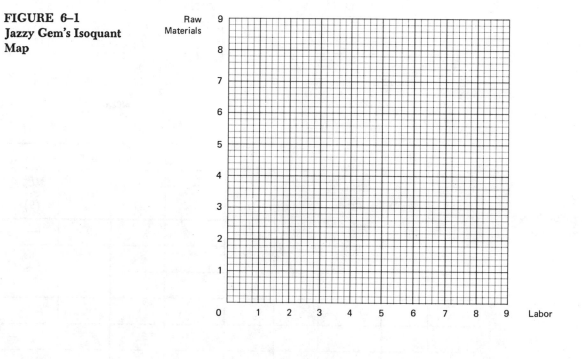

Name

b. The president of Jazzy Gem wants to know something about the marginal productivity (MP) of his inputs. Plot for him in Figures 6–2(a) and (b):

    (1) the MP_L curve when raw material inputs are held constant at 5 units (i.e., for $\bar{R} = 5$),

    (2) the MP_L curve when $\bar{R} = 7$, and

    (3) the MP_R curve when $\bar{L} = 4$.

[Hint: Recall that $MP_L = \Delta q/\Delta L$ and $MP_R = \Delta q/\Delta R$. *Using these* definitions, fill in Table 6–2. Then plot each MP_L figure over the *midpoint* between the two L values you used in calculating ΔL. Also do the same for MP_R. Note you do this because the MP figures you get are *averages* over an interval of input values.]

Is Jazzy Gem's production function characterized by *diminishing returns*

to labor? _____ to raw materials? _____

FIGURE 6–2
Marginal Productivity Curves

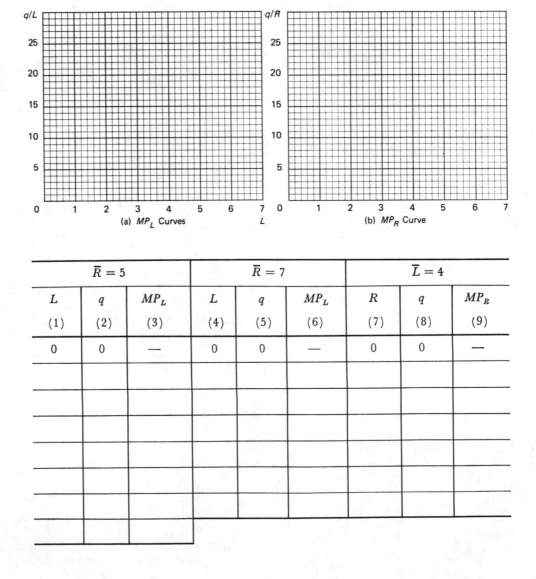

(a) MP_L Curves   (b) MP_R Curve

TABLE 6–2
Marginal Productivity Data for Jazzy Gem

$\bar{R} = 5$			$\bar{R} = 7$			$\bar{L} = 4$		
L	q	MP_L	L	q	MP_L	R	q	MP_R
(1)	(2)	(3)	(4)	(5)	(6)	(7)	(8)	(9)
0	0	—	0	0	—	0	0	—

2. The Mighty Motor Company produces motorcycles using two inputs, capital K and labor L. Their short-run production function can be written in symbols as follows:

$$q = q(L, K)$$

Speed Smith, the company engineer has, through careful investigation of the firm's production function, found that labor inputs are subject in motorcycle production to diminishing returns.

    a. What does it mean for an input to be subject to diminishing returns?

_____

_____

_____

_____

    b. Using an isoquant map, illustrate in Figure 6–3 just what Speed's discovery means; i.e., draw an isoquant map that displays diminishing returns to labor.

FIGURE 6–3
Isoquant Map Displaying Diminishing Returns to Labor

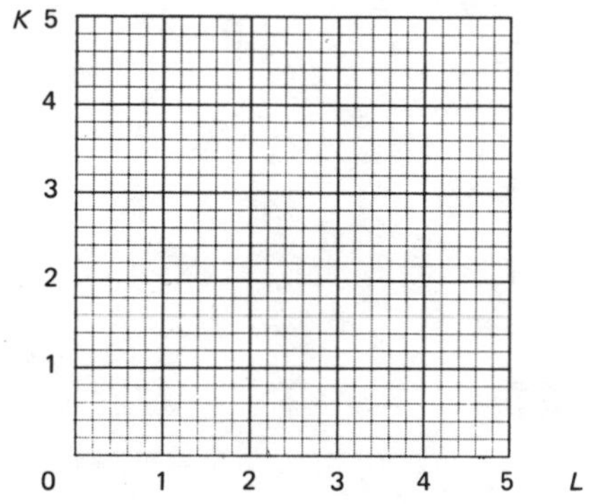

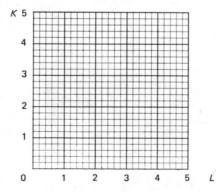

3. Gismos are made with two inputs, laborers and capital. The production function for gismos is characterized by increasing returns to scale but diminishing returns to labor. Draw in Figure 6–4 an isoquant map that might illustrate this production function; i.e., an isoquant map that you show to display simultaneously the above two properties.

FIGURE 6–4
An Isoquant Map Displaying Increasing Returns to Scale and Diminishing Returns to Labor

Name

4. The Russell Raquet Company makes tennis racquets with two variable inputs, raw materials (R) and labor (L). Their production function yields the isoquant map shown in Figure 6–5.

a. Using this map, determine what happens to MP_L as labor is increased when raw material inputs are held constant at one unit. Determine also what happens to MP_R as raw material inputs are increased when labor inputs are held constant at one unit. Record your answers in Table 6–3.

Is labor subject to diminishing returns in racquet production? _____

What about capital? _____

FIGURE 6–5
Russel Raquet's Isoquant Map

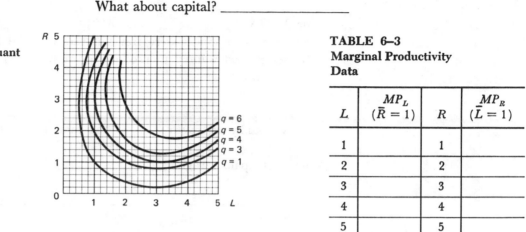

TABLE 6–3
Marginal Productivity Data

L	MP_L $(\bar{R} = 1)$	R	MP_R $(\bar{L} = 1)$
1		1	
2		2	
3		3	
4		4	
5		5	

b. The negative of the slope of an isoquant is called the marginal rate of technical substitution $(MRTS)$, or more simply the rate of factor substitution (RFS). For Russel Raquet, $MRTS$ at any point along one of its isoquants is given by the expression

$$MRTS = MP_L/MP_R$$

From this expression, it is easily determined that *along the isoquant labeled $\bar{q} = 1$:*

(1) $MP_L > 0$ when $L <$ _____ ;

(2) $MP_L = 0$ when $L =$ _____ ; and

(3) $MP_L < 0$ when $L >$ _____ .

Also, *along the isoquant $\bar{q} = 1$:*

(4) $MP_R > 0$ when $R <$ _____ ;

(5) $MP_R = 0$ when $R =$ _____ ; and

(6) $MP_R < 0$ when $R >$ _____ .

c. So long as *MRTS* is decreasing, the isoquant is _____

sloped, but where *MRTS* is increasing the isoquant slope is _____ .

d. No cost-minimizing firm will increase its employment of a variable input to the point the marginal product of that input is negative. Bearing this in mind, sketch in Figure 6–5 *ridge lines;* i.e., lines that divide points on the isoquant map where a cost-minimizing firm might operate from those where it would never operate. At every point through which your

ridge lines pass *either MRTS* = _____ and MP_L = _____

or MRTS = _____ and MP_R = _____ .

e. Suppose labor inputs were free but raw material inputs were not. If Russel Raquet wanted to produce an output level of 5, where would they operate?

_____

How would your answer change if raw material inputs were free but labor

had to be paid a wage? _____

_____

5. *a.* Widgets are made with just two inputs, capital and labor. The widget production function is characterized by constant returns to scale, by diminishing returns to labor, and by fixed factor proportions. Draw in Figure 6–6 an isoquant map that might illustrate this production function (i.e., one that you demonstrate displays each of the above properties).

FIGURE 6–6
The Widget Production Function

K

L

b. Assume that capital inputs are held constant at some specific fixed levels, and draw in Figure 6–7 the corresponding *MP, AP,* and *TP* curves for labor employed in widget production.

FIGURE· 6–7
The *TP, MP,* and *AP* Curves for Labor Employed in Widget Production

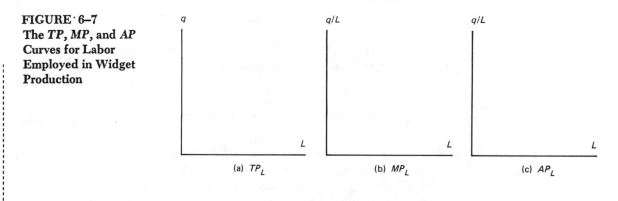

(a) *TP*$_L$ (b) *MP*$_L$ (c) *AP*$_L$

Name

6.* *a.* The XYZ Corporation has the following production function:

$$q = 9L^{2/3}K^{1/3}$$

What sort of returns to scale characterize this production function?

_____ Derive expressions for MP_L and MP_K:

$$MP_L = \text{\underline{\hspace{4cm}}}$$

$$MP_K = \text{\underline{\hspace{4cm}}}$$

b. Prove, using calculus, a result suggested by your answer in (a), namely that, if a firm has a linearly homogeneous (i.e., constant returns to scale) production function of the following sort:

$$f(\lambda L, \lambda K) = \lambda f(L, K)$$

then the marginal product of labor will depend solely on the proportion in which capital and labor are combined; i.e.,

$$f_1(L, K) = f_1(L/K, 1) = g(L/K)$$

where $f_1 = MP_L$. Does a similar result hold for MP_K? _____

---

* Asterisks denote the more difficult problems.

7. Ersatz Ltd. manufactures fake gold by combining two inputs, labor (L) and raw materials (R), whose prices are w and v respectively.

a. Table 6–4 gives three sets of input prices and total expenditures on inputs ($\bar{c}$). Write out the equations of the isocost lines corresponding to each of these sets:

(1) _____

(2) _____

(3) _____

Plot the isocost lines (1), (2), and (3) in Figure 6–8(a). A comparison of these lines shows that increasing the total amount spent on inputs (no change in input prices), shifts the isocost line _____

but has _____ effect on its slope.

TABLE 6–4
Sets of Input Prices and Total Expenditures on Inputs

Case	w	v	$\bar{c}$
1	$2	$4	$ 4
2	2	4	12
3	2	4	20

FIGURE 6–8
Isocost Lines

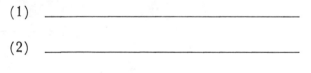

(a) Isocost Lines for Different Levels of Expenditure

(b) Isocost Lines for Different Prices of R

b. Table 6–5 gives four new sets of input prices and total expenditures on inputs ($\bar{c}$). Write out the equations of the isocost lines corresponding to each of these sets:

(1) _____

(2) _____

(3) _____

(4) _____

Plot the isocost lines (1)–(4) in Figure 6–8(b). A comparison of these lines shows that increasing the price of raw materials (no change in w or $\bar{c}$) does what to each of the following: the labor-axis intercept?

_____ the slope of the isocost line? _____

the vertical intercept? _____

TABLE 6–5
Sets of Input Prices and Total Expenditures on Inputs

Case	w	v	$\bar{c}$
1	$2	2	20
2	2	4	20
3	2	10	20
4	2	20	20

8. Smith runs a lawn mowing service using labor (L) and lawn mowers (M). Figure 6–9 shows for Smith four isocost lines (each corresponding to a different level of expenditure on inputs) and four isoquants. Smith wonders how to go about minimizing costs: should he try to produce a given output level at minimum cost *or* should he strive to get the most output possible out of a given level of expenditures on inputs. Explain to Smith the answer to his dilemma. [Hint: If Smith wanted to produce $q = 15$ at minimum cost, where would he operate? If he wanted to spend the amount on inputs corresponding to the isocost line cc and get the maximum output possible where would he operate?]

_____

_____

_____

_____

FIGURE 6–9
Four of Smith's Isocost Lines and Four Isoquants

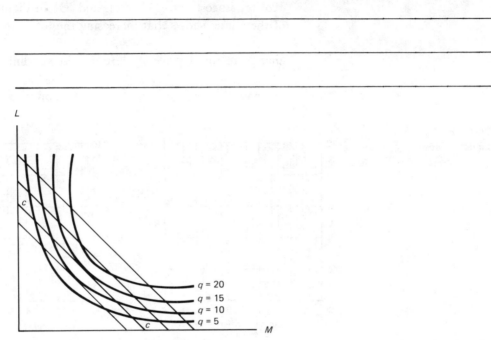

9. Figure 6–10 pictures an isoquant that is concave to the origin. Show that for such an isoquant, the point of tangency with an isocost curve will represent a point of *maximum* cost relative to all other points along the isoquant. Show also that cost minimization in that situation calls for a "corner solution"; i.e., use of just *one* input.

FIGURE 6–10
A Concave Isoquant

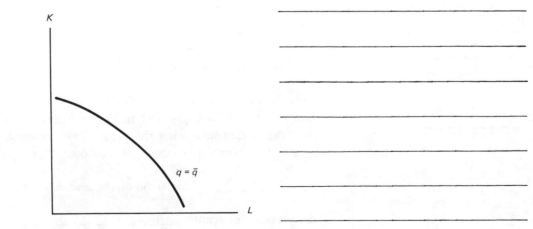

_____

_____

_____

_____

_____

_____

_____

10. The president of the JD Corporation tells you that cost minimization for him has a simple solution. He uses just two inputs x_1 and x_2 and he finds that regardless of input prices or the quantity of output produced, cost minimization always calls for him to use equal amounts of both inputs. What sort of shape must his (x_1, x_2)-isoquant map have? To answer, draw an appropriate diagram.

FIGURE 6–11
An Isoquant Map

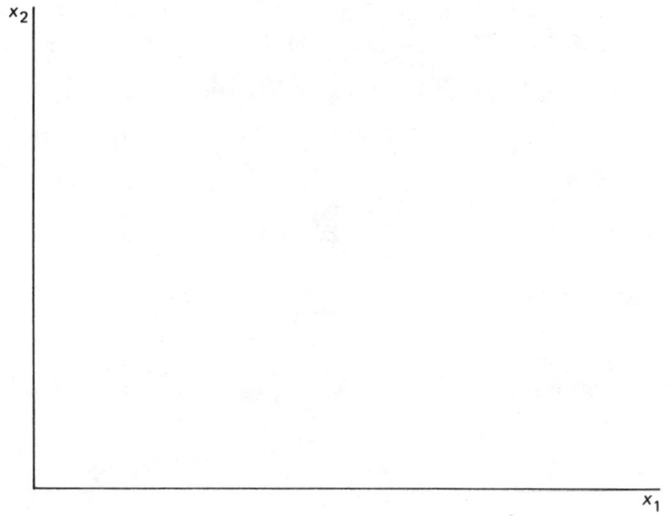

x_2

x_1

11. The MNOP Company's production function yields the isoquant map shown in Figure 6–12.

    a. What does the isoquant map in Figure 6–12 imply about the relation-

ship between the two inputs, x_1 and x_2? _____

    b. What sort of returns to scale does the isoquant map in Figure 6–12

display? _____Is input x_1 subject to diminishing re-

turns? _____ What about x_2?_____

    c. Show, by adding appropriate isocost lines to Figure 6–12, that if the price of x_1 exceeds the price of x_2, MNOP will minimize the cost of producing any output level by using just one input, x_2.

FIGURE 6–12
MNOP's Isoquant Map

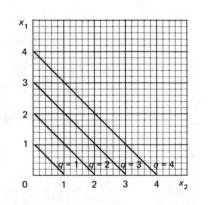

Chapter 7

The Theory of Cost

Name _____

A. DEFINITIONS AND REVIEW

1. In an economy that produces goods q_1 and q_2, the opportunity cost of producing one more unit of q_1 equals _____

_____

2. *a.* A producer is concerned with private costs of production. These include *explicit* and *implicit* costs. Explicit costs are _____

_____

_____

In contrast implicit costs equal _____

_____

b. The layman typically thinks of profit as the difference between a firm's total revenue and its explicit costs. To an economist, profit (which he sometimes calls "pure economic profit") is defined as the difference between a firm's total revenue and its _____.

3. *a.* During any short-run period a firm incurs certain total costs (TC), which can be divided into fixed and variable costs. Fixed costs (FC)

    equal _____ .

    Variable costs (VC) on the other hand are defined as _____

    _____ .

    b. Reducing short-run output will (raise/lower/not change) variable costs but (raise/lower/not change) fixed costs.

4. Besides fixed and variable costs, there are several other important cost concepts, which are defined as follows:

Average fixed cost (AFC) equals _____ ,

average variable cost (AVC) equals _____

_____ , average total cost (ATC), equals _____

_____ , and marginal cost (MC) equals _____

_____ .

5. *a.* A firm's short-run cost curves show the relationship between the above measures of cost and the firm's total output. As output is increased,

    marginal cost may first fall, but eventually it will begin to _____ .

    b. Marginal cost equals the _____ of the firm's TC curve. Thus

    when MC is falling, the TC curve is rising at a _____ rate;

    while when MC is rising, the TC curve is rising at an _____ rate.

    c. If the MC curve first falls and then rises, the AVC curve will _____

    _____ . Also the MC curve will cut the

    AVC curve at the point on the latter curve where it _____ .

    d. An intuitive explanation for this is that _____

    _____

    _____

    _____

    _____ .

6. *a.* For a firm the contrast between the short run and the long run is that

   in the short run _____

   while in the long run _____.

   b. The firm's long-run average cost (*LAC*) curve shows the relationship

   between _____

   _____

   _____.

   c. If we plot the firm's *LAC* curve and a number of its short-run average
   cost (*SAC*) curves, we find that each *SAC* curve (cuts/is tangent to)

   the *LAC* curve; in other words the _____ curve is an envelope

   curve to the _____ curves.

   d. The long-run marginal cost (*LMC*) curve is a companion curve to the
   LAC curve. It cuts the latter curve at the point where the *LAC* curve

   _____. If we compare *LMC* with the short-run
   marginal cost (*SMC*) associated with a particular *SAC* curve, we find
   that *SMC* exceeds *LMC* at all output levels beyond the one at which

   the *SAC* curve in question _____.

7. If we draw the *LAC* curve with a bowl or U shape, we are implicitly assuming that the production function underlying this cost curve is characterized

   first by _____ returns to scale and then by _____ re-
   turns to scale. In contrast the implicit assumption about the production function that we make when we draw the *SAC* curve with a bowl shape is that

   _____

   _____

   _____.

8. To construct the firm's long-run cost curves we need to know _____

   and _____. From this it follows that a *shift* in the firm's long-run cost

   curves must result from a change in either _____ or _____. In
   contrast the firm's short-run cost curves may shift from period to period as a
   result not only of changes of the above two variables, but also as a result of

   a change in the firm's _____.

Name

1. Jones works full-time running a grocery store in which he has invested $25,000. Last year his total revenues were $100,000 and he paid $85,000 for the goods he sold, electricity, and other *explicit* cost items. An economist would calculate his profits for the year as:

   a. $15,000.
   b. $15,000 minus the opportunity cost (i.e., *implicit* cost) he incurred by working full-time in the store.
   c. $15,000 minus the opportunity cost he incurred by tying up $25,000 of capital in the store.
   d. $15,000 minus the opportunity costs he incurred both for his labor and for the capital he had invested in the store.

2. If a firm produces zero output during the short-run, all of the following will be true except:

   a. profits will be zero.
   b. variable costs will be zero.
   c. fixed costs will be positive.
   d. profits will be negative.

3. Increasing short-run output will always lower:

   a. average variable cost.
   b. average total cost.
   c. average fixed cost.
   d. marginal cost.

4. Economists assume that, as short-run output is expanded, marginal cost will eventually begin to rise because:

   a. input prices will rise.
   b. more production means greater fixed costs.
   c. the variable inputs will be subject to diminishing returns because of the existence of fixed inputs.
   d. more production means the firm will get a lower price for its output.

5. The point on any one of the firm's short-run average cost curves where SAC is minimized is *also* a point on the long-run average cost curve:

   a. always.
   b. when LAC is falling.
   c. when LAC is rising.
   d. only at the output level at which LAC is minimized.

6. The long-run total cost curve slopes upward because:

   a. in the long run all inputs are subject to diminishing returns.
   b. all production functions are characterized by decreasing returns to scale.
   c. in any normal production function, higher isoquants correspond to higher levels of output.
   d. as output expands, management gets less efficient.

7. The condition, $LAC = SAC = LMC = SMC$, holds:

   a. at the point on each SAC curve where that curve is tangent to the LAC curve.
   b. at the point on each SAC curve where that curve achieves a minimum.
   c. at the point on the LAC curve where that curve attains a minimum.
   d. nowhere.

8. It is assumed that the *LMC* curve will eventually turn upward because:

    a. labor is subject to diminishing returns.
    b. capital is subject to diminishing returns.
    c. the production function is characterized by decreasing returns to scale at high levels of output.
    d. expanding output eventually forces up input prices.

9. Changing a firm's capital stock will shift:

    a. its *SAC* and *LAC* curves.   *c.* its *LAC* and *LMC* curves.
    b. its *SMC* and *SAC* curves.   *d.* its *SMC* and *LMC* curves.

C. PROBLEMS

1. For a firm that produces output q using both fixed and variable inputs, the key cost measures can be expressed as follows (fill in the blanks):

    a. $TC =$ _____ $+ FC$

    b. $AVC =$ _____ / _____

    c. $AFC =$ _____ / _____

    d. $ATC = AVC +$ _____ $=$ _____ / _____ $+$ _____ / _____

    e. $MC = \Delta TC /$ _____ $=$ _____ / _____

    f. $MC =$ the slope of the _____ and _____ curves.

2. Smith, the financial vice president of the Sparkle Diamond Company, would like to know something about the structure of the firm's costs, so he sent Table 7–1 down to the accounting department. But all the information they could give him was the few figures recorded in the table. Help Smith out and fill in the rest of the table.

TABLE 7–1
Cost Data, Sparkle Diamond Company

Output	FC	VC	TC	AVC	AFC	ATC	MC
0				—	—	—	
							16
1							
							13
2							
							12
3							
							11
4	5						
							10
5							
							10
6							
							11
7							
							13
8							
							17
9							
							24
10							

Name _____

3. The Johnson Floorwaxing Company produces output (waxed kitchen floors) using one fixed input (a big waxing machine) and one variable input (labor). Figure 7–1(a) shows the company's total product of labor (TP_L) curve. Assume that the fixed costs Johnson incurs in connection with owning its waxing machine equal $20 and that labor costs $10 per unit. Derive and plot Johnson's Floorwaxing Company's TC curve in Figure 7–1(b). [Hint: Start by filling in Table 7–2.]

TABLE 7–2
Johnson's Floorwaxing Company: Cost Data

L	q	VC	FC	TC
0				
1				
1.5				
2				
3				
4				
5				

FIGURE 7–1
Johnson Floorwaxing Company's TP_L and TC Curves

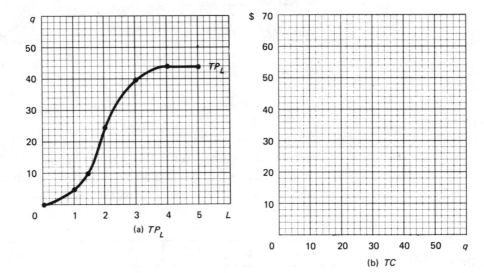

(a) TP_L

(b) TC

4. The Biological Control Company (Fight "bad" bugs with "good" ones) produces a single output, packages of praying mantis eggs, with one piece of capital equipment, a large refrigerator for storing eggs, and two variable inputs, labor and packaging. The fixed costs associated with their refrigerator equal $4. The price of labor is $2 an hour, the price of packaging $2 a pound. Using the isoquant map and isocost curves pictured in Figure 7–2, derive and plot in Figure 7–3 Biological Control's cost curves. [Hint: Sketch Biological Control Company's expansion path, *EE*, in Figure 7–2. Then fill in Table 7–3.]

FIGURE 7–2
Isoquants and Isocost Lines for Praying Mantis Egg Production

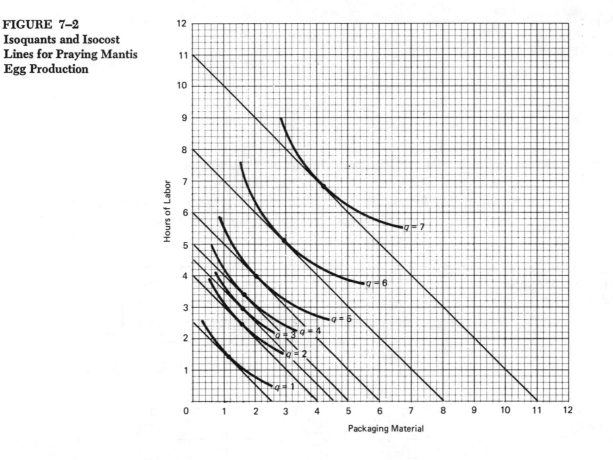

TABLE 7–3
Cost Data for Biological Control

Output	FC	VC	TC	ATC	MC
0				—	
1					
2					
3					
4					
5					
6					
7					

FIGURE 7–3
Biological Control's Cost Curves

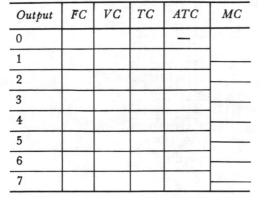

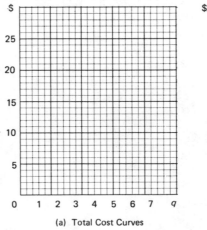

(a) Total Cost Curves

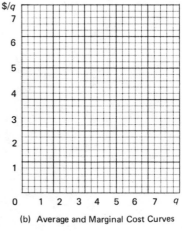

(b) Average and Marginal Cost Curves

5. The B&B Company produces a famous afterdinner drink by combining benedictine and brandy in *equal* proportions. Currently the cost of the company's fixed capital stock plus workers (workers get a guaranteed annual wage and are consequently a fixed cost) equals $20,000. Brandy costs $10 a gallon and benedictine $20 a ballon.

    a. Plot B&B's short-run production function in Figure 7–4. [Hint: Draw isoquants for $\bar{q} = 500$, $\bar{q} = 1,000$, and $\bar{q} = 1,500$ gallons, assuming capital stock and labor are adequate for these levels of output.]

FIGURE 7–4
B&B Short-Run
Production Function

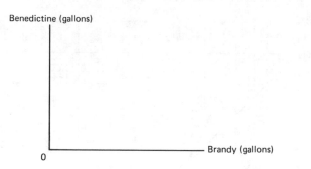

    b. Plot B&B's *FC, TC, AVC, MC,* and *ATC* curves in Figure 7–5(a) and (b). [Hint: Add appropriate isocost lines to Figure 7–4, and fill in Table 7–4.]

TABLE 7–4
Short-Run Cost Data for the B&B Company

q (gallons)	FC	VC	TC	AVC	ATC	MC
0				—	—	
500						
1,000						
1,500						

FIGURE 7–5
B&B's Short-Run Cost Curves

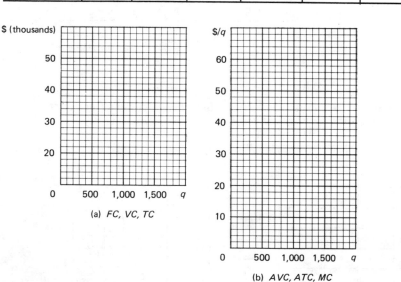

(a) *FC, VC, TC*

(b) *AVC, ATC, MC*

6. Consider a cost-minimizing firm whose position is similar to that of the Biological Control Company (problem 4 in this Chapter). Our new firm combines a fixed input with two variable inputs, which it purchases at fixed prices, to produce—according to a "normal" production function—some output, q. What effects, *if any*, would each of the following changes have on the firm's production function, isoquant lines, expansion path, and on its TC, FC, AVC, and MC curves? Distinguish between shifts of and movements along curves.

a. An increase in the price of one variable input.

_____

_____

_____

_____

_____

_____

b. Discovery of a more efficient production technique.

_____

_____

_____

_____

_____

_____

c. An increase in total output.

_____

_____

_____

_____

_____

_____

_____

Name ----------

7. *a.* Recall the Jazzy Gem Company of problem 1, Chapter 6. They want to produce 30 units of output at *minimum* cost. If labor costs $10/unit and raw materials $10/unit, roughly what quantities of labor and raw materials should they hire? $L = $ _____, $R = $ _____.

What will their total cost be approximately? _____
[Hint: Add approximate isocost lines to Figure 6–1, repeated below.]

FIGURE 6–1
Jazzy Gem's Isoquant Map

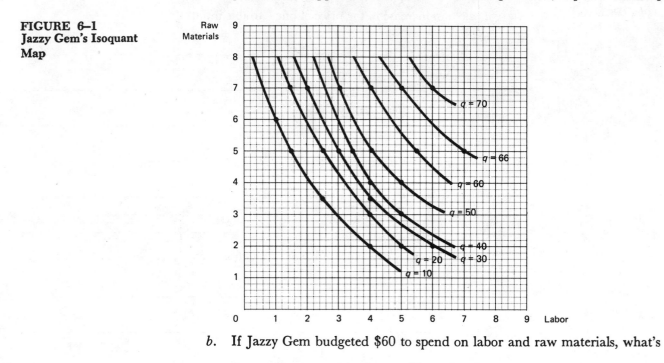

b. If Jazzy Gem budgeted $60 to spend on labor and raw materials, what's the *maximum* output they could produce? _____

8. Figure 7–6 shows the *FC, MC, AVC,* and *AFC* curves for the production of "cold pants," a new midi-length type of ladies' bloomers. Using these curves, sketch in Figure 7–6 the general shape of the *TC* curve. Be sure the shape of your *TC* curve is consistent with that of the other cost curves at q^i, q^{ii}, q^{iii}, q^{iv}.

FIGURE 7–6
Deriving the *TC* Curve from the *MC, AVC, AFC,* and *FC* Curves

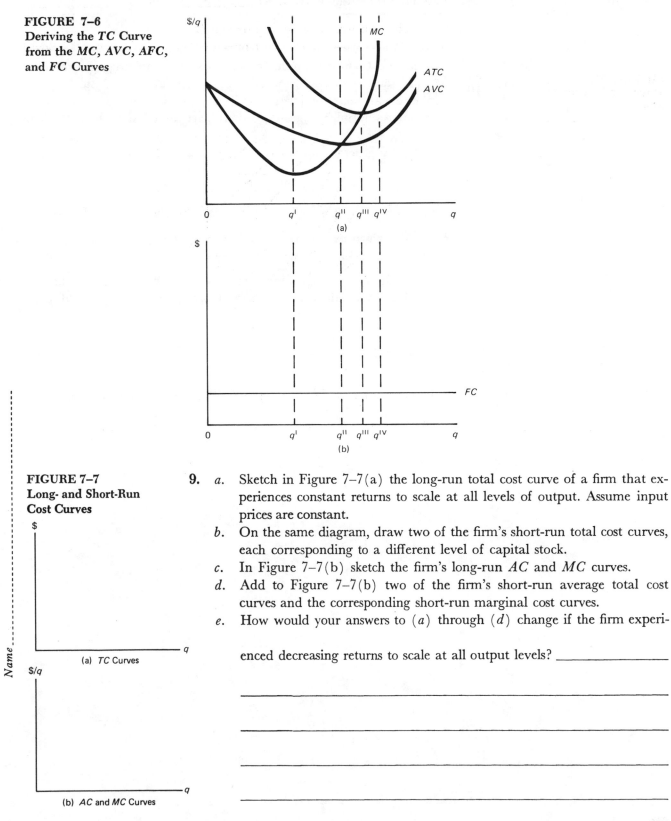

FIGURE 7–7
Long- and Short-Run Cost Curves

(a) *TC* Curves

(b) *AC* and *MC* Curves

9. *a.* Sketch in Figure 7–7(a) the long-run total cost curve of a firm that experiences constant returns to scale at all levels of output. Assume input prices are constant.

b. On the same diagram, draw two of the firm's short-run total cost curves, each corresponding to a different level of capital stock.

c. In Figure 7–7(b) sketch the firm's long-run *AC* and *MC* curves.

d. Add to Figure 7–7(b) two of the firm's short-run average total cost curves and the corresponding short-run marginal cost curves.

e. How would your answers to (*a*) through (*d*) change if the firm experienced decreasing returns to scale at all output levels? _____

_____

_____

_____

_____

If it experienced increasing returns to scale at all output levels?

_____

_____

_____

10.* The Hoolahoop Company produces play toys by combining two variable inputs, labor (L) and plastic (P), with one fixed input, capital stock $(\overline{K})$. Hoolahoop pays $2 an hour for labor and $1 for plastic; the fixed costs (including depreciation and interest) associated with its capital stock total $150 a period.

    a. Write out a general equation for Hoolahoop's total costs.

$$TC = \underline{\hspace{2cm}} + \underline{\hspace{2cm}} + \underline{\hspace{2cm}}$$

    b. Suppose Hoolahoop's short-run production function is given by the expression

$$q = h(L, P, \overline{K}) = 2\,LP$$

where each unit of q represents a thousand plastic toys. Using calculus, determine the minimum total cost at which Hoolahoop could produce 100,000 rubber bands? _____

To achieve minimum cost, what quantities of labor and plastic would

Hoolahoop have to use? _____

Chapter 8

Theory of Price in Perfectly Competitive Markets

A. DEFINITIONS AND REVIEW

1. For a market to be perfectly competitive, a number of conditions must hold.

    a. Buyers must be so numerous that no one of them can through his actions alone perceptibly influence market price, this condition guarantees that buyers will behave as price (setters/takers).

    b. Sellers too must be so numerous that they behave as price _____.

    c. The product sold must be _____.

    d. All buyers and sellers in the market must possess _____ knowledge concerning price and the product sold.

2. In a perfectly competitive market, the equilibrium price p^0 must be the one at which the market demand and supply curves intersect because:

    a. At any price above p^0, market demand would _____ market supply and there would exist a group of unsatisfied sellers whose actions

    would tend to _____ market price.

    b. At any price below p^0, market demand would _____ market supply and there would exist a group of unsatisfied buyers whose actions

    tend to _____ market price.

Name ....

3. *a.* In a perfectly competitive market, the market demand curve is the horizontal sum of _____

_____.

b. The market demand curve is assumed to slope downward because

_____

_____

_____.

c. In contrast, the demand curve facing an individual seller in a perfectly competitive market has an _____ slope; i.e., is _____. The reason for this contrast is that _____

_____

_____

_____.

4. *a.* Any producer selling in a *perfectly competitive* market will maximize profits by adjusting his output to the level at which his marginal cost just equals his marginal _____, which in turn equals

_____.

b. If the producer raised his output above the level that equated *MC* with market price, his marginal cost over the output range in question would be _____ his marginal revenue, and raising output would consequently cause total costs to rise _____ total revenue with the result that profits would _____.

c. Alternatively, if the producer cut his output below the level that equated *MC* with market price, his marginal revenue over the output range in question would be _____ his marginal cost; and cutting output would consequently cause total revenue to fall _____ total cost with the result that profits would _____.

5. *a.* The perfect competitor maximizes profits by operating at the output level at which the vertical distance between his *TR* and _____ curves is greatest. This condition is equivalent to saying that he maximizes profits by operating at the point where *MC* equals market price because the output level at which the vertical distance between the *TR* and *TC* curves is greatest is certain to be the one at which the two curves have the same _____; and the slope of the *TC* curve equals _____ while the slope of the *TR* curve equals _____.

b. If for a perfect competitor, there are two different levels of output at which marginal cost equals market price, one of these output levels must represent a point of _____ while the other will represent a point of _____.

6. *a.* The short-run supply curve of a perfectly competitive firm is identical with its _____ curve for all prices above the level at which the *MC* curve intersects the _____ curve.

b. At prices below this level, the firm would supply _____ output; in this low range of prices the firm's supply curve lies along the _____ axis.

c. The reason the firm chooses to shut down in the short run when price falls below minimum _____ is that, if the firm operated at such a low price, its *TR* would be less than _____ and its losses would be greater than the amount to which the firm could reduce its losses by ceasing production; i.e., greater than _____.

7. To attain long-run equilibrium, a perfectly competitive firm will adjust its capital stock and output so that it operates at a point where the condition

$$p = \text{_____} = \text{_____}$$

holds. At the firm's point of long-run equilibrium, the relationship between the firm's short-run total average cost and long-run average cost is that *LAC* _____ *SAC*.

8. *a.* Consider a perfectly competitive industry in which the production function facing individual firms displays first increasing and then decreasing returns to scale. In this industry each firm's long-run average cost curve

will be _____ shaped; also each firm's long-run marginal cost

curve will, as the firm increases output, eventually turn _____;

and the firm's long-run supply curve will be _____.

b. However, if entry and exit from the industry are free, and if changes in industry output do not affect industry input prices, the industry's

long-run supply curve will be a _____ line; i.e., there will

be some *supply price* at which the industry is willing to supply _____ quantities of output. Looking at the long-run cost curves of individual

firms, we can determine this supply price because it equals _____

_____.

B. MULTIPLE CHOICE

1. For a market to be perfectly competitive, all of the following conditions must hold except:
   a. buyers must behave as price takers.
   b. the market demand curve must be horizontal.
   c. sellers must behave as price takers.
   d. the product sold must be homogeneous.

2. In a perfectly competitive market in which all producers selling output seek to maximize profits:
   a. too little output will be produced to clear the market.
   b. price will be set too high to equate supply and demand.
   c. equilibrium cannot be attained.
   d. equilibrium will be attained during the short run at a price equal to producers' short-run marginal cost.

3. For a producer who sells in a perfectly competitive market and who attains short-run equilibrium by supplying the output level that equates marginal cost with market price, all of the following statements will hold except:
   a. average variable cost is certain to be minimized.
   b. marginal revenue will equal marginal cost.
   c. marginal revenue will equal average revenue.
   d. profits will be maximized.

4. To determine the short-run supply curve of a firm selling in a perfectly competitive market, we need to know which of the following:
   a. the firm's short-run MC curve.
   b. the firm's ATC curve.
   c. the point of minimum average variable cost.
   d. market price for the firm's output.

5. To determine whether a perfectly competitive firm will earn a profit or loss when it attains short-run equilibrium, we need to know which of the following:

   a. the firm's short-run MC curve.
   b. the firm's ATC curve.
   c. the point of minimum average variable cost.
   d. market price for the firm's output.

6. It is not possible to obtain a supply curve for a perfectly competitive industry simply by summing horizontally the supply curves of all firms in the industy if:

   a. the production function facing industry producers is characterized by decreasing returns to scale.
   b. producers in the industry use fixed inputs.
   c. changes in industry output alter the prices of inputs used by the industry.
   d. some firms in the industry attain minimum AVC at lower levels of output than other firms do.

7. If a perfectly competitive industry is in short-run equilibrium, we can be sure that:

   a. all producers in the industry are making a profit.
   b. every producer who is supplying output is making a profit.
   c. all producers who are supplying output are making the same profit.
   d. every producer who is supplying output is producing at a point where market price equals his marginal cost.

8. An upward shift in market demand for a commodity sold in a perfectly competitive market is likely to lead during the *short-run* to which of the following:

   a. a rise in market price.
   b. a rise in quantity produced and sold.
   c. investment by existing producers in new capital stock.
   d. the entry of new producers into the market.

9. An upward shift in market demand for a commodity sold in a perfectly competitive market is likely to lead during the *long-run* to which of the following:

   a. a rise in market price unless the industry is a constant-cost industry.
   b. a rise in quantity produced and sold.
   c. investment by existing producers in new capital stock.
   d. the entry of new producers into the market.

10. When a perfectly competitive firm attains long-run equilibrium, it is certain to be operating at an output level at which its long-run average cost curve:

a. is falling.   *c.* is rising.
b. is falling or attains a minimum.   *d.* attains a minimum or is rising.

11. A perfectly competitive industry can expand its output at constant cost (i.e., have a horizontal long-run supply curve), *only if:*

   a. each firm in the industry faces a constant-returns-to-scale production function.
   b. there are an infinite number of firms in the industry.
   c. the industry uses "unspecialized" resources; i.e., resources whose price won't change as the industry uses more or less of them.
   d. demand for the industry's output is elastic.

C. PROBLEMS

1. *a.* John Greenthumb is a wheat farmer who sells his output in a perfectly competitive market. Assume that Greenthumb's fixed costs equal $2,000 and that he has the *MC* and *AVC* curves pictured in Figure 8–1(a). What quantity of output would Greenthumb choose to sell during the short run and what profits would he earn if the going price offered to him for his wheat were:

Case	Price	q Supplied	Profit Earned
1	$4.00/bu.		
2	$3.00/bu.		
3	$1.75/bu.		
4	$1.50/bu.		
5	$1.00/bu.		

b. Plot Greenthumb's short-run supply curve for wheat in Figure 8–1(b).

c. Greenthumb will choose to shut down (i.e., produce a zero supply) in

the short run whenever his _____ is less than *VC* or, to

put it another way, whenever his price is less than _____.

d. How would a doubling of his fixed costs affect Greenthumb's short-run

supply curve for wheat? _____

e. How would an increase in input prices, that raised Greenthumb's *MC* at all levels of output, affect his short-run supply curve?

FIGURE 8–1
Deriving Greenthumb's
Short-Run Supply Curve

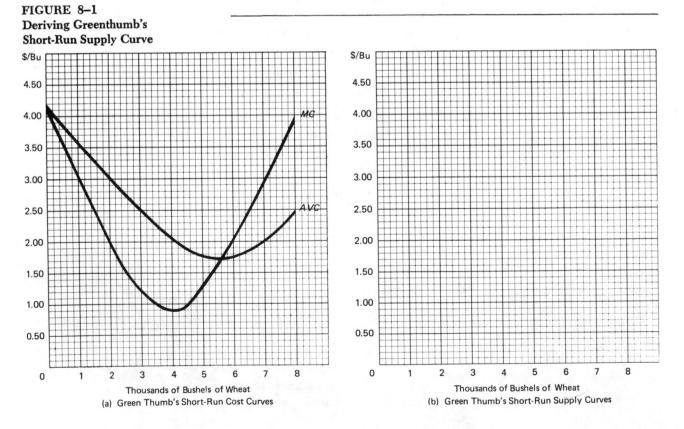

(a) Green Thumb's Short-Run Cost Curves

(b) Green Thumb's Short-Run Supply Curves

2. *a.* Smith, Brown, and Adams are all suppliers of soybeans. Figure 8–2 shows their individual supply curves for this commodity. Construct their joint supply curve for soybeans (i.e., a schedule showing the relationship between the price received and the total quantity all three producers together are willing to supply). Plot this schedule in Figure 8–2(d). [Hint: Begin by filling in Table 8–1.]

TABLE 8–1
Deriving a Joint Supply Curve

Price	Smith's Supply (1)	Brown's Supply (2)	Adams' Supply (3)	Joint Supply (1) + (2) + (3)
4				
3				
2				
1				
0				

FIGURE 8–2
Deriving Smith, Brown, and Adams' Joint Supply Curve

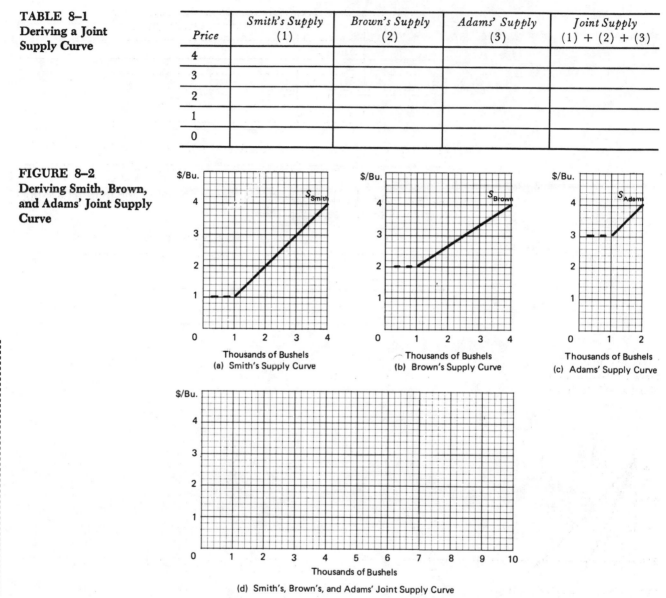

(a) Smith's Supply Curve

(b) Brown's Supply Curve

(c) Adams' Supply Curve

(d) Smith's, Brown's, and Adams' Joint Supply Curve

Name

b. The market supply curve for any commodity is the joint supply curve of *all* producers selling this commodity. Your construction of the joint supply curve in Figure 8–2(d) shows that the market supply curve for any commodity will always slope upward for at least two reasons:

(1) _____

_____

_____

(2) _____

_____

If in addition expansion of an industry's output forces up the prices of inputs used by that industry, the upward slope of the industry's supply curve will be even steeper because

_____

_____

_____

_____

3. *a.* Figure 8–3 pictures supply and demand in a perfectly competitive market. If a price of $5 were initially established in this market, there would be *excess supply E_s* in the market equal to _____,

and this excess supply would exert a _____ pressure on price. The consequent fall in price would tend to reduce excess supply by

_____ quantity demanded and _____ quantity supplied. A downward pressure would continue to be exerted on price

so long as excess supply was _____.

b. If a price equal to $1 were initially established in this market, there would be an *excess demand E_D* in the market equal to _____,

and this excess demand would exert a _____ on price. The

consequent rise in price would tend to reduce excess demand by _____

_____quantity demanded and _____ quantity supplied. An upward pressure would continue to be exerted on price so long

as excess demand was _____.

c. For the market in Figure 8–3, the only price that can be an equilibrium

price is _____ because this is the only price at which $E_D = E_s = $ ____.

At this price, _____ units would be traded.

FIGURE 8–3
Equilibrium in a Perfectly Competitive Market

$/Unit

Thousands of Units

Name

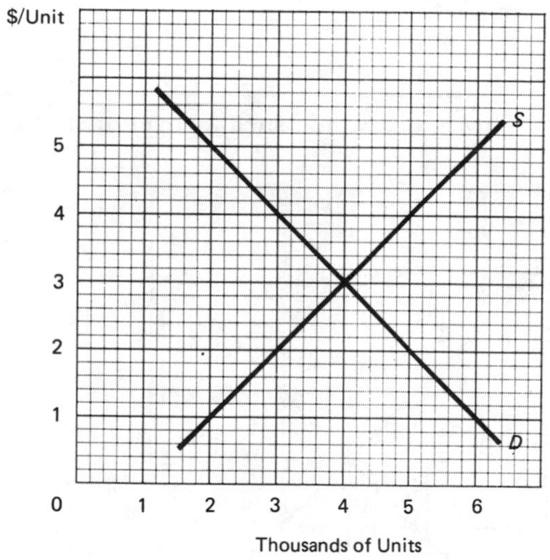

4. *a.* Suppose that a price ceiling were imposed on the market pictured in Figure 8–4 at the level $p = \$2$.

    (1) How would this affect market equilibrium? _____

    _____

    (2) What sort of black market would tend to develop? _____

    _____

    (3) How could rationing be used to limit the development of this

    black market? _____

    _____

    (4) If a free market were to develop for the ration coupons, how much

    would each one be worth? _____

b. Suppose that a price floor were imposed on the market in Figure 8–4 at the level $p = \$4$.

    (1) How would this affect market equilibrium? _____

    _____

    (2) What sort of black market would tend to develop? _____

    _____

    (3) How could government purchases of the commodity sold in the market in question be used to limit the development of this black

    market? _____

    _____

    (4) How much would such a government purchase program cost?

FIGURE 8–4
Supply and Demand in a Perfectly Competitive Market

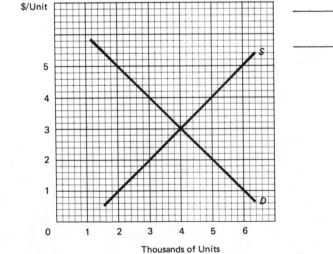

Thousands of Units

_____

5. *a.* Suppose a specific tax of $2 per unit were imposed on every unit *sold* in the market pictured in Figure 8–5 (i.e., that a tax were imposed that is paid by the seller). How would this affect equilibrium in the market? Specifically how would it affect:

(1) The gross price paid by the buyer? _____

(2) The net price received by the seller? _____

(3) Total quantity traded _____

(4) Tax revenue collected by the government? _____
[Hint: To answer, sketch in Figure 8–3 a new market supply curve (S') based on the assumption that sellers pay the tax and regard it as part of their costs.]

b. Suppose alternatively that a specific tax of $2 per unit were imposed on every unit *purchased* in the market pictured in Figure 8–5 (i.e., a tax is imposed that is to be paid by the buyer). How would this affect:

(1) The gross price paid by the buyer? _____

(2) The net price received by the seller? _____

(3) The total quantity traded? _____

(4) Tax revenue collected by the government? _____
[Hint: To answer, sketch in Figure 8–5 a new *net* demand curve (D'), which shows the relationship between the net price received by sellers and total quantity demanded.]

c. When a specific tax is imposed on a commodity sold in a perfectly competitive market, the incidence of the tax (does/does not) depend on who is supposed to pay the tax, the buyer or the seller. Instead it depends on

the _____ of the market supply curve and the _____

_____ of the market demand curve.

FIGURE 8–5
Supply and Demand in a Perfectly Competitive Market

Name

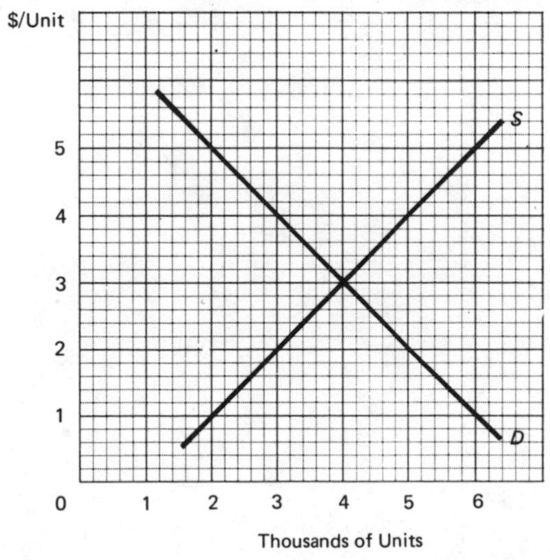

6. *a.* As shown in Figure 8–6, the equilibrium price of cotton in Angolia is currently $300 a bale. In the interest of ensuring that cotton farmers earn an "adequate" return, the Angolian government establishes a price floor for cotton at $500 a bale. By how much will this cause supply to expand? _____ By how much will demand contract? _____ At the $500 price, how much excess supply will exist in the market? _____ If the government decided to deal with the problem of excess supply by setting up a crop purchase program, how much would the program cost? _____

b. To cut the costs of a crop purchase program, the Angolian government decides to limit production to the 30,000 bale level by requiring cotton growers to obtain acreage allotments and issuing such allotments only for those acres that were in production when cotton production was at the 30,000 bale level. Also, the government permits no changes in intensity of cultivation that would increase output per farmed acre. How will these measures affect the supply curve of cotton in Angolia? _____ _____ Sketch in the new supply curve in Figure 8–6 and determine what excess supply under the price-floor-acreage-allotment-crop-purchase program would be. _____ _____ By how much would this program raise the profits of cotton farmers in Angolia *initially?* _____ How much of this rise in profits would consumers pay for through higher prices? _____ _____ How much of it would they pay for through additional taxes? _____

FIGURE 8–6
The Cotton Market in Angolia

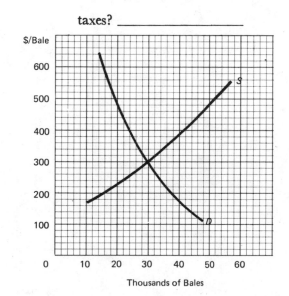

$/Bale

Thousands of Bales

c. If after institution of the program described in (*b*), cotton farmer X wanted to sell land on which cotton growing was permitted, how would

the program have affected the price commanded by this land? _____
How would the program affect the profits earned by the "second gen-

eration" farmer who bought X's land? _____ Over the long run as all cotton farms changed hands, what would be the effect of the program on cotton farmers' profits in general? What group would capture the lion's share of the benefits of the program and how would

they do so? _____

_____

_____

_____

7. *a.* Hansen, who grows corn sold in a perfectly competitive market, has the long-run and short-run cost curves pictured in Figure 8–7. Currently the going price of corn is $5 per bushel, and Hansen is in long-run equilibrium. What quantity of output is Hansen producing? _____

_____ At this output level, what is the relationship between his short-run marginal cost (SMC) and his long-run marginal cost (LMC)?

_____ Between his short-run average total cost (SAC)

and his long-run average cost (LAC)? _____ What

profit is he making? _____

b. If price were to fall to $4 per bushel, what quantity of output would

Hansen produce in the short run? _____ What would

happen to his profits? _____ At the price of $4 per bushel, what quantity of output would Hansen produce when he had time to adjust his capital stock and move to long-run equilibrium?

_____ How would the adjustment in output, as he

moved from short- to long-run equilibrium, affect his profits? _____

_____ Sketch in Figure 8–7 the SAC and SMC curves that Hansen would have if he were in long-run equilibrium at the $4 per bushel price.

FIGURE 8–7
Cost Curves of Hansen's Corn Farm

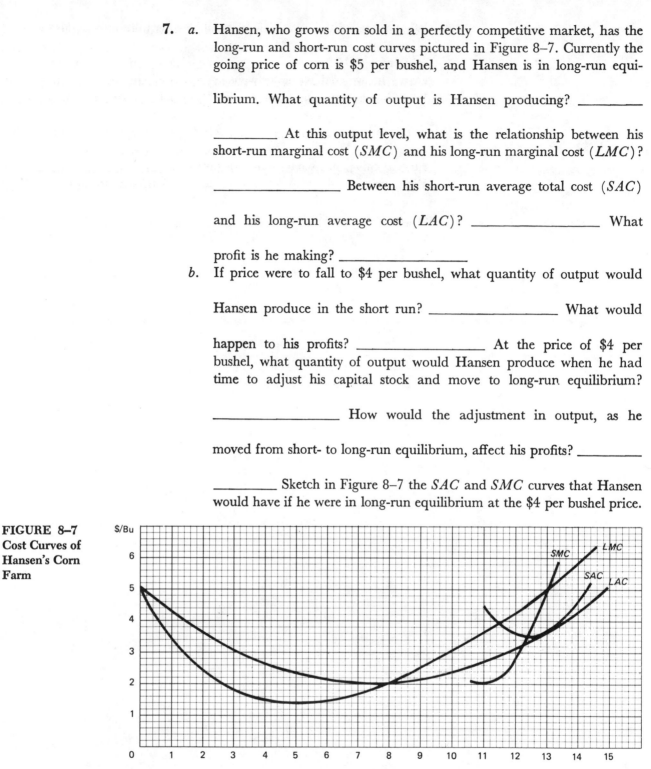

Thousands of Bushels

Name

    c.   What price would lead Hansen to achieve equilibrium at his point of

minimum *LAC?* _____ Sketch in the *SAC* and *SMC* curves he would have if he were in long-run equilibrium at this point. What is the relationship between his *LAC, SAC, LMC,* and *SMC* curves

at this point? _____ If Hansen were in long-run equilib-

rium at this point, what would his profits be? _____
    d.   What price would lead Hansen to achieve long-run equilibrium at the

output level of 3,000 bushels? _____ A perfect competitor will (always/sometimes/never) achieve equilibrium on the downward-

sloping portion of his *LAC* curve because _____

_____

8.* The short-run total cost curve of producer X can be written as follows:

$$TC = q^3 - 4q^2 + 20q + 40$$

    a. Using relationship, derive expressions for the following:

$FC = $ _____ $AFC = $ _____

$VC = $ _____ $MC = $ _____

$AVC = $ _____

    b. At what value of q does producer X achieve minimum $AVC?$ _____

What is the value of AVC at this output level? _____ What is MC

at this output level? _____

    c. Assume that producer X sells in a perfectly competitive market and derive an expression for his supply curve:

_____

    d. What level of price would lead producer X to supply 10 units of

output? _____

Name -

---

* Asterisks denote the more difficult problems.

Chapter 9

Theory of Price under
Pure Monopoly

Name _____

**A. DEFINITIONS
AND REVIEW**

1. A market is said to be characterized by monopoly if _____

_____.

For a product to be under monopoly control, it must have no _____
substitutes.

2. *a.* The demand curve facing a monopolist is identical with the _____

_____ demand curve for his output. Its slope is _____, and

consequently the monopolist's *MR* curve lies _____ his *AR* curve.

   b. If the monopolist faces a downward-sloping linear demand curve, his *TR*

curve will be shaped like an upside-down _____, and his *TR* will

reach a maximum at the output level at which his *MR curve* _____

_____, i.e., at the output level at which $MR =$ _____.

3. *a.* In a particular input market, monopolist X is the sole buyer and the
behavior of sellers can be represented by a market supply curve; such a market

is said to be characterized by _____. In the situation at hand
monopolist X's purchases determine the input's price, and he is said to exercise

_____ power.

   b. Assuming that the input supply curve facing monopolist X is positively
sloped, the marginal cost of the input to him will (be less than/equal/exceed) the
average cost or wage he pays the input.

4. A monopolist maximizes profits by producing the output level at which $MR =$

_____. His profits at this point will be _____ if his

AR curve lies above his ATC curve, _____ if his AR curve is

tangent to his ATC curve, and _____ if his AR curve lies below
his ATC curve.

5. Monopolist X produces his output in two different plants. Let MC_1 denote marginal cost in plant I, MC_2 marginal cost in plant II. To maximize profits, monopolist X should adjust his overall level of output *and* the allocation of this output between the two plants so that the following condition holds:

$$MR = \text{_____} = \text{_____}$$

6. We would expect a profit-maximizing monopolist to respond to an upward

shift in the demand curve for his output:

    a. During the short run by _____

    b. Over the long run by _____

    c. As the monopolist moved from the short-run equilibrium position he achieved after the demand shift to his new long-run equilibrium position,

    his capital stock would _____, his level of output would

    _____, his price would _____, and his profits would

    _____.

7.   *a.* Monopolist Z sells his output in two different markets. Let MR_1 denote marginal revenue in market I, MR_2 marginal revenue in market II. To maximize profits, monopolist Z should adjust his overall level of output *and* the allocation of this output between the two markets so that the following condition holds:

$$MC = \text{_____} = \text{_____}$$

    b. If monopolist Z follows this rule, the prices he charges for output in the two markets will (be the same/probably differ). Whenever a firm charges different prices for the same product in different markets, it is

    said to practice _____.

8. A market is said to be characterized by bilateral monopoly if _____

_____.

A monopolist, who buys an essential input from another monopolist and who is the only buyer of this input, would be able to obtain the maximum profits from his operation if the input seller behaved as a price _____. The input seller, however, would be unlikely to do so, because the profits he would earn by behaving this way would be less than the profits he could earn if he

_____ quantity sold and _____ the price of the input traded.

B. MULTIPLE CHOICE

1. The basis on which a monopolist controls his market might be which of the following:

  a. the monopolist controls vital raw material supplies.
  b. the monopolist's production function is characterized by decreasing returns to scale.
  c. the monopolist's production process is characterized in the short run by diminishing returns to labor.
  d. the monopolist uses a patented production process.

2. The marginal cost of an input to a firm will exceed the average cost of the input:

  a. always.
  b. if the firm operates in a nonconstant-cost perfectly competitive industry.
  c. if the firm is a monopsonist.
  d. if the firm exercises a patent monopoly.

3. To maximize profits, a monopolist should produce at the output level at which:

  a. MC is minimized.   *c.* $MR = MC$.
  b. TR is maximized.   *d.* AVC is minimized.

4. A monopolist with positive MC would never maximize profits by producing at which of the following points:

  a. the one where TR is maximized.
  b. one where AVC is falling.
  c. one where MC is falling.
  d. one where the price elasticity of demand for his output was less than one.

5. A monopoly position is *certain* to offer profits to the firm exercising it in which of the following situations:

  a. the firm is also a monopsonist.
  b. the firm's MR curve intersects its MC curve at the point where MC equals ATC.
  c. the firm's MR curve intersects its MC curve twice.
  d. the firm's ATC curve lies at some output levels below its AR curve.

Name -----------------------------------

6. When a monopolist attains long-run equilibrium, which of the following relations will hold:

a. $SMC = MR$.   c. $LMC = SMC$.

b. $LMC = LAC$.   d. $LAC = SAC$.

7. If firm X attains long-run equilibrium on the downward-sloping portion of its LAC curve, we can be sure that firm X is not:

     a. a perfect competitor.

     b. a monopolist.

     c. maximizing profits.

     d. simultaneously in short-run equilibrium.

8. Persuing a policy of price discrimination will increase the profits of a monopolist who sells in two submarkets:

     a. only if he sells more than one product.

     b. if the price elasticity of demand for his output differs in the two markets.

     c. if buyers in either submarket can easily resell his output to buyers in the other submarket.

     d. only during the short run when capital stock is fixed.

9. If an input is sold under conditions of bilateral monopoly, its price will be:

     a. indeterminate.

     b. determined by the seller.

     c. determined by the buyer.

     d. the same as it would be if the input were traded in a perfectly competitive market.

C. PROBLEMS

1. Three economics students, Smith, Brown, and Adams, are having an argument as usual. Smith says that a profit-maximizing monopolist might operate (i.e., be in equilibrium) on the downward-sloping portion of his long-run AC curve, but that a profit-maximizing perfect competitor never would. Brown says neither ever would. Adams claims both might. Who's right? Illustrate your argument by adding appropriate demand, MR and MC curves in Figure 9–1.

_____

_____

_____

_____

_____

_____

FIGURE 9–1
Profit Maximization under Monopoly and Perfect Competition

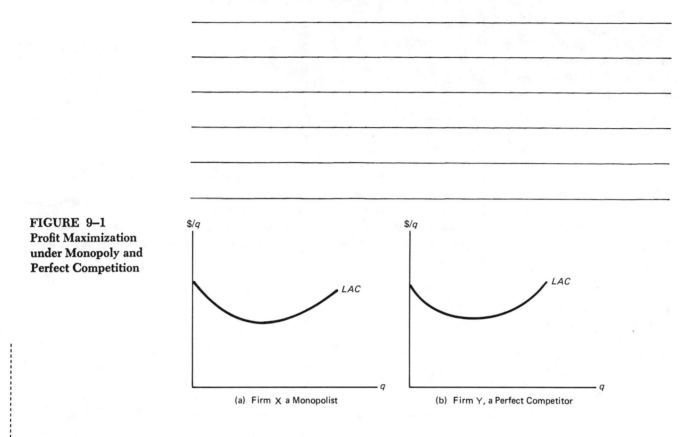

(a) Firm X a Monopolist   (b) Firm Y, a Perfect Competitor

2. *a.* As indicated by the thousands of patented products that have never been produced, monopoly need not be profitable. Whether it is depends on the relationship of demand for the monopolized product to its costs of production. Draw in Figure 9–2 the *AR, MR, AC, MC, TC, TR,* and profit (π) curves of a monopolist whose *maximum*-profit output, q^0, corresponds to a point of *zero* profit. Also label in both diagrams the output level q' at which total revenue is maximized.

FIGURE 9–2
Cost and Revenue Curves of a Monopolist Whose Maximum-Profit Output, q^0, Yields Zero Profits

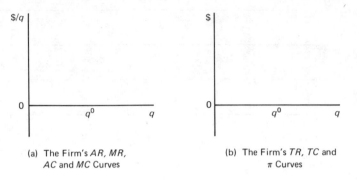

(a) The Firm's *AR, MR, AC* and *MC* Curves

(b) The Firm's *TR, TC* and π Curves

b. Draw in Figure 9–3 the same curves you drew in Figure 9–2 for a monopolist whose *maximum-profit* output, q^0, corresponds to a point of *minimum loss.* Also label q', the output level at which total revenue is maximized.

FIGURE 9–3
Cost and Revenue Curve of a Monopolist Whose Maximum-Profit Position Is a Position of Minimum Loss

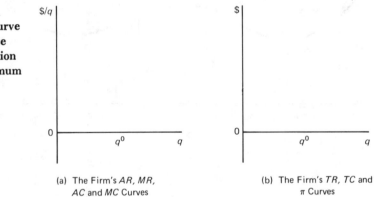

(a) The Firm's *AR, MR, AC* and *MC* Curves

(b) The Firm's *TR, TC* and π Curves

3. *a.* Would a profit-maximizing monopolist ever attain equilibrium by operating at a point along the demand curve for his output where demand elasticity was less than one? Explain your answer by drawing an appropriate diagram in Figure 9–4. [Hint: For simplicity assume that your monopolist faces a linear downward-sloping demand curve.]

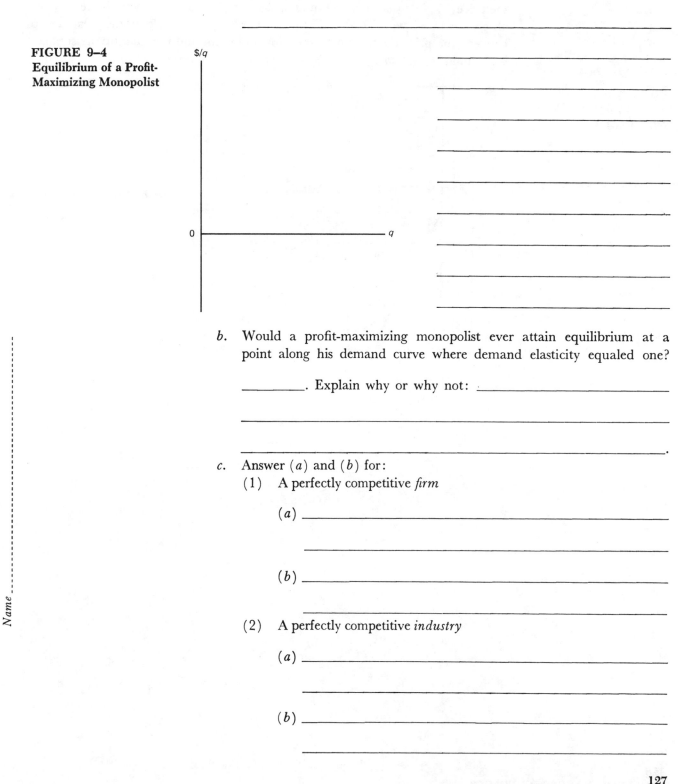

FIGURE 9–4
Equilibrium of a Profit-Maximizing Monopolist

b. Would a profit-maximizing monopolist ever attain equilibrium at a point along his demand curve where demand elasticity equaled one?

_____. Explain why or why not: _____

_____

_____.

c. Answer (*a*) and (*b*) for:
  (1) A perfectly competitive *firm*

   (*a*) _____

   _____

   (*b*) _____

   _____

  (2) A perfectly competitive *industry*

   (*a*) _____

   _____

   (*b*) _____

   _____

Name --

4. The supply curve of a perfectly competitive firm shows the relationship between the price the firm receives for its output and the quantity of output it is willing to supply. *No* such supply curve can be constructed for a monopolist. Figure 9–5 can be used to prove this result. The figure as it stands shows two different demand curves that might face a monopolist. Sketch in the companion *MR* curves. Then add an *MC* curve whose shape is such that the monopolist would, if faced with either of these demand curves, maximize profits by charging the price p^0. Note that since the quantity sold at p^0 would be greater if the monopolist were faced with D' than with D, your graph shows that the relationship between the price the monopolist gets for his output and the quantity he supplies is not unique; i.e., *that the monopolist has no supply curve.*

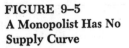

FIGURE 9–5
A Monopolist Has No Supply Curve

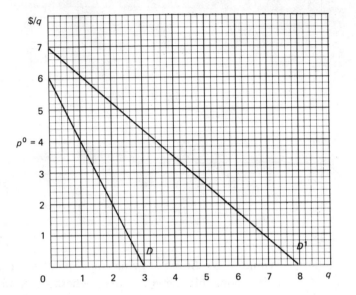

5. Zeon, Inc., is a monopolist. It produces a single product in two different plants. Figure 9–6 shows the *MC* curves in both plants and the demand curves for Zeon's output. Using this information, determine the following:

    a. How much output should Zeon produce to maximize profits? _____

    b. What price should Zeon charge for its output? _____

    c. How much output should Zeon produce in Plant I? _____

    d. How much output should it produce in Plant II? _____
       [Hint: Begin by adding a *joint MC* curve to Figure 9–6(c); i.e., a curve that shows what Zeon's *MC* would be at each level of output if it always allocated output between its two plants so as to *minimize* its total costs of production.]

FIGURE 9–6
Determining the Maximum-Profit Position of a Two-Plant Monopolist

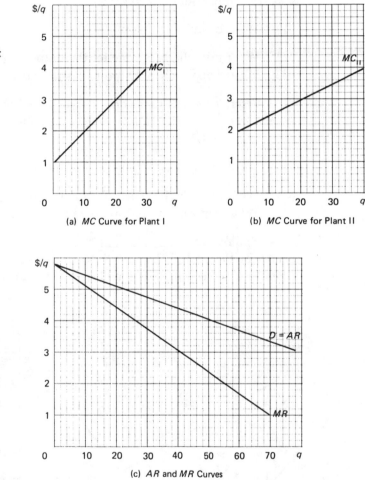

6. Greedy Graham is a happy monopolist. For years demand for his output was such that he faced the revenue curves AR and MR in Figure 9–7. Naturally, being a profit maximizer, he achieved both long- and short-run equilibrium with respect to these revenue curves. Then demand for Greedy's output suddenly shifted up to AR'. Greedy's immediate responses to this shift was to expand output and move to his new short-run equilibrium position. Then as time passed, he expanded capacity and increased output still more to achieve his new long-run equilibrium. Studying Figure 9–7, determine the following:

  a. When Greedy was initially in long- and short-run equilibrium with respect to the revenue curves MR and AR:

   (1) What quantity of output did he produce? _____

   (2) What price did he charge for this output? _____

  b. When demand shifted from AR to AR', and Greedy moved to his new *short-run* equilibrium position:

   (1) What quantity of output did he produce? _____

   (2) What price did he charge for this output? _____
   (3) What happened to his profits as he moved from the equilibrium

   described in (*a*) to the one described in (*b*)? _____

  c. When Greedy moved to a new *long-run* equilibrium with respect to the demand curve AR':

   (1) What quantity of output did he produce? _____

   (2) What price did he charge for this output? _____
   (3) What happened to his profits as he moved from short- to long-run

   equilibrium? _____

  d. Sketch in Figure 9–7 the new SMC and SAC curves faced by Greedy when he achieved long-run equilibrium with respect to the demand curve AR'.

FIGURE 9–7
Short- and Long-Run
Equilibrium of a Profit-
Maximizing Monopolist

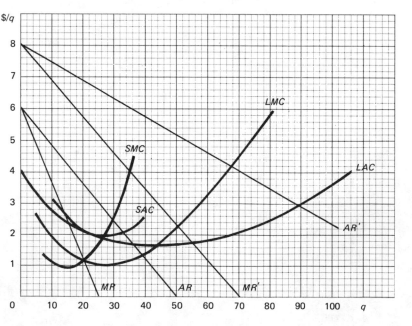

7. Schmoos Ltd. produces a new toy guaranteed to keep babies from crying. As all mothers know, there is no close substitute for such a toy. Consequently, Schmoos Ltd. has a monopoly. Figure 9–8 shows Schmoos Ltd.'s cost curves as well as the demand curves for schmoos in the home and foreign markets. These two markets are effectively separated by transport costs, tariff barriers, etc. Consequently, Schmoos Ltd. is in a position to practice price discrimination; i.e., to sell its output at different prices in the two markets.

Kelly Green, the president of Schmoos Ltd., perceives that price discrimination is the way to profit maximization but he is having a hard time figuring out just how to go about it. Help the poor fellow out by determining for him:

    a. The total output Schmoos Ltd. should produce to mazimize profits.

        ——————————

    b. The price it should charge in the home market. ——————————

    c. The quantity of output it should sell there. ——————————

    d. The price it should charge in the foreign market. ——————————

    e. The quantity of output it should sell there. ——————————

    f. The total profits the company will earn if it follows your strategy.

        ——————————————————————

[Hint: Begin by sketching (1) in Figure 9–8(a) the *MR* curve in the foreign market, (2) in Figure 9–8 (b) the *MR* curve in the home market, and (3) in Figure 9–8(c) a *joint MR* curve; i.e., an *MR* curve that shows the relationship between output sold and *MR* when the firm allocates its output between the two markets so as to *maximize* total revenue from sales in the two markets.]

FIGURE 9–8
Cost and Revenue Curves for Schmoos Ltd.

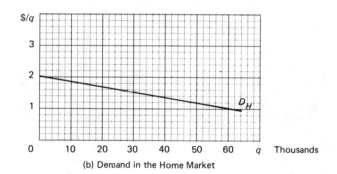

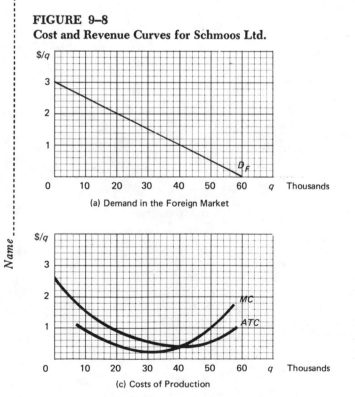

8. Monoprofit, Inc., exercises a monopoly over an unusual product, whatnots. Production of whatnots requires, as indicated by the isoquant map pictured in Figure 9–9, the use of two inputs, capital and labor. In any short-run period, capital inputs are *fixed* but labor inputs are *variable*. Currently, Monoprofits is a price taker in both the labor and capital markets. It pays $2 a unit for labor and $1 a unit for capital.

FIGURE 9–9
Isoquant Map for
Whatnot Production

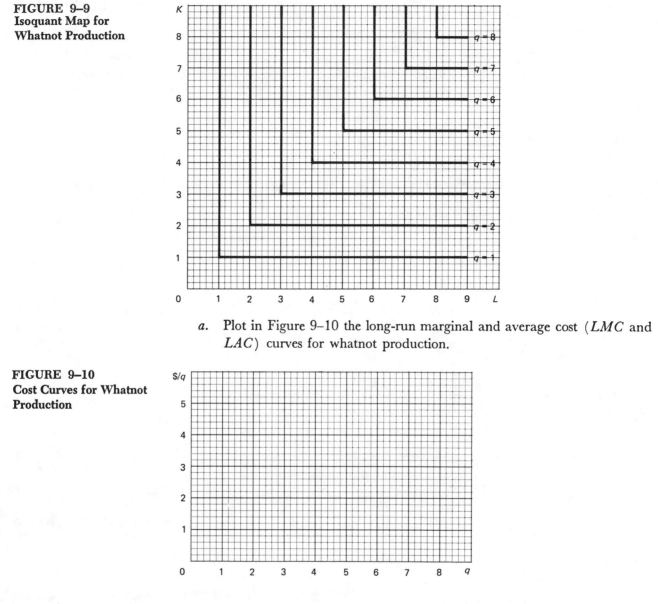

a. Plot in Figure 9–10 the long-run marginal and average cost (*LMC* and *LAC*) curves for whatnot production.

FIGURE 9–10
Cost Curves for Whatnot
Production

b. Assume that the demand curve for whatnots is given by
$$q = 10 - p$$

If Monoprofit, Inc., were in *long-run* equilibrium, what quantity of

output would they produce? _____ At what price

would they sell this output? _____ What profits

would they earn? _____

[Hint: Whatnots can be produced only in discrete units (no halves or thirds), so you'll get the correct *MR* and *MC* figures for answering these questions by filling in Table 9–1.]

TABLE 9–1
Cost and Revenue Figures for Monoprofit, Inc.

p	q	TR	MR	LMC
10	0		—	—
9	1		9	
8		16		
7				
6				
5				

c. In the current period, Monoprofit, Inc., happens to have a fixed capital stock of two units. Add their short-run *MC* and *AC* curves to Figure 9–10. [Hint: Start by filling in Table 9–2.]

TABLE 9–2
Short-Run Cost Figures for Monoprofit, Inc.

q	FC	VC	SMC	ATC
0			—	—
1				
2				
3				
4				

d. With a fixed capital stock of two units, and the demand curve given in

(*b*) above, what is Monoprofit's short-run equilibrium output? _____

_____ What price will they charge for this output? _____

_____ What profits will they earn? _____

Assuming no change is expected in demand or production costs, what change will Monoprofit, a profit maximizer, make in its capital stock

over the long run? _____

9.* *a.* Monoprofit, Inc., of problem 8 becomes discouraged by the high cost of labor and moves to a small town where it is the only employer. In this town Monoprofit is a monopsonist in the local labor market. It faces the supply curve of labor indicated by the first two columns in Table 9–3. Assuming that Monoprofit's current capital stock happens to be five units, what quantity of labor should it hire this period to maximize

short-run profits? _____ What wage will it pay this

labor? _____ What level of output will it produce?

_____ What price will it charge for this output?

_____ What profits will it earn? _____

_____ [Hint: Recall that demand for Monoprofit's output is given by the expression $q = 10 - p$. To maximize short-run profits, Monoprofit, a *monopsonist,* must equate the marginal cost of labor with labor's marginal revenue product MRP_L, so begin by filling in Table 9–3 ($MRP_L = MP_L \cdot MR$).]

TABLE 9–3
Labor's *MC* and *MRP* for
Monoprofit, Inc.

Wage	L	TC_L	MC_L	MP_L	MRP_L
$0	0		—	—	—
0.50	1				
0.75	2				
1.00	3				
1.50	4				
2.00	5				
3.00	6				

b. Is the short-run equilibrium point you located in (*a*) also a point of long-run equilibrium? Explain.

_____

_____

_____

10.* Firm X is a monopolist. Its short-term total costs are given by the expression

$$TC = q^3/3 - 15q^2 + 200q + 2,000$$

Demand for its output q_d is given by the expression

$$q_d = \frac{600 - p}{15}$$

To maximize profits, what quantity of output should this firm produce?

_____ What price should it charge for output?

_____ What profits will it earn at its maximum-

profit position? _____

Chapter 10

Competition and Monopoly: Some Theoretical Exercises

A. DEFINITIONS AND REVIEW

Name ....

1. *a.* If a *unit tax* (say T dollars per unit traded) is imposed on the sale of a product sold in a perfectly competitive market, we can analyze the incidence of this tax either (1) by imagining that the tax is imposed on producers and shifting

vertically upward their _____ curves by an amount equal to

_____ or (2) by imagining that the tax is imposed on buyers and

shifting vertically downward their _____ curves by an amount equal to

_____. Approaches (1) and (2) lead to (different/identical) conclusions with respect to the incidence of the tax.

    b. If we take approach (1), the imposition of the tax causes every

individual producer's short-run supply curve to shift _____

_____, which is equivalent to (an increase/a decrease) in supply, and the

market supply curve shifts _____.

    c. If market demand and supply are both elastic, the result of this shift will be that the *gross* price received by producers (rises/falls), the *net* price (gross price minus tax paid) received by producers (rises/falls), the quantity of output traded in the market (rises/falls), and the government collects revenue equal

to _____.

d. If we take approach (2), the imposition of the tax causes every buyer's net demand curve (i.e., the curve showing the relationship between the net after-tax price producers receive and the quantity the consumer demands) to shift

_____, which is equivalent to (an increase/ a decrease)

in demand. Also as a result of this, the *net market* demand curve shifts _____

_____.

e. In the post-tax situation market equilibrium will be indicated by the

intersection of the market supply curve with the _____
curve. If market demand and supply are both elastic, the result of tax will be to (raise/lower) the gross price received by producers, to (raise/lower) the net price received by producers, and to (raise/lower) the quantity of output traded in the market.

2. An *ad valorem* tax is a sales tax which equals a _____.

_____.

3. *a.* A lump-sum tax is _____.

b. Imposing a lump-sum tax on a firm will over the *short run* have what ef-

fect on each of the following, the firm's marginal cost: _____;

average variable cost: _____; average fixed costs: _____;

marginal revenue: _____; average revenue: _____;

the firm's equilibrium output _____; the firm's profits _____

_____.

c. From this it follows that imposing a lump-sum tax on every firm operating in a perfectly competitive industry will have what effect on each of

the following during the short run: industry output _____; the

price at which industry output is sold _____; profits earned

by producers in the industry _____.

d. Over the *long run* imposing a lump-sum tax on a firm will _____

_____ its average variable cost but have _____ effect on its
marginal cost.

e. Consequently the long-run effect on a perfectly competitive, constant-cost industry of imposing a lump-sum tax on every firm in the industry will be to

cause industry output to _____, the price received for this output to

_____, and the number of firms in the industry to _____

_____; also the output level of each firm that remains in production will (rise/not change/fall).

4. If a price ceiling is imposed in a perfectly competitive market at a level below the price that equates supply and demand, the long-run effect is always to create excess demand at the ceiling price, because the imposition of the ceiling causes

market supply to _____ and market demand to _____.
In the extreme case of a constant-cost industry, imposition of a price ceiling would

have the long-run effect of reducing market supply to _____.

5. Using a price ceiling to force a monopolist to lower price will also cause the

monopolist to *increase* his output so long as _____.

It will create a shortage only if the price ceiling is set _____

_____.

6. Imposing a high price floor in a perfectly competitive market will (increase/decrease) market demand, (increase/decrease) market supply, and thereby

create excess _____ in the market at the support price.

1. The imposition of a tax on the sale of a product traded in a perfectly competitive market will have no effect in the short run on the quantity of output traded in which of the following situations:

   a. the tax is imposed on buyers of the product.
   b. the tax is small.
   c. market demand for the product has zero elasticity.
   d. market supply of the product has zero elasticity.

2. The imposition of a tax on the sale of a product traded in a perfectly competitive market will lower producers' short-run profits by the full amount of the tax in which of the following situations:

   a. the tax is imposed on sellers of the product.
   b. the tax is small.
   c. market demand for the product has zero elasticity.
   d. market supply of the product has zero elasticity.

3. In the long run the imposition of a tax (that sellers are required to pay) on the sale of a product traded in a perfectly competitive market will raise the price to the consumer by the full amount of the tax in which of the following situations:

a. market demand has zero elasticity.   *c.* market supply has zero elasticity.
b. market demand is infinitely elastic.   *d.* market supply is infinitely elastic.

4. The imposition of a unit tax on a commodity traded in a perfectly competitive market might cause which of the following outcomes:

    a. producers incur losses in the short run.
    b. in the long run some producers leave the industry.
    c. producers incur losses in the long run.
    d. in the long run new producers enter the industry.

5. The imposition of a unit tax on the output of a constant-cost, perfectly competitive industry will over the long run:

    a. cause price to increase by the full amount of the tax.
    b. cause the outputs of individual firms in the industry to fall.
    c. cause industry output to fall even more than it fell in the short run.
    d. cause some firms to leave the industry.

6. The long-run effect of imposing a lump-sum tax on a monopolist (one that is less than his equilibrium profits) will be that:

    a. his marginal cost rises.
    b. he raises prices.
    c. he decreases output.
    d. his profits fall by the amount of the tax.

7. A monopolist is likely to respond to a price ceiling that forces down his price by raising his output because:

    a. by doing so he can maintain profits at the pre-tax level.
    b. the price ceiling lowers his MC.
    c. the price ceiling raises his MR over a considerable range of output.
    d. the price ceiling shifts up demand for his output.

8. The imposition of a price floor that forced a monopolist to raise his price would:

    a. raise the monopolist's profits.
    b. force the monopolist to increase output to keep his profits from falling.
    c. lower the monopolist's profits.
    d. cause a shortage in the market for the monopolist's output.

C. PROBLEMS

1. *a.* Figure 10–1 pictures the market for wheat in Germania. This year's crop has just been harvested and S_m, the *momentary supply curve*, represents the relationship between current price and the amount currently supplied. A second curve, S_{sr}, the *short-run supply curve*, represents the relationship between price received and the quantity growers would supply during the next growing season, which is coming up so fast that growers have no time to make major adjustments in capital stock. Finally curve S_{lr}, the *long-run supply curve*, represents the relationship between price received and quantity supplied over the long run when all growers have time to fully adjust their capital stock, and entry and exit from the industry are thus possible. Clearly wheat production in Germania is a constant-cost industry. Also the industry, as shown in Figure 10–1, is in long-run equilibrium with respect to the present market demand curve, D. In this

position of long-run equilibrium, price equals _____

and quantity sold equals _____.

FIGURE 10–1
Impact Over Time of a
Specific Tax in a Perfectly
Competitive Market

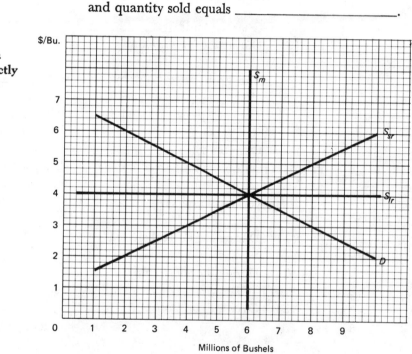

Name - - - - - - - - - - - - - - - - - -

b. Suppose now that the government imposes a tax of $2 a bushel on wheat sold in Germania. (Represent this tax in Figure 10–1 by sketching a new lower *net* demand curve *D'*; see problem 5, Chapter 8.) What will be the effect of this tax:

(1) During the *current* or momentary period on

The gross price paid by consumers? _____

The net price received by growers? _____

Quantity sold? _____

(2) During the *short run* on

The gross price paid by consumers? _____

The net price received by growers? _____

Quantity sold? _____

(3) During the *long run* on

The gross price paid by consumers? _____

The net price received by growers? _____

Quantity sold? _____

c. As a result of imposition of the tax on wheat, what total tax revenue will

the government collect:

(1) During the current period? _____

(2) During the short run? _____

(3) Over the long run? _____

2. Figure 10–2 pictures four perfectly competitive markets that are all initially in equilibrium with 2,000 units being traded at a price of $2. How would imposition of a specific tax of $1 per unit sold affect equilibrium in each of these four markets? Record your answers in Table 10–1. [Hint: To answer, first sketch in *each* part of Figure 10–2 an appropriate D' or S' curve.]

FIGURE 10–2
Incidence of a Specific Tax in a Perfectly Competitive Market

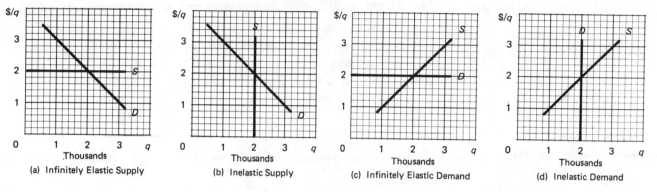

(a) Infinitely Elastic Supply   (b) Inelastic Supply   (c) Infinitely Elastic Demand   (d) Inelastic Demand

TABLE 10–1
Post-Tax Equilibrium in Four Markets

Case (1)	Gross Price Paid by Consumers (2)	Net Price Received by Sellers (3)	Quantity Sold (4)
(a) Supply infinitely elastic			
(b) Supply zero elasticity			
(c) Demand infinitely elastic			
(d) Demand zero elasticity			

Name

3. *a.* The market pictured in Figure 10–3 is in equilibrium. If the government were to disturb this equilibrium by giving a subsidy of $2 per unit on every unit *sold* (i.e., by giving a subsidy *to sellers*), how would this affect:

(1) The net price paid by buyers? _____

(2) The gross price (i.e., net price plus subsidy) received by sellers?

_____

(3) Total quantity sold? _____

(4) Government subsidy expenditures? _____
[Hint: A subsidy per unit sold is simply a *negative* commodity tax. So start by sketching in Figure 10–3 a new market supply curve *S′* based on the assumption that sellers get the subsidy and regard it as part of the gross price they receive for each unit sold.]

FIGURE 10–3
Impact of a Subsidy on a Perfectly Competitive Market

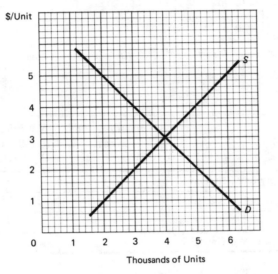

$/Unit

Thousands of Units

b. Suppose alternatively that a subsidy of $2 per unit were given on each unit *purchased* (i.e., that the subsidy were given *to buyers* of the commodity). How would this affect:

(1) The net price (i.e., gross price minus subsidy) paid by buyers?

_____

(2) The gross price received by sellers? _____

(3) Quantity traded? _____

(4) Subsidy expenditures by the government? _____
[Hint: To answer, sketch in Figure 10–3 a new net demand curve *D′*, which shows the relationship between the *total* price received by sellers and quantity demanded.]

c. When a subsidy is given on a commodity sold in a perfectly competitive market, the incidence of the subsidy (does/does not) depend on who is supposed to receive the subsidy, buyers or sellers. Instead it depends

on the _____ of the market supply curve and on the

_____ of the market demand curve.

4. This year's corn crop looks as if it is going to be another bumper one, and corn prices are consequently expected to fall. The government wants to do something to *raise the total revenue* growers will receive when they sell their crop. Jackson, a corn belt senator, says the thing to do is to make every grower destroy a fixed percentage of his crop (say 10%) at harvest time. A colleague of his argues, however, that a better approach would be to give individual corn growers some of the corn the government has in storage and let them sell it; his theory is that by selling more output, growers would get more total revenue. Who is right? On what important factor does the answer depend? _____

_____

_____

_____

5. By restricting the acreage that can be devoted to corn production, the government of Zumie manages to hold total corn production to a fixed sum, 100,000 bushels per year. Corn in Zumie is sold in a perfectly competitive market, and currently market demand is such that Zumie corn commands a price of $4 a bushel. However, the government would like corn farmers to get $5 a bushel. The government could accomplish this either (*a*) by subsidizing corn consumption or (*b*) by setting a $5 price floor in the corn market and buying up excess supply. Either way total output will be 100,000 bushels. Naturally the government wants to implement the cheaper of the two programs. What would you

advise them to do? _____

_____

_____

_____

On what crucial factor does your answer depend? _____
[Hint: Draw a diagram.]

6. A firm called Zee, Inc., exercises monopoly control over product X. Their cost and revenue curves are shown in Figure 10–4.

    a. Assuming that Zee, Inc., is a profit-maximizing firm:

        (1) What price will they charge for commodity X? _____

        (2) What quantity of it will they sell? _____

        (3) What profits will they earn? _____

    b. If the government imposed a price ceiling of $4.50 on product X, how would your answers to (1) through (3) in (*a*) change? [Hint: How does the price ceiling affect Zee's *AR* and *MR* curves?]

        (1) _____ (2) _____ (3) _____

    c. Repeat (*b*) for a price ceiling of $4.00.

        (1) _____ (2) _____ (3) _____

        (4) Is there now a shortage of product X? _____

        (5) Approximately how big is this shortage? _____
        (6) Assuming that the price ceiling is retained, how could this shortage

        be eliminated? _____

    d. What *combination* of measures (price ceiling, lump-sum subsidy, etc.) could the government use to induce Zee, Inc., to produce and sell an

    output level of 7,000? _____

FIGURE 10–4
Cost and Revenue Curves of Zee, Inc.

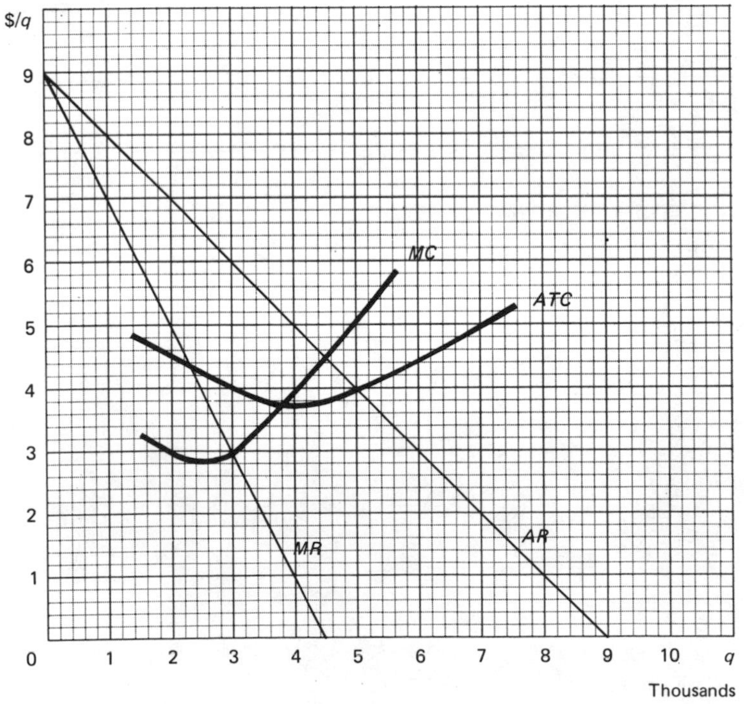

_____

      _____

      _____

      _____

      _____

      _____

      _____

      _____

      _____

      _____

7. Suppose the government were to impose a specific tax of $2 per unit sold on commodity X produced by Zee, Inc., of problem 6 above. (The relevant cost and revenue curves are shown in Figure 10–4.) How would this tax affect:

a. Zee, Inc.'s equilibrium output? _____

b. The *gross* price charged to consumers? _____

c. The net price received by Zee, Inc., after payment of the tax? _____

_____

d. Zee, Inc.'s profits? _____

e. What total tax revenue would the government receive from taxing

commodity X? _____

FIGURE 10–4
Cost and Revenue Curves of Zee, Inc.

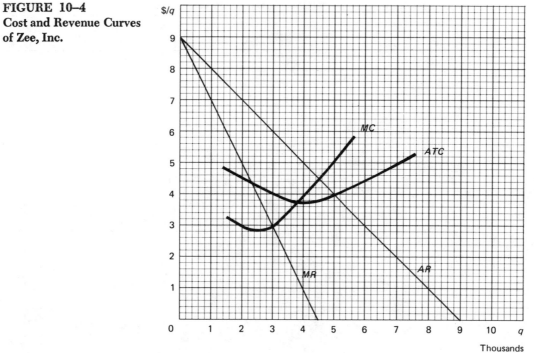

10 / COMPETITION AND MONOPOLY: SOME THEORETICAL EXERCISES

Name -----------------------------

8. The government of Pugwag wants the Greenbelt Corporation, which exercises monopoly control over the local fertilizer production, to increase output. It calls in three "experts" to determine how to do this. One argues that the way to get Greenbelt to raise output is to give the firm a subsidy of X dollars on each ton of fertilizer produced. A second advisor suggests a lump-sum subsidy. A third urges a price ceiling. Who's right? To answer, should you take into account other considerations? [Hint: Draw a few diagrams.] _____

_____

_____

_____

_____

_____

_____

9.* The Zilch Corporation, a monopolist, has the following short-run total cost schedule

$$TC = q^2 + 100$$

Demand for its output, q_d, is given by the expression

$$q_d = \frac{600 - p}{4}$$

a. To maximize profits, what quantity of output should this firm produce?

_____ What price should it charge for output? _____

What profits will it earn at its maximum-profit position? _____

b. Suppose the government were to impose a price ceiling of $200 per unit on Zilch's output. Now to maximize profits, what quantity of out-

put should this firm produce? _____ What price should it

charge for output? _____ What profits will it earn at its

maximum-profit position? _____ How would a price ceiling

of $500 per unit have affected Zilch's operations? _____

Name

---

* Asterisks denote the more difficult problems.

c. Suppose next that the government drops its price ceiling and imposes a specific tax of $60 per unit on Zilch's output. Now to maximize profits,

what quantity of output should the firm produce? _____

What *gross* price will consumers pay for Zilch's output? _____
What *net* price (gross price minus the tax) will Zilch receive for its

output? _____ What profits will Zilch earn? _____

What tax revenue will the government collect? _____

d. If the government were to impose a lump-sum tax of $500 on Zilch, Inc., how would that affect their equilibrium as you described it in (a)?

_____

Chapter 11

Theory of Price under
Monoplistic Competition

A. DEFINITIONS AND REVIEW

1. To say that a product is differentiated means that _____

_____.

2. A market is said to be characterized by monopolistic competition if _____

_____.

3. Perfect competitors and monopolistic competitors both sell in markets in which there are a large number of rival sellers. The perfectly competitive firm faces an infinitely elastic demand curve for its output. The monopolisticly competitive firm faces a _____ demand curve for its output. The reason

for the contrast is that _____.

_____

_____.

4. *a.* A monopolistically competitive firm achieves equilibrium at the output

level at which its marginal cost equals _____. However, a monopolistically competitive firm does not face fixed cost and revenue curves in the same sense that a perfectly competitive firm does; a monopolistically competitive firm, because it produces a differentiated product, is free to vary its product through changes in design, packaging, promotion, etc.; and each such change will alter both its _____

and _____ curves.

b. This fact of life means that, to achieve its maximum-profit position, a monopolistically competitive firm has to make not only the usual price-

output decision, but also decisions concerning optimal product _____

_____, _____, and _____.

5. *a.* Because rival monopolistic competitors produce a differentiated product (i.e., slightly different versions of the same basic output), they will not all have the same cost and revenue curves. Consequently, when a group of rival monopolistic competitors attains equilibrium, they (will/will not) necessarily charge the same prices, (will/will not) necessarily produce the same levels of output, and (will/will not) necessarily earn the same profits.

    b. The size of the difference between the prices charged by monopolist competitors in the same group will depend on how successfully the firms in the group manage to differentiate their products. The greater

    the differentiation, the _____ the price differences will be. If product differentiation were eliminated, the price differences would

    fall to _____, and the competitive situation in the market would

    revert to _____.

B. MULTIPLE CHOICE

1. The principal difference between monopolistic competition and perfect competition is that in a monopolisticly competitive market:

    a. sellers are relatively less numerous.
    b. buyers are relatively less numerous.
    c. the market demand curve is negatively sloped.
    d. the product sold is differentiated.

2. The means by which a producer can seek to differentiate his product from that of his competitors include all of the following but:

    a. changing the ingredients he puts in his product.
    b. changing the price at which he sells his product.
    c. changing the way he packages his product.
    d. changing the properties he attributes to his product in advertising.

3. When a monopolistic competitor attains equilibrium, we can be sure that he is operating at a point where:

    a. his average costs of production are minimized.
    b. his interaction with his rivals has led him to behave as a price taker.
    c. his MR equals his MC.
    d. his price equals his MC.

4. In the special case in which all monopolistic competitors in a given group are assumed to face identical cost and revenue curves, the profits that these firms earn in long-run equilibrium will, assuming free exit and entry:

    a. be substantial if they avoid price competition.
    b. be zero.
    c. be substantial if they avoid nonprice competition.
    d. be substantial if exit from the group is limited.

5. If a group of monopolistic competitors with identical cost and revenue curves moves from a long-run equilibrium position in which there is price competition to one in which there is *only* nonprice competition, all of the following changes will occur in the position of an individual producer except:

    a. his equilibrium output will decline.
    b. his equilibrium price will rise.
    c. his profits will rise.
    d. his average cost of production will rise.

6. If a group of monopolistic competitors with identical cost and revenue curves attains long-run equilibrium via price competition, each firm will end up producing at a point where:

    a. its profits are positive.
    b. its "perceived" or "anticipated" demand curve is tangent to its *LAC* curve.
    c. $LAC = LMC$.
    d. production differentiation has been eliminated.

C. PROBLEMS

1. Product Z, a homogeneous good, is sold in a perfectly competitive market. All actual and potential producers in the industry have the same long-run cost curves—those pictured in Figure 11–1. Currently there are 100 producers in the industry; and if each were—at any price that might prevail—always to get exactly 1/100 of total industry sales, he would face the *proportional demand curve* labeled *D* in Figure 11–1.

    a. What is the equation of the proportional demand curve facing each

    producer? _____ What is the equation of the market

    demand curve for product Z? _____

    b. What is the elasticity of the *proportional demand curve* facing each producer at the point on this curve corresponding to a price of $5?

    _____ What is the elasticity of the *market demand curve* at

    the point corresponding to a price of $5? _____

    [Hint: Use the formula $\eta = \left| \dfrac{\Delta q}{\Delta p} \cdot \dfrac{p}{q} \right|$, where $\Delta q / \Delta p$ equals the inverse of the slope of the demand curve.]

Name --

c. Assuming that each of the 100 producers in the industry during the short run keeps cutting price so long as price exceeds marginal cost, what equilibrium price will be established in the short run? _____

What quantity of output will each firm produce? _____

What quantity of output will the industry produce? _____

What profits will each firm earn? _____

d. Over the long run, assuming no decrease in market demand, the profits earned by existing producers will induce the entry of new firms into the industry. Sketch in Figure 11–1 the new proportional demand curve D' that will face each firm when the industry is in long-run equilibrium. At the point of long-run industry equilibrium, what number of firms will be producing? _____ What quantity of output will each produce? _____ What will total industry output be? _____

_____ What price will prevail in the market? _____

What profits will each firm earn? _____

FIGURE 11–1
Short-Run and Long-Run Equilibrium in a Perfectly Competitive Market

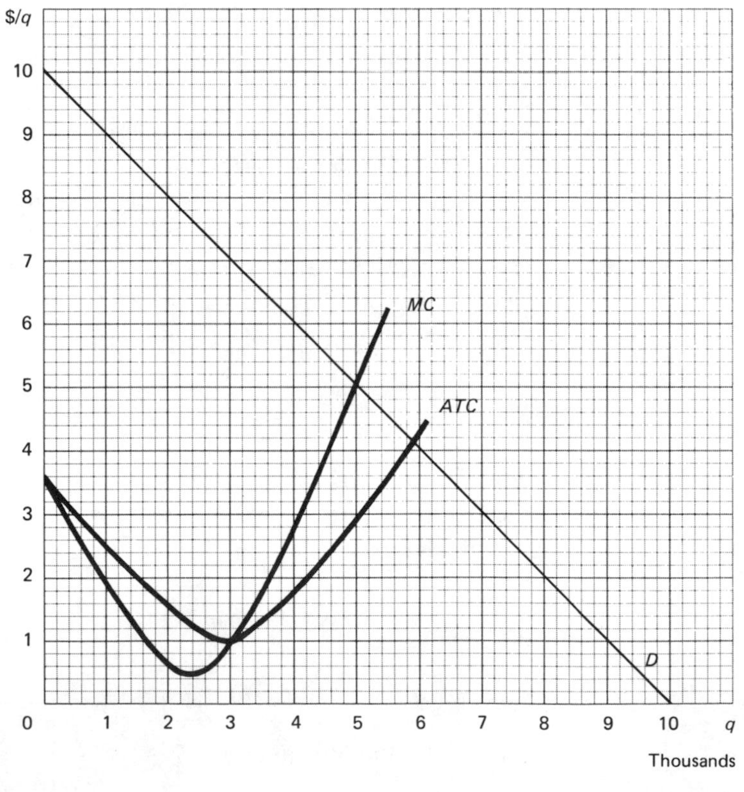

2. A monopolistic competitor, whose rivals all have identical cost curves, faces the two demand curves pictured in Figure 11–2. The *proportional demand curve,* D, shows the relationship between the quantity of output he can sell and the price he charges assuming that all of his rivals charge the same price he does. The *perceived demand curve, d,* shows the relationship between the price he charges and the quantity of output he could sell if all his competitors continued, as he assumes they will, to charge a price of $3. Add to Figure 11–2 an MC, ATC, and MR curve, such that the firm in question would be in short-run equilibrium charging a price of $3 and earning a positive profit. Are the firm's

rivals also in short-run equilibrium? Explain. _____

_____

_____

_____

_____

FIGURE 11–2
Short-Run Equilibrium
of a Profitable
Monopolistic Competitor

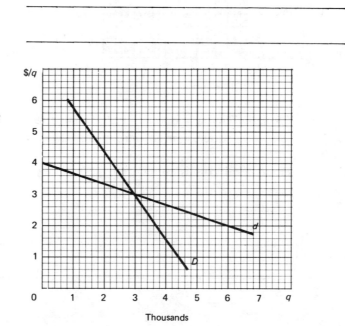

3. *a.* Using *proportional* and *perceived* demand curves, D and d (as defined in question 2 above), draw in Figure 11–3 a diagram picturing a monopolistically competitive firm that attains long-run equilibrium by producing 2,000 units of output and selling this output at a price of $2 per unit. For simplicity assume that the firm and all its rivals have identical cost curves. Also assume that entry into the group is free.

FIGURE 11–3
Long-Run Equilibrium of a Monopolistic Competitor

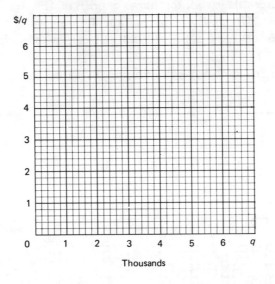

b. Explain why a monopolistically competitive firm would never attain *long-run* equilibrium by producing the output level at which its average total cost is minimized. _____

_____

_____

_____

4. *a.* Assume that producers in a monopolistically competitive group perceive that their rivals will match any price cuts they make. Then they will be concerned only with the *proportional* demand curve D for their output. If entry into such a group is free, and if all firms have identical cost curves, what will the long-run equilibrium of an individual firm look like? To answer, sketch in appropriate *LAC, LMC, D* and *MR* (companion to D) curves in Figure 11–4.

FIGURE 11–4
Long-Run Equilibrium of a Firm in a Nonprice-Competitive Monopolistically Competitive Industry

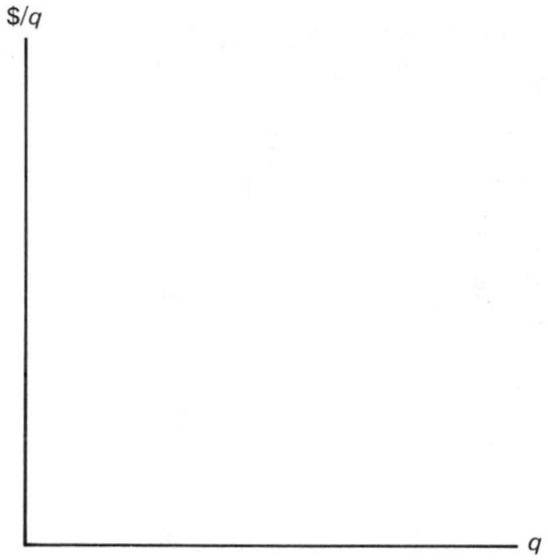

$/q

q

b. Explain why it is that, when monopolistically competitive rivals do not engage in price competition, each individual firm's long-run equilibrium output is lower and its average cost is higher than when price competition is present. _____

_____

_____

_____

_____

_____

_____

Name

Chapter 12

Theories of Prices in Oligopoly Markets

Name --

A. DEFINITIONS AND REVIEW

1. A market is said to be characterized by oligopoly if _____

_____

_____. In pure oligopoly the product sold is (homogeneous/differentiated) while in differentiated oligopoly the product sold is (homogeneous/differentiated).

2. *a.* Duopoly is a special case of oligopoly in which _____.
   The Cournot solution to the duopoly problem is based on the assumption that each seller is a (price/quantity) setter, and that each seller assumes any action he takes will not lead the rival seller to alter his

   _____. Under the Cournot solution to the duopoly problem, output is (larger/smaller) than under the monopoly solution but (larger/smaller) than under the competitive solution.

   b. According to the Edgeworth approach, the rival sellers are (price/quantity) setters. Also each rival assumes that any action he takes will not

   lead the rival to change his _____. The Cournot approach leads to a definite equilibrium. In contrast the outcome of the Edgeworth model is _____.

   c. Under the Chamberlin solution, the rival duopolists recognize their

   _____, and seek to maximize their joint _____ by producing together an output equal to the equilibrium monopoly output.

3. Sweezy argued that an oligopolist will often find himself facing a kinked demand curve. The interpretation of such a demand curve is that, if the oligopolist raises price, his rivals (will/will not) match his price hike, and consequently his sales will fall (sharply/by a small amount). In contrast when he lowers price, his rivals (will/will not) match his price cut, and consequently his sales will rise (sharply/by a small amount).

4.* *a.* Attempts have been made to use game theory to analyze oligopoly behavior. A constant-sum game is one in which _____

_____

_____.

If we view sellers' total revenue as their winnings, then a market in

which demand is _____ illustrates a constant-sum game. A

zero-sum game is one in which _____.

b. A player who follows a minimax strategy seeks to _____

_____.

The Chamberlin duopolist who sets a monopoly price is persuing a

minimax strategy because _____

_____

_____.

c. To say that a player follows a mixed strategy means that _____

_____.

If mixed strategies are permitted, (some/every) constant-sum game has a unique minimax solution.

5. *a.* A cartel is a combination of firms whose object is to _____

_____. Any cartel involves some degree of collusion. When collusion is perfect, the joint profits of the colluding firms are maximized. To achieve the maximization of joint profits, the colluding firms must

agree on _____, _____, _____,

_____, and _____.

b. Maximizing joint profits requires that the colluding firms produce their joint output at minimum cost; to do so, they must allocate total output amongst themselves in such a way that *the following condition* holds:

_____.

---

* Asterisks denote the more difficult problems.

6. *a.* Price leadership is an imperfect form of collusion (i.e., does not lead to joint profit maximization) for several reasons, which include:

_____

_____.

b. In an oligopolistic market in which there is a single dominant seller who sets price, that firm's smaller rivals are likely to behave as price (setters/takers) and to adjust their individual output levels so that their

_____ equals market price p. The dominant firm in contrast

will be operating at output level where its MC is _____p.

c. If a group of oligopolists practicing price leadership shifted their strategy to perfect collusion, the effects on market price, on industry output, on the allocation of that output among firms, on nonprice competition,

and on industry profits would be: _____

_____

_____

_____

_____.

B. MULTIPLE CHOICE

1. If the market for commodity X is oligopolistic, we can be sure that in this market:

   a. the product sold is differentiated.

   b. there are only a few sellers.

   c. nonprice competition has been eliminated through collusive agreements.

   d. there are at least a few sellers who dominate the market in the sense that these sellers can through their own actions significantly influence market price.

2. The price-output combination at which a market characterized by duopoly will attain equilibrium:

   a. always conforms to the Cournot solution.

   b. always conforms to the Edgeworth solution.

   c. always conforms to the Chamberlin solution.

   d. is indeterminate.

3. A duopolist behaves in accordance with the Chamberlin solution to the duopoly problem if he:

   a. recognizes the mutual dependence that links him and his rival.

   b. assumes that his own actions will not influence his rival's decision about how much output to produce.

   c. assumes that his own actions will not influence the price set by his rival.

   d. plays a mixed strategy.

Name _____

4. All of the following statements about the Sweezy oligopoly model are true except:

    a. the model offers an explanation of why an oligopolist might maintain a constant price in the face of cost shifts.

    b. the model implies a discontinuous *MR* curve.

    c. the model explains how the equilibrium price, at which the kink in the oligopolist's demand curve occurs, is determined.

    d. the model assumes that, if the oligopolist cuts his price, his rivals will match his price cut.

5.* The game of matching pennies (heads, you win $1 from me; tails, I win $1 from you) is an example of which of the following:

    a. a constant-sum game.

    b. a zero-sum game.

    c. a strictly determined game.

    d. a game which has a unique minimax solution if mixed strategies are allowed.

6. When rival firms form a cartel, this *always* leads to:

    a. the maximization of the rivals' joint profits.

    b. the elimination of nonprice competition.

    c. the imposition of limits of some sort on interfirm competition.

    d. a price leadership situation.

7. In a market characterized by price leadership, one can be sure that:

    a. the rival firms have adjusted their outputs so that they all have identical marginal costs.

    b. the rival firms are maximizing their joint profits.

    c. the rival firms do not engage in nonprice competition.

    d. price is higher and output lower than would be the case if the rival firms engaged in active price competition.

8. All of the following are forms of nonprice competition except:

    a. product differentiation created through differences in product quality.

    b. advertising by individual firms.

    c. product differentiation created through differences in design.

    d. use of a basing-point price system.

C. PROBLEMS

1. *a.* Figure 12–1(a) pictures the market demand curve for product W, an unusual product which Firm A, whose fixed costs equal zero, can produce at zero marginal cost. Initially Firm A is the only producer of product W. Assuming this firm is a profit-maximizer, what price will it charge for product W? _____ What quantity of output will it produce? _____ What profits will it earn? _____

FIGURE 12–1(a)
The Cournot Duopoly
Case
Firm A

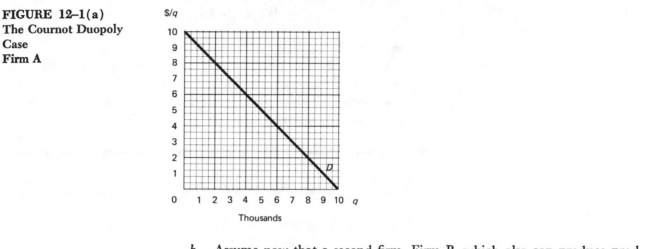

Thousands

b. Assume now that a second firm, Firm B, which also can produce product W at zero marginal cost, enters the market. If Firm B is a Cournot-type oligopolist (that is, if this firm expects that its rival, Firm A, will never alter its output), what demand curve will Firm B believe it faces? Plot this demand curve and the corresponding MR curve in Figure 12–1(b). To maximize profits, given its assumption about A's behavior, what price should Firm B charge? _____ What quantity of output will it sell? _____ What profits will it earn? _____

What will happen to A's profits when B enters the market? _____

FIGURE 12–1(b)
Firm B

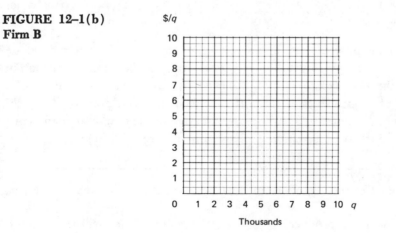

Thousands

Name _____

c. Assume now that A too is a Cournot-type oligopolist; i.e., that it believes that B will never alter its output. What demand curve will Firm
A assume it faces? Plot this demand curve and the corresponding *MR*
curve in Figure 12–1(c). To maximize profits, given its assumption

about B's behavior, what price should Firm A charge? _____

What quantity of output will it sell? _____ What profits will

it earn? _____ What will happen to B's profits when A alters

its output level? _____

d. Assuming that B continues its Cournot-type behavior, how will it respond to the adjustment made by A in (c)? Specifically what demand
curve will firm B now assume it faces? Plot this curve in Figure 12–1(d).
To maximize profits, given its assumption about A's behavior, what price

should Firm B charge? _____ What quantity of output will it

sell? _____ What profits will it earn? _____ What

will happen to A's profits when B alters its output level? _____

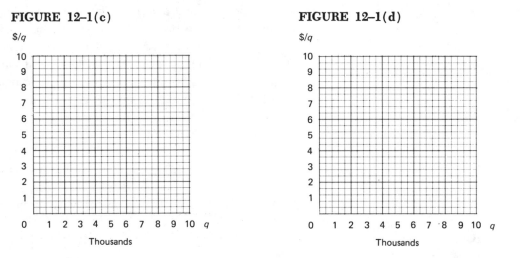

FIGURE 12–1(c)

FIGURE 12–1(d)

e. It can be proved that, if two Cournot duopolists face a market demand curve given by $p = a - bQ$ where Q is their joint total output,
then the equilibrium output achieved by *each* rival as a result of a
series of adjustments of the sort described in (a) through (d) of this
problem will equal $a/3b$. Write the equation of the market demand curve
for product W. This curve is pictured in Figure 12–1(a):

_____

In final Cournot equilibrium how much output will each of the rival

firms A and B produce? _____ What price will they charge?

_____ What profits will each earn? _____

2. Chamberlin has argued that two duopolists of the sort described in problem 1 would be likely to recognize their mutual dependence and decide that the best solution is to maximize and split joint profits. If they did, what level of output would they produce together? _____ What level of output would each produce? _____ What price would they charge? _____

What profits would each earn? _____ Is the Chamberlin equilibrium more profitable than the Cournot equilibrium? _____

3.* *a.* Using calculus, prove the result cited in problem 1(*c*); i.e., that if two *Cournot* duopolists who produce at zero marginal cost face a market demand curve given by

$$p = a - bQ$$

where Q is their joint total output, then the equilibrium output achieved by *each* rival as a result of a succession of quantity adjustments of the sort outlined in problem 1 will equal $a/3b$.

b. Prove that, if both duopolists have the same variable cost functions, $VC = c(q)$, where q represents their own output and $c'(q) > 0$, then the equilibrium level of output achieved by each rival will equal $[a - c'(q)]/3b$.

Name ....

4. The XYZ Company produces hand calculators in Germania. The local market in which it sells is characterized by oligopoly. Currently XYZ and its rivals are all selling their product at a price of $60. If XYZ were to raise its price, its rivals would not follow and its sales would drop sharply. But if XYZ were to cut price, its rivals, fearing a loss of market share, would match the price cut with the result that XYZ's sales would not increase as much from a price cut as they would decrease from a price hike. Consequently XYZ faces the kinked demand curve pictured in Figure 12–2.

  a. Sketch XYZ's *MR* curve in Figure 12–2.

FIGURE 12–2
Equilibrium of an Oligopolist Facing a Kinked Demand Curve

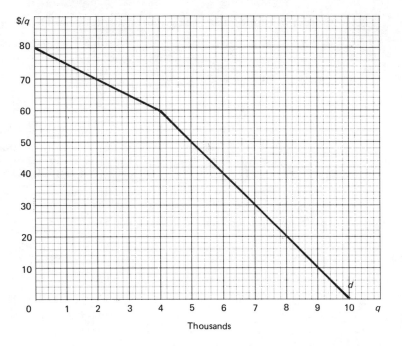

  b. If XYZ had fixed costs of $20,000 and produced output at a constant marginal cost of $25 per unit, what would be their equilibrium level of

  output? _____ What would be their equilibrium price? _____

  _____ What profits would they earn? _____

  c. If a rise in labor costs increased XYZ's marginal cost to $30 per unit,

  how would this affect their equilibrium output? _____

  Their price? _____ Their profits? _____

  d. How would a tripling of XYZ's fixed costs affect their equilibrium

  position? _____

5.* Two duopolists, A and B, are selling a product they both produce at constant and identical marginal costs. The price they charge for this product is set at the government-imposed ceiling of $70 a unit, and demand for this output at that price equals exactly 10,000 units. The total profit payoff of the two firms is thus a fixed amount, which currently equals $15,000. How total sales and thus total available profits are divided between the two firms depends on the design and packaging strategies (all of which cost roughly the same) adopted by the two firms.

    a. Table 12–1 shows what payoff A would earn for each possible combination of strategies A and B might pursue. B's profits will equal the total amount to be earned, $15,000, minus what A gets. What strategies

will the two firms select? _____ [Hint: Fill in the row minimum and column maximum figures in Table 12–1. Then assume that A seeks to maximize the minimum it earns; i.e., that it "maximins." Assume also that B follows similar strategy (see Table 12–1) which means that it seeks the strategy that will minimize the column maximums.]

    b. Suppose now that, due to a change in consumer preferences with respect to design, A's strategy *c* pays off better than before when B pursues strategy *b'*. See the payoff matrix in Table 12–2. Suppose also that each firm selects a strategy for the current period and holds it so long as the other firm does not alter its strategy. What strategy would firm A

choose in the initial period? _____ In response to that

choice, what strategy would firm B choose in period 2? _____
In response to B's period 2 choice, what strategy would firm A pick

in period 3? _____ And how would firm B react in period

4? _____ What would be firm A's response in period 5? ____

_____ Is the outcome of the game (i.e., the strategies the two

firms select) now determinate as it was above? _____

    c. What condition must hold in a two-firm, constant-sum game for the

game to have a determinate outcome? _____

TABLE 12–1
Payoff Matrix for a Constant-Profit Duopoly Game

A's Strategies	B's Strategies a'	b'	c'	d'	Row Minimum
a	0	8	7	4	
b	11	10	12	15	
c	8	6	4	3	
d	11	2	15	12	
Column Maximum					

TABLE 12–2
Payoff Matrix for a Constant-Profit Duopoly Game

A's Strategies	B's Strategies a'	b'	c'	d'	Row Minimum
a	0	8	7	4	
b	11	10	12	15	
c	8	14	4	3	
d	11	2	15	12	
Column Maximum					

6. Three rival oligopolists who produce a homogeneous commodity and whose *MC* curves are pictured in Figure 12–3(a–c) decide that the best policy for them is to set total output, price, and the allocation of production amongst themselves so as to *maximize their joint profits* which they then agree to redistribute amongst themselves according to some "fair" formula. If market demand for their product is given by the demand curve *D* in Figure 12–3(d), what total output will

the three firms produce? _____ What price will they charge? _____

_____ How much output will be produced by Firm I? _____

By Firm II? _____ By Firm III? _____ What sort of profit

redistribution would you expect the three firms to adopt? _____ [Hint: To maximize *joint* profits, the three firms have to produce output at the lowest possible total cost, which implies that any level of output produced should be allocated among the three firms so that all producing firms have identical marginal costs and all nonproducing firms could not produce at that low a marginal cost. Thus step one in the solution is to construct and plot in Figure 12–3(d) a *joint MC* curve, that is a curve that shows the relationship between the level of output produced and the marginal cost incurred by the group when output is allocated so as to minimize joint total cost. The next step is to derive an *MR* curve from the market demand curve *D*, and find the price-output combination that equates *MR* with joint *MC*.]

FIGURE 12–3
Perfect Collusion

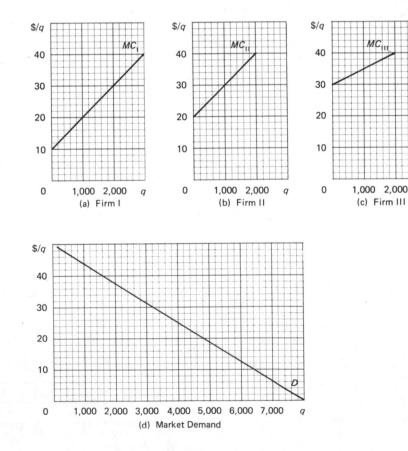

(a) Firm I   (b) Firm II   (c) Firm III

(d) Market Demand

7. Suppose that the colluding oligopolists of problem 6 could sell their output both in the home market and the foreign market and that demand in the two markets was as shown in Figure 12–4(a–b). Now maximization of joint profits could call not only for a collective decision on output, price, and the allocation of production, but also for *price discrimination*.

Given the *MC* curves in Figure 12–3 and the demand curves in Figure 12–4, what total output should the three firms produce to maximize joint profits?

_____ How much should they sell in the home market? _____

At what price? _____ How much should they sell in the foreign market?

_____ At what price? _____ How much will Firm I produce? _____ How much will Firm II produce? _____ How much will Firm III produce? _____ [Hint: Start by sketching in Figure 12–4(c) the joint *MC* curve you plotted in Figure 12–3(d). Then (see problem 7 in Chapter 9) add an appropriate joint *MR* curve.]

FIGURE 12–3
Constructing a Joint *MC* Curve

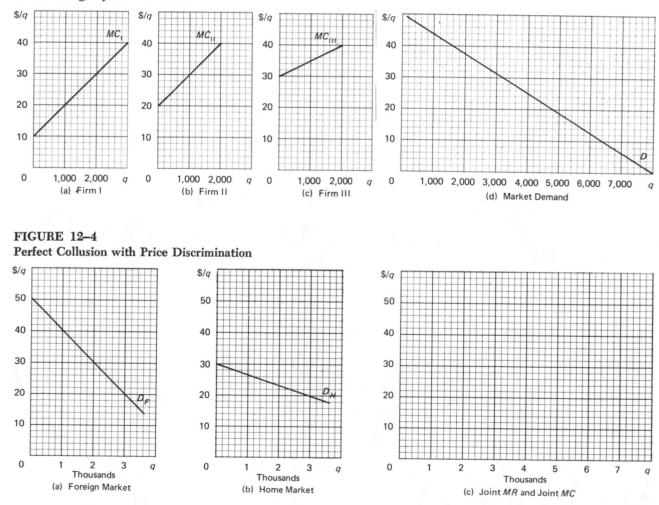

FIGURE 12–4
Perfect Collusion with Price Discrimination

8. *a.* In Angolia widget production is controlled by a group of rival oligopolists, one of these is a large low-cost dominant firm, the others are smaller and higher cost producers. Figure 12–5 pictures the market demand D in Angolia for widgets as well as the marginal cost curve of the dominant firm, MC_D. The dominant firm would like to use its cost advantage to drive its smaller rivals out of the market and establish a monopoly

position. If it did, it would charge a price of _____ and sell

an output level of _____ [Hint: To answer, add an appropriate MR curve to Figure 12–5.]

FIGURE 12–5
Price Leadership

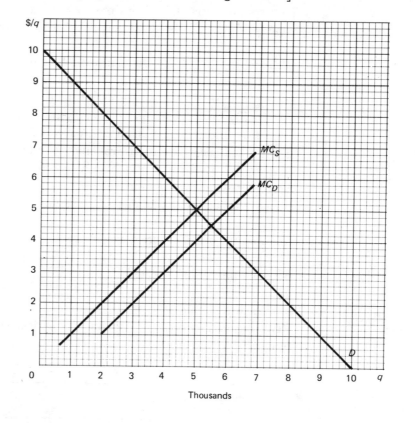

b. In fact the dominant firm cannot drive its rivals out of the market because of local antitrust policy. Suppose that the dominant firm decides to adopt the following strategy for coexisting with its rivals. It will set price—act as the industry *price leader*—and permit its rivals to sell all they wish to at the established price. MC_s is the joint marginal cost curve of the smaller firms (see problem 6 above); it shows the relationship between the joint output of these firms and the marginal cost they would all incur if they always expanded their individual outputs to the point where their marginal costs were identical.

With the dominant firm setting price, the smaller firms will presumably view themselves as price takers, and MC_s will in effect be their joint supply curve. Given this response on the part of the smaller firms, what price should the dominant firm set in order to maximize its own

profits? _____ At that price, how much will it sell? _____

How much will the small firms together sell? _____ [Hint: Plot in Figure 12–5 the *net* demand curve $(D\text{–}MC_s)$ facing the dominant firm and the companion MR curve.]

c. Is price leadership the most profitable solution for these live-and-let-live oligopolists? To answer, sketch in a new joint MC curve, MC_{s+D}, and figure out what the equilibrium position of these firms would be if they engaged in perfect collusion; i.e., maximized joint profits. In such an

equilibrium position, price would be _____, the output of

the dominant firm would be _____, and the output of the

smaller firms would be _____.

d. Referring to Figure 12–5, explain why perfect collusion would be more profitable for the group than the scheme of price leadership outlined in

(b). _____

_____

_____

_____

_____

Chapter 13

Marginal Productivity Theory of Distribution in Perfectly Competitive Markets

A. DEFINITIONS AND REVIEW

1. *a.* For any variable input, the *value of the marginal product* (*VMP*) equals

    the input's _____ multiplied times _____. In contrast, an input's *marginal* revenue product (*MRP*) equals the input's

    _____ multiplied times _____.

    b. For a firm selling in a perfectly competitive market, *VMP* (is less than/equals/exceeds) *MRP*.

    c. Consider a firm combining a single variable input, labor, with a fixed input, capital. If this firm is a perfect competitor, the value of labor's marginal product to the firm VMP_L (and MRP_L too) will decrease,

    as the firm hires more labor, because _____

    _____

    _____.

    d. Assume that labor can be purchased at the going wage rate, *w*. A perfectly competitive firm using a single variable input labor will maximize profits by adjusting its employment of labor so that the following condition (choose >, =, or <) holds:

    $$w \left(\begin{smallmatrix} > \\ = \\ < \end{smallmatrix}\right) MRP_L \left(\begin{smallmatrix} > \\ = \\ < \end{smallmatrix}\right) VMP_L$$

2. *a.* For a perfectly competitive firm using a single variable input labor,

the firm's demand curve for labor coincides with labor's _____ curve. Since VMP_L declines as more labor is used, the firm's demand

curve for labor is _____ sloped. If a firm uses more than one variable input, deriving its demand curve for labor is more compli-

cated but the curve obtained is still _____ sloped.

b. The demand curve for labor of a firm that combines several variable inputs with a fixed input will *shift* whenever changes occur in any of

the following: _____, _____,

_____, and _____. A change in the going wage rate (will/will not) cause the firm's demand curve for labor to shift.

3. If an input is traded in a perfectly competitive market, the market supply

curve will normally have a _____ slope, the market demand curve

a _____ slope, and the market will attain equilibrium at the input price

at which _____.

4. To derive an individual's supply curve of labor we need to know his _____

_____ (and/but not) what the going wage rate is. Normally an individual will respond in only one way to a decrease in the price of a consumption good,

by buying _____ of it. In the case of labor supply, however, an in-

dividual may respond to a rise in the wage rate by supplying either _____

or _____ labor.

5. The return earned by fixed inputs during the short run is referred to in the

jargon of economists as a _____. Any quasi-rent can be broken into

two parts _____ and _____.

6.* If a firm, whose production function is homogeneous of degree one, adjusts its employment of *all* inputs so that the *real* wage paid each input equals that input's marginal product, the firm's total wage bill will (be less than/equal/be greater than/bear no relationship to) the total product it produces. In other words, if a firm whose production function is homogeneous of degree one, pays all its inputs a real wage equal to their marginal product, its profits will necessarily

be _____.

---

* Asterisks denote the more difficult problems.

7.* *a.* For a firm employing two inputs, capital and labor, Hicks' elasticity of substitution (σ) measures the responsiveness of the firm's capital-labor ratio (K/L) to changes in the marginal rate of technical substitution

of capital for labor ($MRTS$). Specifically it is defined as _____

_____

In symbols we can write this as

$$\sigma = \underline{\hspace{6cm}}$$

b. An increase in the absolute return earned by a factor of production is likely to alter its share of total income. It will increase this share if the

elasticity of substitution is _____ one, decrease this a share

if the elasticity of substitution is _____ one, and have no

effect on this share if the elasticity of substitution _____ one.

8.* *a.* According to Hicks' definition, technological progress is capital-using if, as a result of a change in technology, the marginal rate of technical substitution of capital for labor (diminishes/remains unchanged/increases) at the originally prevailing capital-labor ratio. If technological change is capital-using, it increases the marginal product of capital (more than/less than/the same amount that) it increases the marginal

product of labor, and consequently the firm _____ its capital-labor ratio.

b. If most technological change is capital-using, the relative share of capital in total income will tend to (increase/remain unchanged/decrease) over time.

B. MULTIPLE CHOICE

1. Consider a firm that produces output with a *single* input labor and which faces a constant-returns-to-scale production function. The firm sells its output in a perfectly competitive market at a price of $1 per unit. The marginal product of labor is five units and the wage rate is $4. To maximize profits, this firm should hire:

a. zero workers.

b. some number of workers but the information is insufficient to know how many.

c. an infinite number of workers.

d. probably five workers, but you need to know fixed costs to be sure.

Name _____

2. The preceding question illustrates this important point:

   a. only firms facing a downward-sloping demand curve attain equilibrium by employing a finite number of workers.

   b. a perfectly competitive firm, using a single variable input labor, will attain equilibrium by hiring a positive, but finite, number of workers only if labor is subject to diminishing returns.

   c. a firm that sells its output in a perfectly competitive market does not have a demand curve for labor.

   d. a perfectly competitive firm will attain equilibrium by employing a finite number of workers only if in its operations VMP_L exceeds MRP_L.

3. A firm's demand curve for labor is likely to *shift* upward in response to any of the following changes except:

   a. a rise in the price it gets for its output.

   b. a rise in the price of substitute inputs.

   c. a labor-using technological change in its production function.

   d. a fall in the going wage received by labor.

4. Assume that unskilled labor is sold in a perfectly competitive market in which the market demand curve is negatively sloped and the market supply curve positively sloped. To finance health services, the government imposes a tax on employers of T dollars for each worker employed. The effects of this tax will include which of the following:

   a. raise the gross cost to employers of hiring a worker by exactly T dollars.

   b. lower the net wage received by workers by something less than T dollars.

   c. cut the equilibrium level of employment.

   d. raise government tax revenues by T dollars times the pre-tax equilibrium level of employment.

5. An individual's supply curve of labor will shift in response to:

   a. a rise in the wage rate.

   b. a change in his labor-leisure preferences.

   c. a downward shift in the market demand curve for labor.

   d. none of the above.

6.* Quasi-rents, as defined by Marshall:

   a. must always be nonnegative.

   b. typically rise as the firm moves from short-run to long-run equilibrium.

   c. are exactly equal to the pure economic profit attributable to the use of fixed inputs.

   d. equal the difference between the firm's total revenue and its variable costs.

7.* The product exhaustion theory—namely that paying each input a real wage equal to its marginal product will exhaust total product:

    a.   applies only to the long run when all inputs are variable.

    b.   holds only if technological change is unbiased.

    c.   holds only if the production function is characterized by constant returns to scale.

    d.   holds only if short-run quasi-rents are zero.

8.* For production functions of the sort $q = f(L,K)$, the marginal product of labor is certain to depend *solely* on the capital-labor ratio in production (i.e., not also on the scale of ouput):

    a.   always.

    b.   only if the production function is linearly homogeneous.

    c.   only if the elasticity of substitution equals one.

    d.   only if neither capital nor labor are subject to diminishing returns.

9.* Firm X combines capital and labor to produce output. If after a technological change in Firm X's production function, we find that this firm has the same marginal rate of transformation between capital and labor *and* the same capital-labor ratio as before the change, we can infer that:

    a.   the firm's equilibrium level of output did not change.

    b.   the technological change was neutral.

    c.   the technological change was labor-using and capital-using.

    d.   the firm's production function is linearly homogeneous.

Name ---

C. PROBLEMS

1. *a.* Johnson, a sole proprietor, produces a new product, zips, using one *fixed* input, capital (K), and one *variable* input, labor (L). Currently zips are sold in a perfectly competitive market at a price of $1 each. While Johnson is a whiz at producing zips, he is poor at profit calculations and isn't sure how much labor he should hire during the current period to maximize short-run profits. Can you help him out? The relationship between the inputs of labor and capital that Johnson uses and the output he gets is depicted by the isoquant map in Figure 13–1. Johnson's current stock of capital totals four units and costs $500 per period. The price of labor is $1,500 per worker. To maximize short-run profits, how much labor

should Johnson hire? _____ What level of output should

he produce? _____ What profits will he earn? _____

_____ [Hint: Start by filling in columns 2 through 11 in Table 13–1.]

FIGURE 13–1
The Production Function for Zips

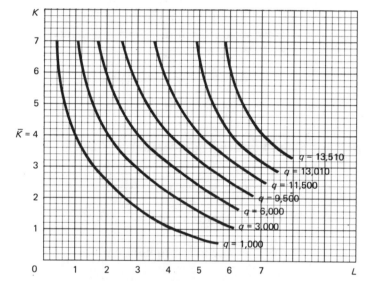

TABLE 13–1
Cost and Revenue Data for Zip Production

L (1)	q (2)	MP_L (3)	p (4)	VMP_L $(p \cdot MP_L)$ (5)	w (6)	VC $(w \cdot L)$ (7)	FC (8)	TC (9)	TR (10)	π (11)	ARP_L $(p \cdot AP_L)$ (12)
0	0	—		—		0					—
1											
2											
3											
4											
5											
6											
7											

b. Your calculations in (*a*) show that, to maximize profits, Johnson should hire labor up to the point where the wage (w_L) he has to pay approximately equals the *value of labor's marginal product, VMP_L.* Explain

why this is so. _____

_____

_____

_____

_____

c. Derive Johnson's demand curve for labor during the current period (i.e., his demand curve based on a capital stock of four) and plot it in Figure 13–2. [Hint: The *average revenue product* of labor is given by: $ARP_L = p \cdot AP_L = TR/L$; using this relationship fill in column 12 of Table 13–1; then plot the VMP_L curve in Figure 13–2. Part (which part?) of this curve corresponds to the firm's demand curve for labor.]

d. How would the firm's short-run demand curve for labor be altered by each of the following:

(1) A rise in fixed costs (property taxes go up)? _____

(2) A rise in the price of labor? _____

(3) A change in technology that altered the firm's production function?

_____

(4) A change in size of the firm's capital stock? _____

(5) A rise in the equilibrium price of zips? _____

FIGURE 13–2
Deriving the Demand-for-Labor Curve in Zip Production

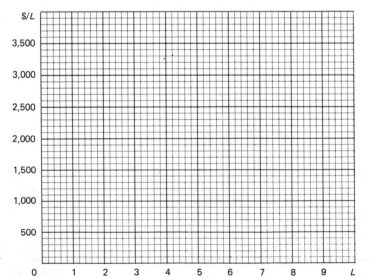

2. *a.* Jones, a not atypical consumer, derives utility from income, which permits him to buy things, and from leisure, which gives him time to do things; all of which faces Jones with a difficult tradeoff—the more hours he works, the greater his income *but* the less his leisure, and vice versa. Just how Jones resolves his labor-leisure tradeoff depends both on his preferences with respect to labor and income and on the wage rate—which determines the terms on which he can trade one for the other.

Figure 13–3 pictures Jones' labor-leisure preference map. From it derive Jones' *supply curve of labor;* i.e., a schedule showing the relationship between the wage he receives and the number of hours he is willing to work per day. [Hint: The appropriate budget constraint is:

$$Y = w_L(24 - F)$$

where Y denotes income, w_L is the wage rate per hour, 24 equals the number of hours available per day, and F is the amount of time Jones devotes to leisure or free time. To solve the problem, plot a family of the above budget lines, each corresponding to a different value of w_L. Then record your results in Table 13–2, and plot the resulting figures in Figure 13–4.]

FIGURE 13–3
Deriving Jones' Supply Curve of Labor

TABLE 13–2
Deriving Jones' Supply Curve of Labor

w_L $/Hour (1)	F Hours (2)	$S_L = 24 - F$ Hours (3)
0.50		
1.00		
1.50		
2.00		
2.50		

Name ....

b. (1) The supply curve of labor you plotted in Figure 13–4 is *backward bending* indicating that, as the wage rate increases, Jones' initial response is what one might expect, he works more. But as the wage rate continues to increase, eventually he responses to such increases by working less; i.e., by demanding more leisure. Whenever the wage rate increases, this price change alters the consumer's *equilibrium consumption of income* via both an income and a substitution effect. In Figure 13–5 identify the income and substitution effects generated by a rise in the wage rate that shifts the consumer's budget line from *bb* to *b'b*. Substitution effect:

_____ Income effect: _____ Over the range of w_L considered, what is the slope of the S_L curve?

_____

(2) When w_L rises, what will always be the impact via the substitution effect on the consumer's willingness to supply labor?

_____ What will be the normal impact via

the income effect? _____

(3) Explain why for a consumer a negatively sloped supply curve of labor is plausible while a positively sloped demand curve for a commodity is highly unlikely.

_____

_____

_____

_____

FIGURE 13–5
The Income and the Substitution Effect When S_L Is Negatively Sloped

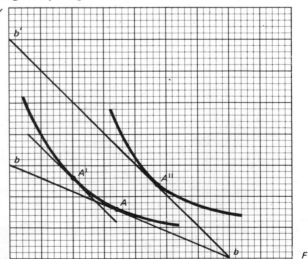

FIGURE 13–4
Jones' Supply Curve of Labor

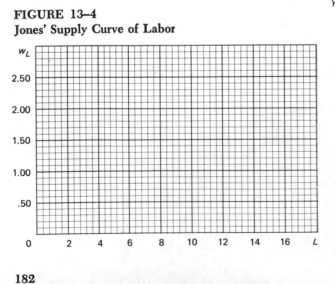

3. *a.* The city of Old York, like lots of other cities, is facing a fiscal crisis—expenditures exceed tax receipts. To fill its budget deficit, the city council decides to impose a tax on firms employing unskilled labor. To "protect" workers it decrees that the tax of 50¢ per hour for each worker employed will be paid by employers. Referring to Figure 13–6, which pictures the market for unskilled labor in Old York, determine what the effect of the tax will be both on employers and workers. Specifically what is:

(1) The pre-tax equilibrium wage? _____

(2) The pre-tax equilibrium level of employment? _____

(3) The post-tax equilibrium *gross* wage paid by the employer?

_____

(4) The post-tax net wage received by workers? _____

(5) The post-tax equilibrium level of employment? _____
[Hint: To answer sketch in a new *net* demand curve in Figure 13–6 (see problem 5, Chapter 8).]

FIGURE 13–6
Imposition of a Specific
Tax on the Labor Market

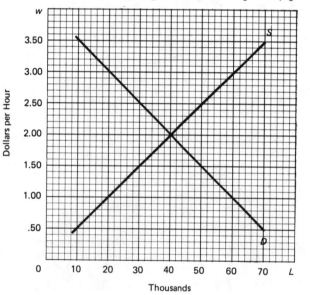

b. How would your answers in (*a*) have been affected, if initially there had been a minimum wage of $2.50 per hour in Old York:

(1) _____

(2) _____

(3) _____

(4) _____

(5) _____

4. The return earned by any fixed factor during the short-run, $TR - VC$, is often referred to as *quasi-rent*. Any quasi-rent can in turn be broken into two components: (*a*) *the opportunity cost* incurred by the firm in using the input, and (*b*) pure economic profit; i.e., the short-run profits earned by the firm through production.

Figure 13–7 pictures the short-run cost curves of a perfectly competitive firm. Referring to this diagram, determine for each of the prices listed in Table 13–3 what the firm's equilibrium output would be, what quasi-rents the firm's fixed inputs would earn, and how big the two components of quasi-rent would be. Record your answers in Table 13–3.

FIGURE 13–7
Quasi-Rents

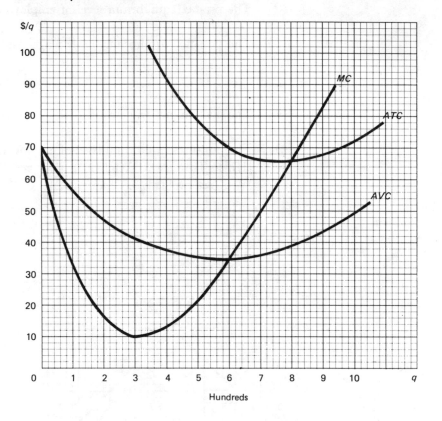

TABLE 13–3
Determining Quasi-Rents and Their Components

Output Price (1)	Equilibrium Output (2)	Quasi-Rent (3)	Opportunity Cost (4)	Pure Economic Profit (5)
$82		$	$21,600	$
66				
50				
35				
30				

5. *a.* Figure 13–8 pictures the $q = 1$ isoquant from a production function in which output (q) is produced by combining capital (K) and labor (L). Any improvement in technology will shift the $q = 1$ isoquant closer to the origin. If after such a shift, the firm were to continue producing one unit of output at the *originally prevailing capital-labor ratio,* it would find the marginal productivities of capital and labor $(MP_K$ and $MP_L)$ were higher. If the proportionate increases in MP_L and MP_K were identical, the technological change would be said to be *neutral.* If the proportionate increase in MP_L were greater than the proportionate increase in MP_K, the technological change would be said to be *labor-using.* Finally, if the proportionate increase in MP_L were less than the proportionate increase in MP_K, the technological change would be said to be *capital-using.* In Figure 13–8 sketch in new isoquants $[q'(L,K) = 1]$ corresponding to neutral, capital-using, and labor-using technological changes. [Hint: What counts is the slope of the q'-isoquant at the originally prevailing capital-labor ratio.]

FIGURE 13–8
Technological Change—
Neutral and Biased

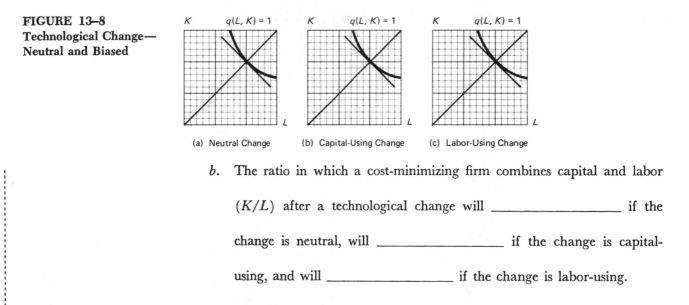

(a) Neutral Change   (b) Capital-Using Change   (c) Labor-Using Change

b. The ratio in which a cost-minimizing firm combines capital and labor (K/L) after a technological change will _____ if the change is neutral, will _____ if the change is capital-using, and will _____ if the change is labor-using.

6.* Product q is produced by combining capital K and labor L. The production function for this production process, $q = f(L,K)$, is linearly homogeneous. Prove that with such a function

$$q = Lf_1 + Kf_2$$

i.e., paying inputs returns equal to their marginal products exhausts the product. [Hint: Start from the definition of a linearly homogeneous production function: $\lambda f(L,K) = f(\lambda L, K)$. Note also that f_1 denotes $\partial q/\partial L$ and f_2 denotes $\partial q/\partial K$.]

Chapter 14

Theory of Employment in Imperfectly Competitive Markets

A. DEFINITIONS AND REVIEW

1. *a.* For any variable input, we define the values of the marginal product and the marginal revenue product as follows:

$$VMP = \underline{\hspace{1cm}} \cdot \underline{\hspace{1cm}} = \underline{\hspace{1cm}} \cdot \underline{\hspace{1cm}}$$

$$MRP = \underline{\hspace{1cm}} \cdot \underline{\hspace{1cm}}$$

b. For an imperfect competitor (i.e., for a firm facing a downward-sloping demand curve), VMP (is less than/equals/exceeds) MRP.

c. Consider a firm combining a single variable input, labor, with a fixed input, capital. If this firm is an imperfect competitor, labor's marginal revenue product (MRP_L) will decrease as the firm hires more labor, because \underline{\hspace{2cm}}

\underline{\hspace{4cm}} and because \underline{\hspace{6cm}}

\underline{\hspace{9cm}}.

d. Assume that labor can be purchased at the going wage rate, *w*. A monopolist using a single variable input, labor, will maximize profits by adjusting his employment of labor so that the following condition holds:

$$w \left(\genfrac{}{}{0pt}{}{>}{\genfrac{}{}{0pt}{}{=}{<}} \right) MRP_L \left(\genfrac{}{}{0pt}{}{>}{\genfrac{}{}{0pt}{}{=}{<}} \right) VMP_L$$

e. The key way in which a monopolist's equilibrium position with respect to the labor market differs from that of a perfect competitor is that for a monopolist in equilibrium, VMP_L \underline{\hspace{2cm}} MRP_L; while for a perfect competitor in equilibrium, VMP_L \underline{\hspace{2cm}} MRP_L.

2. *a.* The demand curve for labor of a *monopolist* who uses a single variable

input labor, coincides with labor's _____ curve. Since MRP_L declines as the firm employs more labor, the firm's demand curve for labor will be

_____ sloped. It is also true that, if the firm uses more than one variable input, its demand curve for any one of these variable inputs will be

_____ sloped.

    b. The demand curve for labor of a monopolist who uses several variable

inputs will *shift* whenever changes occur in any of the following: _____

_____ , _____ , _____ , and

_____. A change in the going wage rate (will/will not) cause a monopolist's demand curve for labor to shift.

3. *a.* When economists say that an input is subject to monopolistic exploitation, what they mean is that the input is employed at a wage that is less than its

_____. The rule that profits are maximized when labor is hired to the point where

$$w = MRP_L$$

holds for *both* perfectly competitive firms and monopolists using a single variable input, labor. However, a monopolist (does/does not) practice monopolistic exploitation of labor while the perfect competitor (does/does not). The explanation

of the contrast is that _____

_____ .

    b. When a firm practices monopolistic exploitation of labor, it hires too (much/little) labor and produces (much/little) output for resource allocation to be efficient. An effective measure for correcting this situation is to (force the firm to pay a higher wage rate/force the firm to lower its output price).

4. *a.* A market is said to be characterized by *monopsony* if _____

_____. It is said to be characterized by oligopsony if

_____.

b. When a firm is a monopsonist in an input market, the input supply curve

represents for him the relationship between _____

_____.

Whenever a producer is a monopsonist in the market for a particular input, the relationship between the average cost to him of this input (i.e., the wage he pays it) and the input's marginal cost is that

$$AC \underline{\hspace{1cm}} MC$$

Using an input's AC (or supply) curve, we can construct for the input an MC

curve which shows the relationship between _____

_____.

c. Suppose that the input in question is the only variable input that the monopsonist uses. Then the quantity of it that he employs in equilibrium will be

determined by the intersection of the _____ curve and the

_____ curve. To figure out what wage the monopsonist will

pay the input in equilibrium, we _____

_____.

d. Let w denote the wage rate, r the return earned by capital. A firm that is a price taker in both the labor and capital markets will minimize costs by adjusting its capital and labor inputs so that the following condition holds:

$$\frac{MP_L}{w} \left(\genfrac{}{}{0pt}{}{>}{\genfrac{}{}{0pt}{}{=}{<}} \right) \frac{MP_L}{MC_L} \left(\genfrac{}{}{0pt}{}{>}{\genfrac{}{}{0pt}{}{=}{<}} \right) \frac{MP_K}{MC_K} \left(\genfrac{}{}{0pt}{}{>}{\genfrac{}{}{0pt}{}{=}{<}} \right) \frac{MP_K}{r}$$

In contrast, a firm that is a monopsonist in both the labor and capital markets will minimize costs by adjusting its capital and labor inputs so that this relationship holds:

$$\frac{MP_L}{w} \left(\genfrac{}{}{0pt}{}{>}{\genfrac{}{}{0pt}{}{=}{<}} \right) \frac{MP_L}{MC_L} \left(\genfrac{}{}{0pt}{}{>}{\genfrac{}{}{0pt}{}{=}{<}} \right) \frac{MP_K}{MC_K} \left(\genfrac{}{}{0pt}{}{>}{\genfrac{}{}{0pt}{}{=}{<}} \right) \frac{MP_K}{r}$$

e. A monopolist, who is a price taker in input markets and who uses one variable input labor, maximizes profits by operating at the point where

$$w \left(\genfrac{}{}{0pt}{}{>}{\genfrac{}{}{0pt}{}{=}{<}} \right) MC_L \left(\genfrac{}{}{0pt}{}{>}{\genfrac{}{}{0pt}{}{=}{<}} \right) MRP_L \left(\genfrac{}{}{0pt}{}{>}{\genfrac{}{}{0pt}{}{=}{<}} \right) VMP_L$$

Such a firm engages in monopolistic exploitation of labor because, at its maximum-profit position,

$$w \left(\genfrac{}{}{0pt}{}{>}{\genfrac{}{}{0pt}{}{=}{<}} \right) VMP_L$$

Name _____

f. In contrast a firm which uses one variable input, labor, and which is a monopolist in the output market and a monopsonist in the labor market, maximizes profits by operating at the point where

$$w \quad \left(\genfrac{}{}{0pt}{}{>}{\genfrac{}{}{0pt}{}{=}{<}}\right) \ MC_L \ \left(\genfrac{}{}{0pt}{}{>}{\genfrac{}{}{0pt}{}{=}{<}}\right) \ MRP_L \ \left(\genfrac{}{}{0pt}{}{>}{\genfrac{}{}{0pt}{}{=}{<}}\right) \ VMP_L$$

In doing so the firm engages in something *more than* monopolistic exploitation of labor because, at its maximum-profit point,

$$w \quad \left(\genfrac{}{}{0pt}{}{>}{\genfrac{}{}{0pt}{}{=}{<}}\right) \ MRP_L \ \left(\genfrac{}{}{0pt}{}{>}{\genfrac{}{}{0pt}{}{=}{<}}\right) \ VMP_L$$

An effective means for eliminating exploitation of labor due solely to the exercise of monopsony power would be to (force the firm to pay a higher wage rate/ force the firm to lower its output price).

B. MULTIPLE CHOICE

1. When a monopolist hires an additional worker his total revenue rises by an amount equal to:

a. VMP_L.   c. $AR \cdot MP_L$.

b. $MR \cdot MP_L$.   d. w

2. A monopolist who uses a single variable input, labor, and who is a price taker in the labor market, is currently operating at his point of maximum profit. Which of the following conditions must hold for him?

a. $MR = MC$.   c. $MRP_L = MC_L$.

b. $w = MC_L$.   d. $MRP_L = w$.

3. If it is possible to construct a producer's demand curve for a variable input, this curve will be negatively sloped:

    a. only if the producer is a monopolist.

    b. only if the producer is a perfect competitor.

    c. only if the producer is a monopsonist.

    d. regardless of market organization in the output market.

4. Forcing a monopolist to charge a price for his output below the price that would maximize his profits will tend to reduce monopolistic exploitation of labor because:

    a. it would lower VMP_L without altering MRP_L, and the gap between VMP_L and MRP_L would thereby be narrowed.

    b. it would reduce monopoly profits.

    c. it would raise MR and thus MRP_L in the neighborhood of the firm's equilibrium position and thus induce the firm to hire more workers.

    d. with a price ceiling the firm would no longer maximize profits by operating at a point where $MR = MC$.

5. For a monopsonist who can hire nine workers at a wage of $5 but has to pay a $6 wage to get ten workers, the marginal cost of the tenth worker would be:

    a. $15.

    b. MC_L would equal AC_L which isn't given.

    c. $6.

    d. you need revenue and productivity data to answer the question.

6. For a firm that is a monopolist in the output market and a monopsonist in the labor market, which of the following conditions will hold at the point of maximum profit:

a. $MC_L < w$.   c. $AC_L < MRP_L$.

b. $MC_L = MRP_L$.   d. $MRP_L < VMP_L$.

7. Raising the minimum wage that a firm, which is a monopsonist in the labor market, must pay for labor, will tend to decrease exploitation of labor due to the exercise of monopsony power because:

    a. it will cause the monopsonist to raise the price he charges for output, which in turn will give him more money to pay to workers.

    b. it will cause the monopsonist to operate at a point where $MRP_L = VMP_L$.

    c. it will lower the marginal cost of labor in the neighborhood of the monopsonist's initial (i.e., pre-minimum-wage) equilibrium position and thereby cause him to hire more labor.

    d. it will cause the monopsonist to lower output, which will raise MRP_L.

8. Initially the market for unskilled workers is perfectly competitive, and the going wage for such workers is w^0, the wage that equates market demand and supply. Then a union organizes unskilled workers and through bargaining raises the wage above w^0. As a result, which of the following will occur:

    a. the number of unskilled workers employed will decrease unless market demand for labor is infinitely inelastic.

    b. the total wages earned by employed unskilled workers will rise if market demand for such labor is elastic.

    c. the total wages earned by employed unskilled workers will rise if market demand for such labor has unit elasticity.

    d. the total wages earned by employed unskilled workers will rise only if market demand for such labor is inelastic.

9. By raising the wage rate, unions can eliminate:

    a. monopolistic exploitation of labor.

    b. the portion of total monopsonistic exploitation of labor that is uniquely attributable to monopsony in the labor market.

    c. the portion of total monopsonistic exploitation of labor that is uniquely attributable to the monopoly power that the monopsonist exercises in his output market.

    d. any and all exploitation of labor in which a monopsonist engages.

Name ....

C. PROBLEMS

1. The Flower People Co., produces its output, dried daisies, with a single variable input, labor. Figure 14–1 shows the MRP_L and ARP_L curves for labor employed in dried daisy production.

a. (1) $MRP_L = MR \cdot$ _____ $= \Delta TR/\Delta L$
$ARP_L = AR \cdot AP_L = TR/L$

$VMP_L =$ _____ $\cdot$ _____

(2) In terms of sales revenue received by the firm, the distinction

between MRP_L, VMP_L, and ARP_L is _____

_____

_____

_____

_____.

(3) For a perfectly competitive firm MRP_L _____ VMP_L

because under perfect competition MR _____ AR.
However, for an imperfectly competitive firm, MRP_L is always

_____ VMP_L because under imperfect competition,

MR is _____ AR.

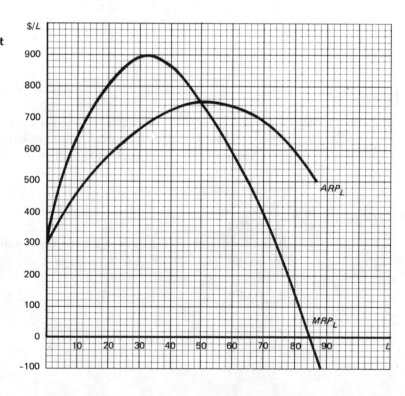

FIGURE 14–1
Average Revenue Product and Marginal Revenue Product Curves for Labor Employed by the Flower People Co.

b. The MRP_L curve for labor employed in a firm that uses fixed inputs and sells its output in an imperfectly competitive market, is certain to turn down *eventually* as labor inputs are increased. Give two reasons for this:

(1) _____

_____

(2) _____

_____

c. The MRP_L curve in Figure 14–1 rises initially (i.e., is positively sloped)

at low levels of labor inputs. What's the explanation for this? _____

_____

_____

d. The MRP_L curve in Figure 14–1 intersects its companion ARP_L curve where the latter attains a maximum. Is this the normal relationship be-

tween the two curves? _____ Explain why

or why not: _____

_____

_____

_____

e. Assuming that the Flower People Co. is a profit maximizer, what quantity of labor would it hire at each of the following wage rates w_L that might

prevail in the labor market? $w_L = 900$ _____; $w_L = 750$ _____;

$w_L = 400$ _____; $w_L = 150$ _____.

f. If the fixed costs of the Flower People Co. equaled \$3,000, what profits (or losses) would they earn at each of the above possible wage rates?

$w_L = 900$ _____; $w_L = 750$ _____; $w_L = 400$ _____;

$w_L = 150$ _____.

g. How would your answers to (*e*) and (*f*) change if the firm's fixed costs were doubled? _____

_____

_____

h. What portion of the MRP_L curve in Figure 14–1 constitutes the Flower People Co.'s short-run demand curve for labor? _____

_____

_____

Why is it that this firm would shut down in the short run if the prevailing wage rate were so high that w_L exceeded ARP_L at all levels of labor inputs? _____

_____

_____

i. We have been considering the short-run case where labor is the only variable input. Why is it, that for a perfectly competitive firm, it's a portion of the VMP_L curve that constitutes the firm's demand curve for labor, while for a monopolist it's a portion of the MRP_L curve that corresponds to the firm's demand for labor? _____

_____

_____

_____

_____

_____

Name ------------------

2. *a.* The Johnson firm described in problem 1 of Chapter 13 was assumed to sell its output in a perfectly competitive market at a price of $1 per unit. (Data on this firm are given in the partial repeat of Table 13–1.) *Now let us suppose that this firm, instead of being a perfect competitor, is a monopolist* and that the maximum prices at which it can sell the various quantities of output it would produce at different levels of labor employment are those recorded in column 3 of Table 14–1. Assuming no changes in any other of the givens of the problem (i.e., the relationship between labor inputs and total output that is given in Table 13–1, $FC = \$500$, and $w_L = \$1,500$), how many workers should the firm now

employ to maximize profits? _____ At this profit-maxi-

mizing level of employment, what total output will the firm produce?

_____ What price will it charge for its output? _____

_____ What profits will it earn? _____ [Hint: Begin by filling in Table 14–1.]

TABLE 13–1
Cost and Revenue Data for the Johnson Firm Which Produces Zips and Sells Them in a *Perfectly Competitive* Market

L	q	MP_L	p	w	VC $(w \cdot L)$	FC	TC	TR	π
0	0		$1	$1,500	$ 0	$500	$ 500	$ 0	$ −500
1	1,000	1,000	1	1,500	1,500	500	2,000	1,000	−1,000
2	3,000	2,000	1	1,500	3,000	500	3,500	3,000	−500
3	6,000	3,000	1	1,500	4,500	500	5,000	6,000	1,000
4	9,500	3,500	1	1,500	6,000	500	6,500	9,500	3,000
5	11,500	2,000	1	1,500	7,500	500	8,000	11,500	3,500
6	13,010	1,510	1	1,500	9,000	500	9,500	13,010	3,510
7	13,510	500	1	1,500	10,500	500	11,000	13,510	2,510

TABLE 14–1
Optimal Labor Inputs under *Monopoly*

L (1)	q (2)	p (3)	TR (4)	MRP_L (5)	w_L (6)
0	0	$4.50	$	$ —	$1,500
1	1,000	4.00			1,500
2	3,000	3.50			1,500
3	6,000	3.00			1,500
4	9,500	2.50			1,500
5	11,500	2.20			1,500
6	13,010	2.00			1,500
7	13,510	1.50			1,500

Name _____

b. The monopolist described in this problem gets a better price in equilibrium for his output than did the perfect competitor described in problem 1 of Chapter 13 ($2.20 versus $1.00). Given this, how can you explain the fact that the monopolist does not choose to produce more output than the perfect competitor did? Note both have the same cost structure.

3.* BIM, Inc., is a monopolist that produces output in the short run with a single variable input, labor. Figure 14–2 shows the MRP_L and ARP_L curves for labor employed by BIM. The going wage BIM pays for labor is w^0, and initially BIM attains equilibrium by employing L^0 of labor.

Suppose now that the government disturbs BIM's equilibrium by imposing a price ceiling which forces BIM to lower its output price. How would this move affect (*a*) the general shape of BIM's MRP_L and ARP_L curves and (*b*) the quantity of labor BIM employs in its post-ceiling equilibrium? To answer, note that in Figure 14–2, A is the point on the ARP_L curve that corresponds to the initial equilibrium output price p^0, and B is the point on this curve you are to assume corresponds to the post-ceiling price, p_c; now sketch in Figure 14–2 new MRP_L and ARP_L curves (MRP_L' and ARP_L') consistent with your ideas about how these curves will change. Also show the new equilibrium employment of labor, L'. [Hint: It will help you to think first about how a price ceiling affects the firm's AR and MR curves as well as its equilibrium price and output as determined in the standard MR-AR-MC-AVC diagram of profit maximization. Also assume that the relationship between the firm's revenue and cost curves is such that, at the ceiling price, the firm choose to meet full market demand for its output.]

FIGURE 14–2
The Effect on a
Monopolist's Demand for
Labor of Imposing a
Price Ceiling
on His Output

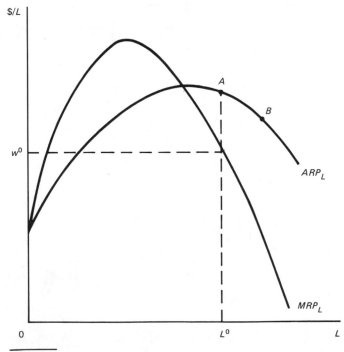

4. *a.* An input is said to suffer from *monopolistic exploitation* if it is paid a wage less than the value of its marginal product (*VMP*).

Zap, Ltd., produces an output it sells in an imperfectly competitive market at a price of $10 per unit. The marginal product of labor employed by Zap equals 50 units, the average product is 70 units. Zap pays its workers a wage of $400.

Currently Zap is operating at its point of maximum profit. For this firm:

$$MRP_L = \text{_____} ;$$

$$ARP_L = \text{_____} ; \text{ and}$$

$$VMP_L = \text{_____}$$

(For definitions of these terms, see problem 1 in this chapter.)

b. Does Zap engage in monopolistic exploitation of labor? _____

Explain why or why not. _____

_____

_____

_____

Name --

5. *a.* Howard Blum of Blum, Inc., produces blips with some fixed inputs (plant and equipment) and a single variable input, labor. Blum is a monopolist in his output market and a monopsonist in the labor market, which sounds like a surefire receipe for profits. Unfortunately for Blum at the moment he's not doing so well. He employs seven workers and earns profits (π) of only $54 per week. Using the data in Table 14–2, which is all Blum has, show him how he could do better. Specifically to

maximize weekly profits, Blum should hire _____ workers;

this will cost him _____, bring him total revenue of _____

_____, and earn him profits of _____. [Hint: Start by filling in all the missing numbers in Table 14–2.]

TABLE 14–2
A Numerical Example of Profit-Maximization by a Monopsonist

L (1)	$w = AC_L$ (2)	VC (3)	MC_L (4)	MRP_L (5)	ARP_L (6)	TR (7)	FC (8)	π (9)
0	—		—	—	—			
1	5				50			
2	8				80			
3	12				90			
4	16				90		100	
5	20				80			
6	24				70			
7	28				50			

b. From your figures in Table 14–2, it is clear that to maximize profit Blum, a monopsonist, should expand his labor force so long as MRP_L

_____ MC_L; conversely he should cut back his work force

whenever MRP_L _____ MC_L. Blum can't hire workers by the fraction (i.e., he can't hire say 5.2 workers); if he could, he'd maximize

profits by operating at the point where MRP_L _____ MC_L.

6. The Tripp Corp. is a monopsonist. Figure 14–3 shows the supply curve of labor it faces as well as the firm's MRP_L curve which, over the range shown, coincides with its demand curve for labor.

    a. To maximize profits, what quantity of labor should Tripp, Inc., hire?

_____ What wage will it pay? _____

and what will be its marginal cost of labor? _____

[Hint: The S_L curve constitutes the firm's average cost of labor (AC_L) curve. Use this curve to sketch the firm's marginal cost of labor (MC_L) curve in Figure 14–3.]

FIGURE 14–3
Equilibrium with
Monopsony

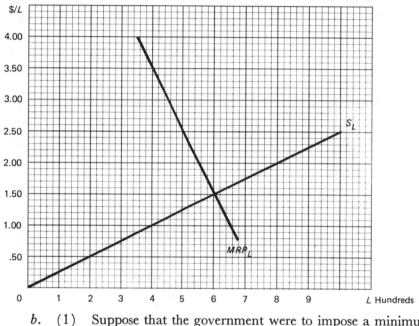

    b. (1) Suppose that the government were to impose a minimum wage of $1.50. How would this affect Tripp's equilibrium employment?

_____the wage rate the firm pays? _____

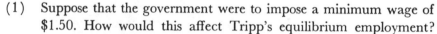 the firm's profits? _____ Usually a firm will respond to an increase in an input price by buying less of that input. Why is it that Tripp in the case at hand responds to a rise in the wage rate it has to pay by *increasing* its labor inputs?

_____

_____

    (2) Would Tripp respond in the same way if the minimum wage were

raised again from $1.50 to say $2.50? _____

Why or why not? _____

_____

_____

Name ------

c. Suppose that the government were to impose a tax of $1.50 on every unit of labor purchased by Tripp, Inc. How would this affect the firm's

employment of labor? _____ The wage rate received

by labor? _____? The marginal cost of labor to the

firm? _____ Under the tax, how much revenue

would the government collect on Tripp's purchases of labor? _____
[Hint: Shift the MC_L curve vertically upward or the MRP_L curve vertically downward by the amount of the tax.]

d. Suppose alternatively that the government were to subsidize the employment of labor by giving Tripp, Inc., a subsidy of $1.50 on every unit of labor employed by the firm (say the government wants to increase employment in the area where Tripp operates). How would this

affect the firm's employment of labor _____

and the wage rate received by labor _____? How

much would the subsidy end up costing the government? _____

e. (1) Tripp, Inc., is an imperfect competitor in its output market. Consequently, it faces a downward-sloping demand curve for this product and in equilibrium sells it at a price that exceeds marginal cost. How would the imposition of a price ceiling on Tripp's output market, one that forced it to lower price, affect the firm's demand curve for labor?

_____

_____

_____

(2) How would it affect the quantity of labor employed by the firm

_____ and the wage rate paid by the firm

_____? A firm that sold its output in a perfectly competitive market would respond to imposition of a price ceiling that forced it to lower price by cutting back on production and its employment of inputs. Tripp in contrast responds to an output price ceiling by hiring more labor. Explain the contrast:

_____

_____

_____

_____

7. Firms X and Y are almost twins. Both are profit-maximizing monopolists who produce their output with a single variable input, labor, and both have MRP_L and ARP_L curves of the general shape shown in Figure 14–1. The principal difference between the two firms is that X is a price taker in the labor market while Y is a monopsonist who faces upward-sloping supply curve, S_L, in its labor market. In problem 1, you showed that a firm such as X would never attain equilibrium at a labor-input level at which MRP_L exceeded ARP_L. Is the

same true for a firm such as Y? _____ Explain why or why not:

_____

_____

_____

[Hint: Sketch a few diagrams illustrating Firm Y's equilibrium position under different possible configurations of the MRP_L, ARP_L, S_L, and MC_L curves.]

8. *a.* Firm X produces its output q by combining two inputs, labor (L) and capital (K). Currently, the firm purchases both inputs in competitive markets at prices w and r respectively. Write out the firm's condition for long-run cost minimization in terms of MP_L, MP_K, w, and r.

_____

b. Repeat (a) this time assuming that the firm is a monopsonist in the labor market. Note in this case $w = AC_L$ and $MC_L > w$.

_____

c. Repeat (a) this time assuming that Firm X is a monopsonist in both the labor and capital markets.

_____

d. Which of the conditions you wrote in (a) through (c) is a general condition that holds in all cases? _____. Explain: _____

_____

_____

Name ----------------------------

9.* Firm M produces output during the short run with a fixed capital stock, $\overline{K}$, and a single variable input labor, L. Its production function can be expressed as follows:

$$q = f(L, \overline{K})$$

Firm M is a monopolist, and the price it gets for its output is given by the relationship

$$p = g(q),$$

where $g'(q) < 0$.

Currently, Firm M pays the competitive determined wage rate, w, for labor. Show that to maximize profits it should adjust its labor inputs so that

$$MRP_L = w$$

[Hint: Begin by writing Firm M's total revenue as a function of its labor inputs; then differentiate this expression to get an equation for MR and determine MRP_L. Next write profits as a function of the firm's labor inputs, differentiate this expression with respect to L, and set it equal to zero.]

10.* Using the production function introduced in problem 9,

$$q = f(L, \bar{K}),$$

shows that $ARP_L = MRP_L$ at the point where ARP_L attains a maximum. [Hint: Express ARP_L as a function of the firm's labor inputs; then differentiate this expression with respect to L, and set it equal to zero.]

Name ---

Theory of General
Economic Equilibrium

**A. DEFINITIONS
AND REVIEW**

1. A multimarket economy is said to be in *general equilibrium* when _____

_____ .

Walras' Law states that if, in an economy in which there are n markets, $n - 1$ markets are in equilibrium, the nth market (must/may/cannot) also be in equilibrium.

2. *a.* We can use an *Edgeworth box* to illustrate the trading possibilities that exist between two individuals holding stocks of two goods. The *con-*

tract curve through such a box is the locus of all points at which _____

_____ . The significance of the contract curve is this: whenever the two consumers' commodity stocks are divided between them in such a way that they are at a point on the contract curve, their marginal rates of substitution in consumption (will/will not) be equal, and, consequently there (will/will not) exist possibilities for mutual beneficial trades between them (i.e., trades that would increase simultaneously the utility of both of them); in contrast if the two consumers are at a point off the contract curve, their marginal rates of substitution in consumption (will/will not) be equal, there (will/will not) exist possibilities for mutual beneficial trades.

b. The allocation of consumption goods among a group of consumers is

said to be *Pareto optimal* whenever _____

_____

_____ .

If we use an Edgeworth box to picture a two-person, two-good, exchange

economy, all Pareto optimal points will lie along _____ .

3.* In a two-person economy the utility-possibility frontier shows the relation-

ship between _____

_____.

If our two-person economy is a pure exchange economy, a movement from one point on the utility-possibility frontier to another corresponds to a movement

within the Edgeworth box from one point along _____

_____ to _____.

4. The Edgewood box can also be used to illustrate a situation in which fixed stocks of two inputs are allocated between the production of two outputs. In this

situation the contract curve is the locus of all points at which _____

_____. If production occurs at a point on the contract curve, the rate of technical substitution between the two inputs in the production of one good (will/will not) equal the rate of technical substitution between the two inputs in the production of the other good. At any point along the contract curve, production is said to be Pareto

optimal, which means that _____

_____

_____

5. *a.* In a two-output economy the production possibility frontier shows the

relationship between _____

_____

_____.

  b. If the two outputs are produced using fixed stocks of two inputs, every point on the production possibility curve will correspond to a point

_____ within the Edgeworth box.

  c. To get from the contract curve to the production possibility frontier,

we need to determine for both outputs the _____ corresponding to each isoquant lying within the Edgeworth box. If for some reason production in the economy occurs at a point off the con-tract curve, the economy will be operating at a point (above/on/below) its production possibility curve.

6. In a perfectly competitive economy, production and consumption will both

be Pareto optimal if the economy operates at a point of _____.

---

* Asterisks denote the more difficult problems.

B. MULTIPLE CHOICE

1. Economists have shown that a perfectly competitive economy operating under ideal conditions will, if it attains general equilibrium, allocate resources efficiently. From this it follows that an efficient allocation of resources is not inconsistent with which of the following modes of behavior:

    a. producers seek to maximize profits.

    b. consumers seek to maximize utility.

    c. some people choose not to work at the going equilibrium wage rate.

    d. the government repeals minimum wage laws "protecting" the unskilled worker.

2. If we draw an Edgeworth box to illustrate the possibilities for trade between two individuals holding stocks of two goods, the dimensions of the box will be determined by:

    a. consumer I's endowment of both goods.

    b. consumer II's endowment of both goods.

    c. both consumer's endowments of both goods.

    d. the amounts of the two goods that it is socially desirable for the two consumers to receive.

3.* To move in a two-good, two-person economy from the contract curve in the Edgeworth box to the utility-possibility frontier, we need to know:

    a. the initial endowments possessed by both consumers of both goods.

    b. the competitive structure of the market in which the two goods are traded.

    c. the point on the contract curve the two consumers reach through trading.

    d. the level of utility that corresponds to each one of both consumers' indifference curves.

4. If a two-input, two-output economy is operating at a point along its production possibility curve, we know which of the following:

    a. production is Pareto optimal.

    b. consumption is Pareto optimal.

    c. all producers in both industries have identical rates of technical substitution between both inputs.

    d. the output of one good could not be increased without decreasing the output of the other good.

5. In a two-input, two-output economy, the production possibility curve will shift whenever which of the following occurs:

    a. technology in one or both industries changes.

    b. the fixed input supplies available for production are increased.

    c. producers within the economy move from a point on the contract curve to a point off the contract curve.

    d. producers within the economy move from one point on the contract curve to another point on this curve.

1. Two days ago, the pirate ship, Black Phantom, sank on a reef not far from a small tropical island. Two of its mates, Pete and Paul, each managed to make it ashore with a few provisions, some beer and dried beef. Since the island is small and lacks resources, there are no opportunities for Pete and Paul to engage in productive activities. In fact about the only useful thing they can do is to trade dried beef for beer. Since neither pirate has a pistol and neither wants to be alone, we will assume that all trading bargains made by the two are struck in a friendly and noncoercive fashion. In sum our pirates, unbeknownst to them, constitute a perfect example of a classic economic model: the two-person, two-good, exchange economy.

The Edgeworth box in Figure 15–1(a) portrays Pete and Paul's situation in an economically accurate, if rather colorless, fashion. Paul's holdings of beer and beef are measured out of the lower left-hand origin, denoted 0_{Paul}; while Pete's are measured out of the upper right-hand origin labeled 0_{Pete}. The dimensions of the box correspond to the total quantities of beef and beer Pete and Paul carried to shore; just how these goods are initially divided between the two individuals is indicated by the endowment point E in Figure 15–1(a).

FIGURE 15–1
Our Friendly Pirates
Exchange Economy

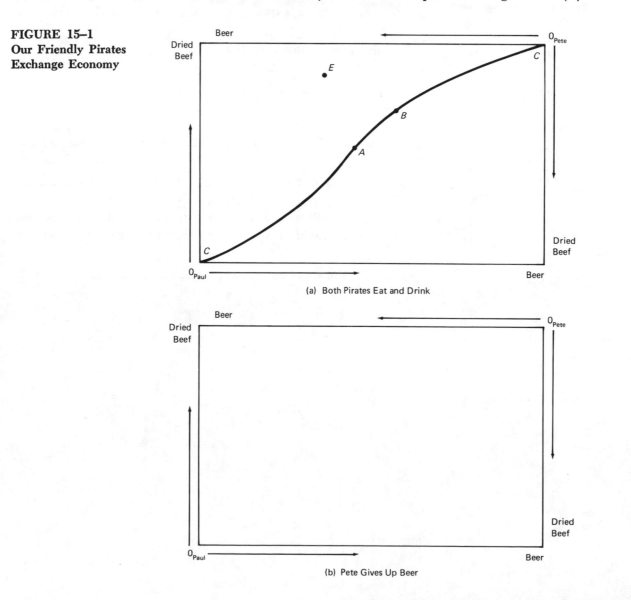

(a) Both Pirates Eat and Drink

(b) Pete Gives Up Beer

a. If Pete and Paul reached through one trade or a series of trades a point in the Edgeworth box at which there existed no further feasible trades of beer for beef that would increase the utility of one of them without decreasing the utility of the other, they would be on what economists call the *contract curve*. Some omniscient economist tells you (1) that *CC* in Figure 15–1(a) is the contract curve for Pete and Paul in the situation at hand and (2) that, given that all trades are made voluntarily, the only points on the contract curve that the two might reach lie in the range *A* through *B*. What does this tell you about Pete and Paul's preferences for beer and beef? Specifically sketch in Figure 15–1(a) four or five indifference curves for each individual that are consistent with the above information.

b. (1) Suppose that Pete, foreseeing a speedy demise, decides to give up drinking, but Paul does not. In Figure 15–1(b) redraw the situation pictured in 15–1(a) allowing for Pete's change in preferences. Now what possibilities exist for trading? Specifically denote in Figure 15–1(b) the range of points *A–B* that Pete and Paul might now reach through trading with a line segment *AB*. Also where

is the new contract curve? _____

_____

_____

    (2) What possibilities for trading would exist between Pete and Paul

if teetotaling Pete had not brought any beer to shore? _____

_____ What possibilities for trading would exist between Pete and Paul if they both had endowments of beer but both

gave up drinking? _____

2. Suppose that our shipwrecked pirates of problem 1 build a raft and drift to a larger island where they find a limited (i.e., fixed) supply of raw materials with which they can produce two goods, shelter and clothing. Suppose also that the amount of labor each pirate is willing to supply is fixed (say each agrees to work 40 hours a week). Finally, assume that given technologies for producing shelter and clothing are available to our pirates and that in both technologies labor and raw materials can be substituted for each other.

If our pirates are industrious types who always employ their limited resources fully (and we assume they are), we can portray their situation with respect to production, again in a colorless but accurate way, with an Edgeworth box. Figure 15-2(a) pictures such a box. The vertical dimension of the box corresponds to the labor endowment available to our pirates, the horizontal dimension to their endowment of raw materials. The isoquant map corresponding to the shelter-production function is plotted out of the lower left-hand origin labeled $0_{shelter}$, while the clothing isoquant map is plotted out of the upper right-hand origin labeled $0_{clothing}$. The number on each isoquant denotes the amount of output to which this isoquant corresponds.

FIGURE 15-2
Deriving Our Pirates Production Possibility Curve

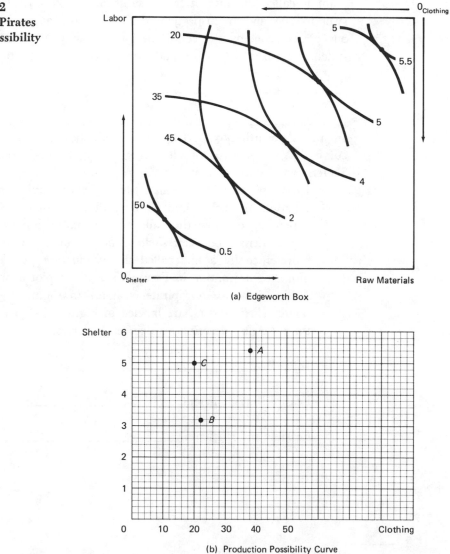

(a) Edgeworth Box

(b) Production Possibility Curve

Name

a. From the Edgeworth box it is clear that the fixed input supplies and fixed technologies available to Pete and Paul place upper limits on the quantities of the two goods they can produce simultaneously. For example, if our pirates chose to produce two units of shelter, then—depending on the proportions in which they allocated their resources between shelter and clothing production—they could produce the following amounts of clothing: _____ units, _____ units, or _____ units.

b. If our pirates produce two units of shelter, is there any way they could, with their fixed input supplies, produce more than 45 units of clothing?

_____

c. Production of two (or many) goods is said to be *efficient,* if there exists no feasible reallocation of inputs that would permit an increase in the production of one output without requiring a decrease in the production of the other output. The negative of the slope of an isoquant at any point is called the rate of factor substitution (*RFS*).[1] From your answer to (*b*) and an inspection of Figure 15–2(a), it is clear that in our pirate economy the condition for efficiency in production can be stated in terms of input use and rates of factor substitution as follows:

_____

_____

In an Edgeworth box portraying a production situation, the contract curve *CC* is the locus of all points at which production is efficient. Sketch in the contract curve in Figure 15–2(a).

d. (1) In our pirate economy, all of the different maximum-output combinations of shelter and clothing that the mates could produce, depending on how they allocated available inputs of labor and raw materials between shelter and clothing production, can be represented by a line called the *production possibility curve.*

(2) Use the information in Figure 15–2(a) to plot a production possibility curve for our pirate economy in Figure 15–2(b). Three points, *A, B,* and *C,* are labeled in Figure 15–2(a). To which of the following descriptions does each correspond?

Infeasible: _____

Feasible but inefficient: _____

Feasible and efficient: _____

---

[1] See problem 4 in Chapter 6.

3.* The small country of Mazul produces two outputs, q_1 and q_2, with two inputs, labor and capital. Currently Mazul has fixed supplies of both inputs, 100 units of labor and 30 units of capital. The production functions for both q_1 and q_2 are characterized by fixed factor proportions.[2] To produce one unit of q_1 requires five units of labor and two units of capital; to produce a unit of q_2 requires ten units of labor and two units of capital. Plot in Figure 15–3 the production possibility curve for Mazul; i.e., a curve that shows, for each possible output of q_1, the maximum feasible output of q_2. [Hint: Plot first a *labor constraint* curve that shows the maximum combinations of q_1 and q_2 that could be produced in Mazul with the given supply of labor and unlimited capital inputs. Next, plot a *capital constraint* curve that shows the maximum possible outputs of q_1 and q_2 that could be produced with Mazul's fixed supply of capital and unlimited inputs of labor.]

FIGURE 15–3
A Production Possibility
Curve with Fixed Input
Coefficients

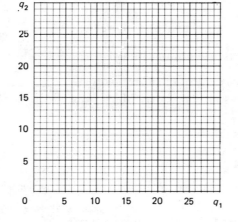

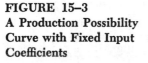

Name

---

[2] See problem 5 in Chapter 6.

4. A given pattern of resource allocation is said to be efficient (or Pareto optimal) if there exists no feasible reallocation of available goods that would increase the welfare of one consumer without decreasing that of another. Pedro and Marco, two mature mountain climbers, go out hiking and get lost. Unfortunately, water and chocolate bars are the only provisions either brought along. Which of the following allocations of resources are efficient? Which are inefficient?

 a. Pedro is twice as big as Marco and, consequently, needs more water and chocolate to keep going. Currently, both have the same holdings of water and chocolate and both have identical rates of commodity substitution[3]

 between these two goods. _____

 b. Pedro has more water than Marco, and Marco has more chocolate than Pedro. Nevertheless, both have the same rates of commodity substitutions between water and chocolate. _____

 c. Pedro has all the water and all the candy. Also seeing Marco get hungry and thirsty doesn't bother Pedro. _____

 d. Pedro has all the water, Marco has all the candy. Pedro is hungry and Marco is thirsty. _____

 e. Same situation as (d) except now the two hikers discover a stream that provides unlimited quantities of drinking water. Marco still has all the candy, and Pedro is still hungry. _____

---

[3] See problem 1 above.

5. An economy in which both production and exchange occur is said to be in *general equilibrium* if all markets in the economy are simultaneously in equilibrium. The economy is said to be at an *efficient point* if there exists no feasible reallocation of either inputs or outputs that would increase the utility of one person without decreasing that of another.

For each of the following situations, determine (1) whether the economy in question could attain a position of general equilibrium and (2) whether such a point, if attained, might correspond to an efficient point. Explain your answer. [Hint: For an economy to operate at an efficient point, it is necessary (but not sufficient) that consumption be efficient (as defined in problem 1 above) *and* that production be efficient (as defined in problem 2 above).]

    a. In economy A, all markets are perfectly competitive and

        (1)   all consumers pay identical lump-sum taxes (say a head tax of

            $10 per person). (*a*) _____ (*b*) _____

            _____

            _____

        (2)   all consumers pay lump-sum taxes of varying amounts, the exact amount of each consumer's tax being determined by a random

            drawing. (*a*) _____ (*b*) _____

            _____

            _____

    b. In economy B, the national labor market is divided into two parts. In the mountainous north there is just a single monopsonist buying labor. In the south the labor market is perfectly competitive. Because labor is immobile between the two regions, wage rates in the north remain consistently below those in the south. All other input markets are

        perfectly competitive. (1) _____ (2) _____

        _____

        _____

    c. In economy C, production of one consumption good, gismos, is controlled by a monopolist who practices price discrimination. All other

        markets are perfectly competitive. (1) _____ (2) _____

        _____

        _____

Name _____

d. In economy C, all markets are perfectly competitive. The government, however, imposes a high minimum wage on firms engaged in interstate commerce but not on firms engaged only in intrastate trade. The result is that different firms pay different wages. (1) _____

(2) _____

_____

_____

e. Economy E consists of a pair of bilateral monopolists, Farmer X who grows apples and Farmer Y who grows pears. Naturally, at the end of the growing season X and Y trade apples and pears. (1) _____

(2) _____

_____

_____

f. In economy F all markets are perfectly competitive. However the government, which wants to place the tax burden on those best able to pay, requires consumers with high incomes (over $20,000 a year) to pay a sales tax of 5 percent on purchases of luxury goods. Low income consumers who can purchase these goods don't have to pay the tax. (1) _____ (2) _____

_____

_____

6. In Zilch two goods are produced, q_1 and q_2. These goods are traded in perfectly competitive markets at prices (p_1 and p_2) determined by the following market supply and demand equations:

$$D_1 = 5 - p_1 - 2p_2$$
$$D_2 = 5 - p_1 - p_2$$
$$S_1 = p_1$$
$$S_2 = -1\frac{1}{2} + 2p_2$$

a. Using the above equations, determine what the equilibrium values of p_1, p_2, q_1, and q_2 would be if the Zilch economy attained a point of general

equilibrium. p_1^0: _____; p_2^0: _____; q_1^0: _____; q_2^0: _____.

b. Plot in Figure 15–4 the demand and supply curves that would prevail in the markets for q_1 and q_2 if the Zilch economy were in a position of general equilibrium. Do the equilibrium values for p_1 and p_2 indicated by your diagrams correspond to those in your answer to (*a*) above?

_____ In a single-market (partial equilibrium) problem, it is possible to use market supply and demand curves to locate the equilibrium price in the market. In a multimarket (general equilibrium) problem such as the one at hand, it is necessary to solve for an equilibrium set of prices before the final point of equilibrium can be illustrated with market supply and demand curves. Explain the contrast:

_____

_____

_____

FIGURE 15–4
General Equilibrium in a
Two-Market Economy

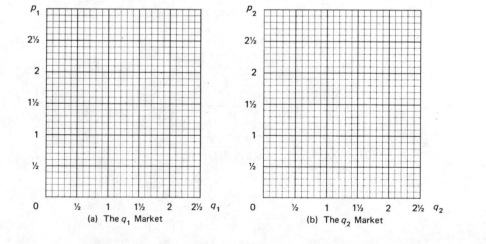

(a) The q_1 Market

(b) The q_2 Market

c. Suppose that a shortening of the growing season causes a decrease in supply in the market for q_1. If the new market supply curve, S', in the market for q_1 is given by $S'_1 = -1 + p_1$ what will be the new equilibrium p and q values determined in the two markets? p'_1: _____;

p'_2: _____; q'_1: _____; q'_2 _____.

d. Add to Figure 15–4 the S'_1, D'_1, and D'_2 curves needed to locate the new equilibrium point. Do the new equilibrium prices, p'_1 and p'_2 shown on your diagram, correspond to the values you solved for in (*c*)? _____.

FIGURE 15–4

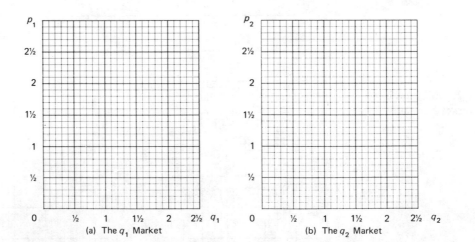

(a) The q_1 Market   (b) The q_2 Market

7.* Consider an economy in which a single good, Q, is produced by combining a fixed supply of land with one variable input, labor. In this economy the utility of any consumer (call him X) depends solely on the quantity of the consumption good he demands Q_D and on the quantity of labor he supplies L_S; i.e., for consumer X,

$$U = U(Q_D, L_S)$$

Assume also that consumer X faces a budget constraint of the following sort: each period he spends on the consumption good an amount equal to his labor income, wL_S, plus the rent he earns on his land R. Presumably the rent on the land will be a function of the wage rate w established. Thus, if p equals the price of Q, the budget constraint is as follows:

$$pQ_D = wL_S - R(w)$$

Using calculus, prove that consumer X will attain equilibrium (i.e., maximize his satisfaction) by adjusting his purchases of output and the amount of labor he supplies so that he is operating at a point on his budget line where this line is tangent to one of his indifference curves between consumption and labor; i.e., that in equilibrium

$$(\partial U/\partial Q_D)(\partial U/\partial L_S) = p/w$$

Sketch a diagram depicting consumer X's equilibrium in Figure 15–5.

FIGURE 15–5
Equilibrium of
Consumer X

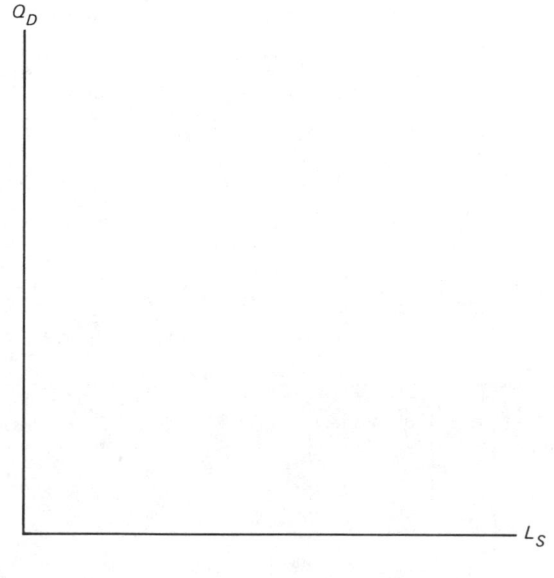

Q_D

L_S

Chapter **16**

Theory of Welfare Economics

A. DEFINITIONS AND REVIEW

1. For the allocation of resources within a production economy to be efficient (i.e., Pareto optimal), it is necessary that the following three conditions hold:

    a. In consumption: _____

_____

_____

_____.

    b. In production: _____

_____

_____.

    c. Between producers and consumers: _____

_____

_____

_____

Name _____

2. *a.* In a two-output economy, for consumption to be efficient, all consumers must have identical rates of commodity substitution. We can be sure that, if both outputs are traded in perfectly competitive markets, this

condition will hold because _____

_____

_____

_____

_____.

b. In a two-input economy, for production to be efficient all producers must have identical rates of technical substitution between the two inputs. We can be sure that, if both inputs are traded in perfectly competitive markets, this condition will hold because _____

_____

_____

_____

_____.

3. * *a.* In a two-person economy the *grand utility-possibility frontier* is the curve

showing the relationship between _____

_____.

b. Consider an economy in which technology and input supplies are fixed. For such an economy there will exist a unique production possibility curve. Production at each point along this curve generates a different Edgeworth box for trading between consumers. To each such Edgeworth box corresponds a unique contract curve, and to each such contract curve corresponds a unique utility-possibility frontier. Each of these utility-possibility curves yields *one* point on the grand utility-possibility frontier. The point at which each individual utility-possibility curve touches the grand utility-possibility curve is the point at which the

following conditions holds: _____

_____.

c. Whenever the economy is operating at a point on the grand utility-possibility frontier, the overall allocation of resources (inputs and out-

puts) within the economy must be _____.

---
* Asterisks denote the more difficult problems.

4.* *a.* To determine which point on the grand utility-possibility frontier maximizes social welfare (i.e., which Pareto optimal point is the best point),

we have to make value judgments that are incorporated in a _____

_____ function, which orders different points in utility space. The

economy's *point of constrained bliss* is the point _____

_____

_____.

b. A perfectly competitive economy operating under ideal conditions is likely to be able to attain general equilibrium at a multiplicity of points, each of which will correspond to a different allocation of resources. Each possible point of general equilibrium (is/is not) certain to be a Pareto optimal point, but (only some/only one) point will be a point of constrained bliss. It (is/is not) possible that the social welfare function will rank some inefficient points higher than some efficient points.

5. Two producers are said to be linked by external diseconomies in production whenever an increase in production by one producer causes the cost curves of

the other producer to _____. Whenever a producer imposes external diseconomies on another producer, the marginal *social* cost of his production (is less than/equals/is greater than) his *private* marginal cost. In such a situation if the producer expands his output to the point where his private marginal cost equals the market price of his output, resource allocation (will/will not) be efficient because his production will (just equal/exceed/be less than) the amount necessary for an efficient allocation of resources. For resource allocation to be efficient in the presence of externalities in production, every output must be sold

at a price equal to _____.

B. MULTIPLE CHOICE

1. In any economy in which all markets are perfectly competitive, the allocation of consumption goods is efficient (i.e., Pareto optimal) because:

  a. in such an economy production is efficient.
  b. all consumers will be maximizing their satisfaction relative to the same set of commodity prices, and, consequently, they will all have identical rates of commodity substitution between any pair of consumption goods.
  c. the social welfare function is defined in such a way that any point of general equilibrium in a competitive economy maximizes social welfare; i.e., corresponds to a point of constrained bliss.
  d. perfect competition permits the economy to consume at a point beyond (i.e., above) the production possibility frontier.

2. A perfectly competitive economy would not achieve a Pareto optimal allocation of resources in production in the presence of which of the following conditions:

    a. the government requires large producers to pay a tax on the labor they employ but exempts small firms from the tax.

    b. the government imposes a minimum wage that exceeds the wage that would equate the supply of and demand for unskilled labor.

    c. externalities exist in consumption; i.e., the utility of some consumers depends in part on the goods consumed by other individuals.

    d. the economy, while it is operating at a point on its production possibility frontier, is not operating at *the* point necessary for obtaining constrained bliss.

3. With respect to *any* point along the grand utility-possibility frontier, which of the following statements is certain to hold:

    a. production is Pareto optimal.

    b. consumption is Pareto optimal.

    c. the rate of substitution in consumption between any two goods equals the rate of substitution between these two goods in production.

    d. the economy is enjoying constrained bliss.

4. Smith and Jones, two students of economics, have both been studying the same economy and have each identified what they believe to be *the* point of constrained bliss for that economy. Assuming no errors in their calculations, Smith's point must correspond to Jones' point:

    a. under all conditions.

    b. only if Smith and Jones both have the same social welfare function.

    c. only if Smith and Jones have the same individual utility functions.

    d. only if Smith and Jones both use the Lange-Lerner rule to move along the grand utility-possibility frontier.

5. Every utility-possibility frontier is tangent at one point to:

    a. the economy's production possibility curve.

    b. the grand utility-possibility frontier.

    c. the Edgeworth-box contract curve.

    d. the national budget constraint.

6. In a certain economy, producers of commodity X impose external diseconomies on producers of other outputs. For resource allocation in this economy to be Pareto optimal:

    a. production of commodity X must be halted altogether.

    b. consumption of commodity X must be discouraged.

    c. commodity X must be sold at a price equal to its social marginal cost.

    d. commodity X must be made a public good.

C. PROBLEMS

1. *a.* Sam Small constitutes a rather lonely one-man economy. Sam is endowed with 24 hours of time per day that he divides between labor L, which he dislikes, and free time F, which he enjoys. When Sam labors, he produces a single output q according to the production function, $q = f(L)$. This production function is subject to diminishing returns to labor, (i.e., $f''(L) < 0$).

Show that for Sam to operate at an efficient point (i.e., at a point where there is no feasible change in the division of his time between labor and leisure that would increase his utility), Sam has to operate at a point where the marginal product of his labor equals his rate of commodity substitution (i.e., the negative of the slope of his indifference curve) between leisure and output. [Hint: Add indifference curves and an appropriate production possibility curve to Figure 16–1.]

b.* (1) Suppose that we now expand Sam's economy to one in which there are many consumers who supply the one available input labor and demand the one output produced, q. Suppose also that there are many firms that demand L and supply q. Finally assume that q is traded for L in a perfectly competitive market. In this situation what condition must hold for resource allocation to be efficient: _____

_____

(2) Will it hold? _____ Explain: _____

_____

_____

_____

_____

_____

_____

_____

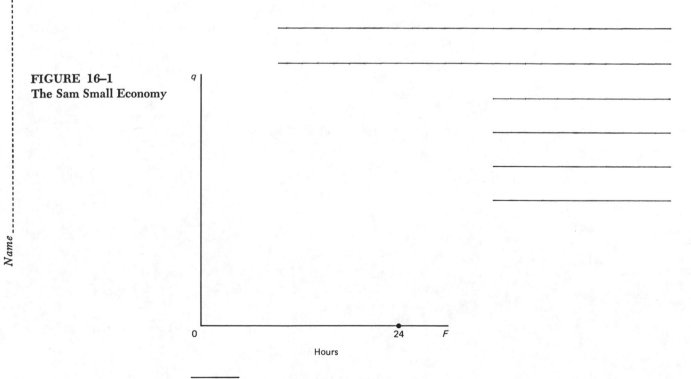

FIGURE 16–1
The Sam Small Economy

Name ....

* Asterisks denote the more difficult problems.

2.* Consider a two-person economy that possesses fixed input supplies and fixed technology and produces two outputs, q_1 and q_2. For such an economy we can easily construct a production possibility curve. Suppose that the economy is operating at one point on this curve, producing the output levels q_1^0 *and* q_2^0. A large number of different allocations of q_1^0 and q_2^0 between the two consumers would lead to efficiency in consumption; i.e., to a situation where both consumers had the same rate of commodity substitution between q_1 and q_2. However, only one such allocation of output would correspond to a point on the grand utility-possibility frontier. In a two-person economy, the grand utility-possibility frontier is the locus in utility space of all points at which one consumer's utility is maximized given production possibilities and the level of utility enjoyed by the other consumer.

   a.   What point on the consumption contract curve corresponding to the output levels q_1^0 and q_2^0 would be the one that also represented a point on the grand utility-possibility frontier?

   _____

   b.   Explain why no other point on the contract curve in question would also correspond to a point on the grand utility-possibility frontier.

   _____

   _____

   _____

   _____

3. If a society can attain more than one efficient point, the question arises of how society should order such points to determine which is best. Any such ordering calls for a strong value judgment. In a democratic society operating under majority rule, it might seem that the logical judgment would be this: the proper ordering is the one that society operating under majority rule would select. Unfortunately, this appealing solution to constructing social preferences may not always work because, as Kenneth Arrow has shown, the preferences of the majority may be inconsistent even when the preferences of all individuals in society are consistent. This paradox is illustrated in the following problem:

a. The town of Syosset has a rather outdated high school building. Three obvious alternatives present themselves: (1) do nothing; (2) remodel the old school; and (3) construct a new school. Suppose that one third of the population prefers 1 to 2 and 2 to 3, that a second third prefers 1 to 3 and 3 to 2. Would majority votes by the population yield a consistent

ordering of the three alternatives? _____ What would it be?

_____.

b. Suppose, alternatively, that the preferences of the townspeople are as follows: one third prefers 2 to 3 and 3 to 1, the second third prefers 1 to 2 and 2 to 3, and the last third prefers 3 to 1 and 1 to 2. Now would

majority rule yield a consistent ordering of 1, 2, and 3? _____

Why not? _____

What is the explanation of this paradoxical result? _____

_____.

4. For resource allocation to be efficient, every firm has to sell at a price equal to marginal cost. The government of Tanzu wants to force its five local monopolists to expand production to the point where $p = MC$. Also in the interests of social justice, it wants to eliminate any remaining monopoly profits with lump-sum taxes. Of course the government can't force a firm to incur continuing losses without forcing that firm out of business; so in cases where marginal cost pricing leads to losses, a subsidy is required.

Table 16–1 shows selected figures on the costs and revenues that each of the five monopolists would incur and receive if they were forced to sell at a price equal to marginal cost and satisfy full market demand at that price. Which of the following policy recommendations would be appropriate for each monopolist:

   a. require to operate at the point where $p = MC$.

   b. require to operate at the point where $p = MC$ and give a subsidy equal to

   _____.

   c. require to operate at the point where $p = MC$ and impose a lump-sum

   tax equal to _____.

   d. a nonsense case because _____.

   (1) _____

   (2) _____

   (3) _____

   (4) _____

   (5) _____

TABLE 16–1
Cost and Revenue Data for Five Monopolists at the Point Where $p = MC$

Monopolist	q	TR	TC	AR	ATC	MR	MC
1	20,000	$20,000	$18,000			$ 1.50	
2		60,000			$2.00	1.00	$ 3.00
3	40,000	20,000			2.00	0	2.00
4	20,000		25,000	$1.00			1.00
5	20,000	20,000			1.00	−.50	−.50

5. *a.* (1) Figure 16–2(a) shows the cost and revenue curves of Monopolist I. If Monopolist I were unregulated, what quantity of output

would he sell? _____ What price would he charge?

_____ What profits would he earn? _____
What would be the relationship between his price and *MC?*

_____

(2) If Monopolist I were permitted to maximize profits, he would engage in what economists call *monopolistic restriction of output;* i.e., produce too little output for resource allocation to be efficient. Could a price ceiling be used in the case at hand to eliminate monopolistic restriction of output? _____

At what level should it be set? _____ After imposition of the price ceiling, what quantity of output would Monop-

olist I produce? _____ What profits would he earn?

_____ What would be the relationship between his

price and *MC?* _____
(3) What measure could the government use that would eliminate Monopolist I's remaining profits but not interfere with the effi-

ciency of resource allocation? _____

FIGURE 16–2(a)
Regulating a Monopolist
Monopolist I

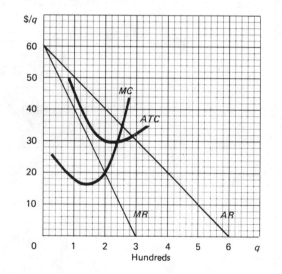

(4) If the government were to impose a price ceiling at the level such that Monopolist I's AR would equal his ATC if he satisfied full market demand, what would be Monopolist I's

new equilibrium output? _____ What profits would he

earn? _____ Would his new equilibrium be consistent

with an efficient allocation of resources? _____ Explain:

_____

_____

_____

If Monopolist I were required to satisfy full market demand at the price ceiling in question ($AR = ATC$), what would happen to his profits? _____ Would his new equilibrium position be consistent with an efficient allocation of resources?

_____ Explain: _____

_____

_____

(5) If the government set a price ceiling at the level determined by the intersection of Monopolist I's MC and ATC curves, what

level of output would he produce? _____ What profits

would he earn? _____ Would his equilibrium position

be consistent with an efficient allocation of resources? _____

Explain: _____

_____

b. (1) Consider now Monopolist II, whose cost and revenue curves are pictured in Figure 16–2(b). If Monopolist II were unregulated, what price would he charge? _____ What ouput would he supply? _____ What profits would he earn? _____ Would he engage in monopolist restriction of output? _____

(2) To eliminate monopolistic restriction of output in the case at hand, the government would have to set a price ceiling of _____ and give Monopolist II a subsidy equal to approximately _____ .

FIGURE 16–2(b)
Monopolist II

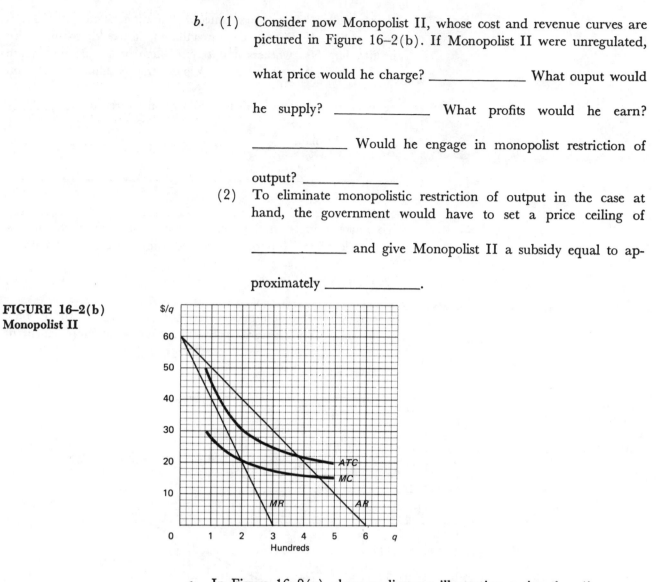

c. In Figure 16–2(c), draw a diagram illustrating a situation (i.e., configuration of cost and revenue curves) in which the imposition of a price ceiling p_c on a monopolist would eliminate simultaneously monopolistic restriction of output *and* monopoly profits.

FIGURE 16–2(c)

$/q

q

Name

d. (1) Problem 6 in Chapter 14 concerned a monopsonist, the Tripp Corporation. If Tripp were unregulated, it would, to maximize profits, hire 500 workers and pay a wage of $1.25; see Figure 14–3, which is repeated here. Would this equilibrium position

be consistent with an efficient allocation of resources? _____

_____ Explain: _____

_____

_____

(2) To make Tripp's employment practices consistent with an efficient allocation of resources, should the government impose a

wage ceiling or a wage floor? _____ At what level

should it set the minimum wage? _____ In response to the minimum wage, Tripp would increase its employment of

workers from 500 to _____.

FIGURE 14–3
Equilibrium of the Tripp Corporation, a Monopsonist

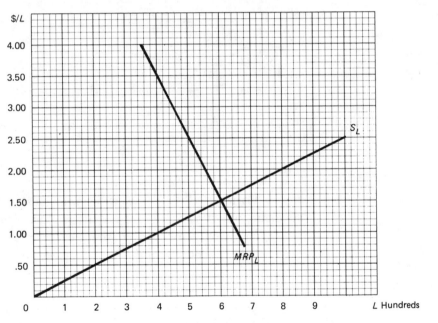

6. Most reasonable premises for defining the optimal economic state imply that this state will, among other things, represent an efficient allocation of resources. However, society may be able to attain many different efficient points, and some of them may be far from optimal as suggested by the following examples.

a. (1) Consider a situation in which the market for unskilled labor is perfectly competitive. Initially, the wage rate prevailing is that determined by supply and demand, and it so happens that this equilibrium wage is so low that all workers receiving it live in poverty. Is this situation consistent with an *efficient* allocation

of resources? _____

(2) Because the equilibrium wage yields a poverty income, the government steps in and institutes a high minimum wage. Now fewer workers have jobs, but those that do have escaped poverty. Is the new situation in the labor market consistent with an efficient

allocation of resources? _____ Explain: _____

_____

_____

(3) How could the government raise the incomes of unskilled workers without interfering with the efficiency of resource allocation?

_____

b. The market for wheat is perfectly competitive, and currently wheat is selling at a price that equates market supply and demand. Is this situa-

tion consistent with an efficient allocation of resources? _____
The government decides that farm income is too low, so it sets a high price floor in the wheat market and buys up for storage all excess supply generated at that price. Farmers now enjoy a much higher standard of living. Is the new situation consistent with an efficient allocation of re-

sources? _____ Explain: _____

_____

_____

c. Milk is sold in a perfectly competitive market. The government believes that it is good for people to drink lots of milk, so it subsidizes milk consumption. Is such a subsidy consistent with an efficient allocation of re-

sources? _____ Explain: _____

_____

_____

7. When externalities link firms, the costs of one firm will depend not only on its own level of output but also on the level of output of some other firm; i.e., the costs incurred by the ith firm will depend not only on its output level, q_i, but also on the output level of the jth firm. In symbols,

$$c_i = f(q_i, q_j)$$

In the absence of externalities, efficiency requires that the output of every firm be sold at a price equal to private marginal cost. In the presence of externalities, efficiency requires that outputs be sold at a price equal to *social* marginal cost.

The government of a small underdeveloped country is building a railroad to link its highlands with the coastal plain. The railroad will be used primarily to haul raw materials from the highlands to coastal manufacturers. Once the railroad is completed, the transportation of such materials will be much faster and more dependable. As a result the cost curves of coastal manufacturers will fall since they will be able to hold smaller inventories of raw materials. The costs of raw material producers will also decline since dependable transportation will reduce losses through spoilage and damage in transit.

The government wants to promote economic efficiency, and for this reason it plans to price railroad services at marginal cost as measured in terms of the money paid out by the railroad for inputs. Will such a policy in the situation at

hand be consistent with an efficient allocation of resources? _____ Will it lead to too much, too little, or just the right amount of production of

railroad services? _____ Explain: _____

_____

_____

What pricing policy should the government follow? _____

_____ Explain: _____

_____

_____

8. Frequently pollution involves externalities of the sort described in the introduction to problem 7 above. Here's one example.

Two firms are located on the Sweet Flow River. The upstream Firm A is a paper mill that uses large quantities of river water in its production process and then returns this water laden with pollutants to the river. The downstream Firm B also needs water to carry out its production process. Normally it could use untreated river water but because of all the pollutants A is dumping into the river, B has to incur considerable expenses in purifying the water it uses.

Both firms are oligopolists, and the government, which wants to promote an efficient allocation of resources, has decided to require both firms to price at marginal cost. Will that measure suffice to make the activities of the two firms

consistent with an efficient allocation of resources? _____

Explain: _____

_____

_____

If the paper mill in pricing its output uses private MC instead of social MC

will it produce too much, too little, or just the right amount of output? _____

Explain: _____

_____

_____

9.* *a.* For consumption to be efficient, it is necessary that there be no feasible reallocation of consumption goods that would increase the utility of one consumer without decreasing that of another. Put alternatively, a point will be efficient only if each consumer's utility is at a maximum given the levels of utility enjoyed by other consumers. Consider an economy in which there are two goods, q_1 and q_2, and two individuals with utility functions: $U_1(q_{11}, q_{12})$ and $U_2(q_{21}, q_{22})$, where q_{11} denotes consumer one's consumption of good one, q_{12} his consumption of good two, etc. The supplies of these goods are fixed at q_1^0 and q_2^0 and

$$q_{11} + q_{21} = q_1^0$$
$$q_{12} + q_{22} = q_2^0$$

Prove, for the economy in question, that consumption will be efficient only if both consumers have the same rates of commodity substitution *RCS;* i.e., that the two consumers reach through trading a point on the Edgeworth-box contract curve. [Hint: Maximize U_1 subject to the constraint that U_2 equal some fixed amount U_2^0. The first-order conditions for this maximum imply that at the point of maximum U_1,

$$\frac{\partial U_1/\partial q_{11}}{\partial U_1/\partial q_{12}} = \frac{\partial U_2/\partial q_{21}}{\partial U_2/\partial q_{22}}$$

i.e., that the two consumers have identical *RCS*s.]

b. In an economy with a large number of consumers, efficiency in consumption would require that all consumers have identical rates of commodity substitution between q_1 and q_2. If the markets in which q_1 and q_2 were traded were perfectly competitive, would this condition be fulfilled?

_____ Explain why: _____

_____

_____

_____

Answers Section

CHAPTER 1

A. Definitions and Review

1. *A. B.* he derives no utility from consuming q_1. *A. C.*

2. the locus of all points in commodity space (i.e., commodity bundles) that yield the consumer the same level of satisfaction. of the different levels of utility he could experience by consuming at different points in the relevant commodity space. higher levels of utility.

3. cardinal. ordinal. ordinal.

4. negative. the consumer derives no utility from one of the goods. transitive.

5. the negative of the slope of his indifference curve through that point. diminishes.

B. Multiple Choice

1. *c*; **2.** *b*; **3.** *c*; **4.** *a*.

C. Problems

1. *a.*

The indifference curve through *A* must run through the two unshaded areas, which implies in turn that the slope of the curve will be negative.

b. To show this, note that any indifference curve corresponding to a higher level of utility than the curve through *A* must pass through points in the "more preferred" region of the diagram; i.e., pass through points upward and rightward from *A*.

3. Point A_1 offers Cassius more of both goods than point A_3; consequently, A_1 is more preferred than A_3. However, because of the intersecting indifference curves, transitivity implies that A_3 and A_1, which are *both* equally preferred to A_2, must also be equally preferred to each other. Since this cannot be, intersecting indifference curves are ruled out.

5. The two goods are perfect substitutes (e.g., white eggs and brown eggs if you are making omelettes and not Easter eggs).

7.* *MRS* is diminishing along the indifference curve in Figure 1–7(a) since it equals 4 at point A, 1 at B, and ¼ at C. *MRS* is not diminishing along the indifference curve in part (b) since it equals 1 at point A, 1 at B, and 1 at C. The set of points more or equally preferred to the bundle (2,2) is convex in (a) but not in (b). With respect to (b), note that points A and C are equally preferred to B, but a line drawn between them lies, except at points A and C, outside the set of points preferred or equally preferred to B.

CHAPTER 2

A. Definitions and Review

1. *a.* the locus of all points (i.e., commodity bundles) that the consumer could purchase at prevailing commodity prices with the sum he's budgeted for consumption.

$$M = p_1 q_1 + p_2 q_2$$

b. M/p_2; M/p_1; Δq_1; negative.

c. less; negative.

d. terms on which the consumer can trade q_1 for q_2 and still remain on his budget line.

e. upward and rightward. no.

f. make steeper; leftward toward the origin. no.

2. tangent. his marginal rate of substitution in consumption.

$$MRS = p_2/p_1$$

satisfaction.

3. *a.* the change in total utility he experiences as a result of a one-unit change in his consumption of q_1.

$$MU = \Delta U/\Delta q_1$$

b. the marginal utility of q_2.

$$MRS = (\Delta U/\Delta q_1) / (\Delta U/\Delta q_2)$$

c. $(\Delta U/\Delta q_1)/(\Delta U/\Delta q_2) = p_1/p_2$.

4. *a.* the relationship between the income he has budgeted for consumption and the amounts of q_1 and q_2 he would purchase at the prevailing values of p_1 and p_2.

b. the relationship between the income he has budgeted for consumption and the amount of one good, q_1 or q_2, that he would purchase at prevailing goods prices.

5. *a.* the percentage change in the amount of q_1 he purchases divided by the percentage change in the amount he has budgeted for consumption.

$$\eta_M = \frac{\% \Delta q_1}{\% \Delta M}$$

b. the absolute value of the percentage change in the amount of q_1 he purchases divided by the percentage change in p_1.

$$\eta = \left| \frac{\%\Delta q_1}{\%\Delta p_1} \right|$$

c. negative. positive. less.

6. a. his preference, his budget M. p_2. p_1. the relationship between the price, p_1, charged for q_1 and the quantities of q_1 and q_2 he purchases given the fixed values of his budget, M, and p_2.

   b. the relationship between the price, p_1, charged for q_1 and the quantity of q_1 he demands.

$$q_d = f(p)$$

Where q_d denotes quantity demanded.

7. a. is greater than one; b. equals one; c. is less than one.

B. Multiple Choice

1. d; 2. c; 3. c; 4. b; 5. d; 6. c; 7. a; 8. a; 9. b; 10. b; 11. b.

C. Problems

1. a. $\$4 = \$1C + \$.50T$ or, solving for T, $T = -2C + 8$
   b. $T = -2C + 12$
   c. $T = -2C + 4$
   d. higher; does not
   e. $T = -C + 4$
   f. $T = -2.5C + 10$
   g. slope; T-intercept; steeper; higher; does not.

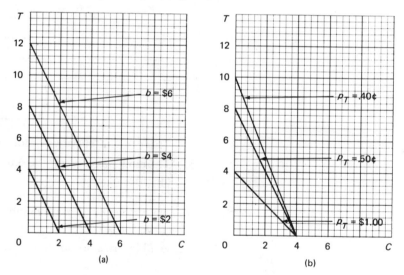

(a)

(b)

3. a.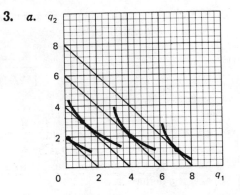

b. For Smith, q_2 is an inferior good for money levels above 20.

c.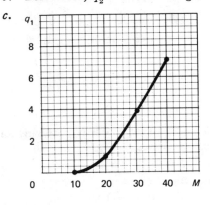

d. No.

5. a.

p_{beans}	$q_{\text{beans demanded}}$
2.40	0.5
1.20	2.0
.80	4.0
.60	6.0
.48	8.0

The demand curve you plot in Figure 2–5(b) should slope downward.

b. Thumb's preferences, the amount of money Thumb has to spend and the price of beef.

c. Shift.

d. No. It would cause Thumb to move up or down *along* his demand curve for beans.

7. She would purchase 4 units of q_2 and no q_1.

9.

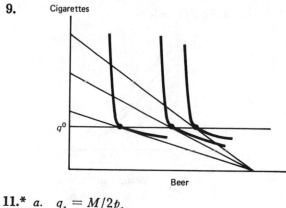

Cigarettes

q^0

Beer

11.* *a.* $q_1 = M/2p_1$

      b. $q_1 = \$100/2(\$5) = 10$

CHAPTER 3

A. Definitions and Review

1. *a.*   the number of dollars of income he receives.

    b.   the size of the bundle of goods and services he can buy with his money income, i.e., his purchasing power.

2. *a.*   the change in relative goods prices caused by the change in p_1.

    b.   the change in his *real* income caused by the change in p_1.

    c.   more.   inferior.

3. *a.*   he will respond to a rise in his money income (no change in goods prices) by buying less of that good.

    b.   when the price of the good rises, consumer X responds by buying more of it.

    c.   (1) the good must be an inferior good. (2) the income effect generated by a change in the price of this good must outweigh the substitution effect.

    d.   consumers do not typically spend large quantities of money on inferior goods; consequently, the income effect generated by a change in the price of an inferior good is likely to be small.

4. *a.* $\eta_{11} = \left| \dfrac{\% \Delta q_1}{\% \Delta p_1} \right|$ $\eta_{12} = \dfrac{\% \Delta q_1}{\% \Delta p_2}$

    b.   substitute. complementary. independent.

B. Multiple Choice

1. *b;* 2. *b;* 3. *c;* 4. *b;* 5. *c;* 6. *d;* 7. *b;* 8. *a;* 9.* *c;* 10.* *c.*

1. *a.* Gucci Clothes

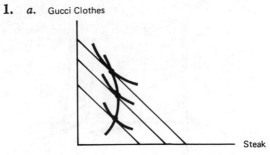

Steak

b. Nothing. Being an inferior good is a necessary but not a sufficient condition for a good to be Giffen good.

c. Gucci Clothes

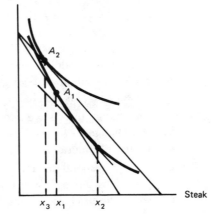

Steak

A_1 is the initial equilibrium, A_2 the final equilibrium. The substitution effect, x_1 to x_2, increases demand for steak. The income effect, x_2 to x_3, decreases demand for steak and swamps the substitution effect.

d. p Steak

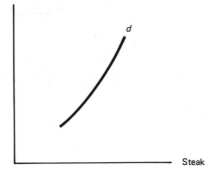

Steak

3. *a.* The missing q_1 values in Table 3–1 are from top to bottom: 0, 0, 0 or 6 (which is indeterminate), 8, 10.

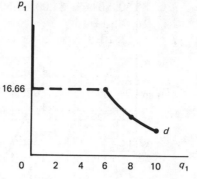

b. The discontinuous segment of Sally's demand curve results from a sharp; one-shot substitution effect. As the price of q_1 drops from just above \$16.66 to just below, Sally responds to the change in relative prices by switching all her spending from q_2 to q_1. As p_1 drops still lower, the income effect *alone* is responsible for the further increases that occur in Sally's demand for q_1.

5. *a.* The missing q_{Coke} figures are from top to bottom: 2, 2.5, 3.3, 5, and 10.

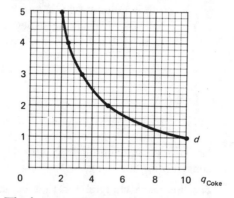

b. The income effect alone.

c. You do not need to know the price of cigarettes since Jones' preference map tells you that he will always spend *all* of his income on Coke.

d. + 1. 0.

7. *a.* $\eta_{12} = p_2/q_1 > 0$. Substitutes

b. $\eta_{12} = -p_2/q_1 < 0$. Complements.

9. *a.* $Y = w(24 - F)$.
   b. The missing figures in Table 3–5 are from top to bottom as follows:
      w: $0.50, $0.66⅔, $1.00, $1.50
      F: 16, 12, 14, 16
      L: 8, 12, 10, 8

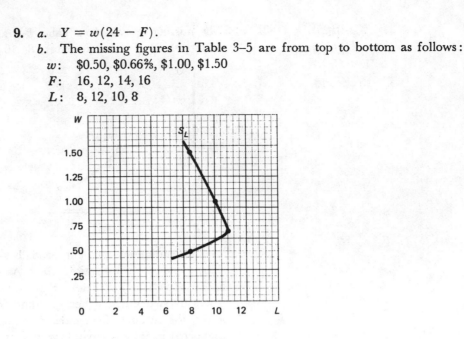

   c. ————

11. *a.* The missing figures are $+10\%$ in column one, and from top to bottom in column two, ⅙ and ⅚.
   b. No. By diversifying Riley reduces the chance of a 10% loss from ⅓ to ⅙ but he also reduces his chance of a 10% gain from ⅔ to ⅚.

CHAPTER 4

A. Definitions and Review

1. Giffen. p_1. consumer X's preferences, the amount he has budgeted for consumption spending, or p_2.

2. the price charged for that commodity and the quantity of it demanded by all consumers in the marketplace. horizontally the individual demand curves of all consumers in the market.

3. *a.* $\eta = \left| \dfrac{\%\Delta q}{\%\Delta p} \right|$

   the responsiveness of quantity demanded to price.
   b. greater than one. increase.

4. *a.* the change in total revenue received by the seller as a result of a one-unit change in the quantity of output sold.
      $MR = \Delta TR / \Delta q$
   b. slope.

5. *a.* positive. positively sloped.
   b. zero. attains a maximum.
   c. negative. negatively sloped.

6. *a.* negative. greater than one, equal to one, less than one.
   b. infinite. infinite. In a perfectly competitive market the demand curve facing the individual seller appears to him to be horizontal because he meets only a negligible part of total market demand and consequently his sales have no perceptible effect on market price.

B. Multiple Choice

1. *d*; 2. *c*; 3. *b*; 4. *b*; 5. *a*; 6. *a*; 7. *c*; 8. *a*; 9. *c*; 10. *b*; 11. *d*.

C. Problems

1. *a.* The missing figures in Table 4–1 are as follows from top to bottom:
    Column 1: 0, .5, 1, 1.5, 2, 2.5, 3, 3.5, 4, 4.5, 5
    Column 2: 0, 0, 0, 0, 0, 0, 1, 2, 3, 4, 5
    Column 3: 0, 0, 0, 0, 0, 0, 0, 0, 1, 2, 3
    Column 4: 0, .5, 1, 1.5, 2, 2.5, 4, 5.5, 8, 10.5, 13

 b. As price falls (1) more consumers enter the market as active buyers, (2) consumers already in the market respond by increasing their purchases.

3.* It has a constant value of 1, which is what you should expect since the demand curve in question implies that total spending on *q* will be the same amount, 10, at all values of *p*.

5. *a.*

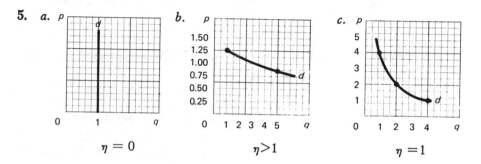

$\eta = 0$ $\eta > 1$ $\eta = 1$

 d. No demand curve.

7. *a.* $TR = p(q) \cdot q = \left(\dfrac{a-q}{b}\right) q = \dfrac{aq - q^2}{b}$

   $MR = \dfrac{dTR}{dq} = \dfrac{a - 2q}{b}$

 b. $TR = p(q) \cdot q$

   $MR = p + q\dfrac{dp}{dq}$

 c. Yes. $MR = \dfrac{a - 2q}{b} = \dfrac{a-q}{b} + q\left(-\dfrac{1}{b}\right) = p + q \cdot \dfrac{dp}{dq}$.

CHAPTER 5

A. Definitions and Review

1. whose usage cannot be changed in the short run. whose usage can be increased or decreased during the short run. physical plant and equipment. factory labor.

2. *a.* a relationship showing, for each possible bundle of inputs the firm might use, the *maximum* output that could be obtained with that bundle of inputs.

 b. if all inputs used are to be fully employed, they must be combined in some fixed ratio. one input can be substituted for another; i.e., inputs can be combined in various ratios.

3. a. total output produced divided by the number of units of the input used. the change in total output that would occur as a result of a one-unit change in the input.
   b. $q = f(L, \bar{K})$. $AP_L = q/L$. $MP_L = \Delta q/\Delta L$.
   c. reaches a maximum, falls, negative.
   d. exceeds. equals. is less than.

4. a. the marginal product of the variable input will eventually fall.
   b. each unit of the variable input has less and less of the fixed input to work with and consequently its productivity falls.

5. slope. increasing. falling.

6.* an equiproportional increase in all inputs leads to an increase in output of the same proportion. constant. ratio.

B. Multiple Choice

1. d; 2. d; 3. c; 4. b; 5. a; 6. b; 7. b.

C. Problems

1. a. Column (3) should read from top to bottom: 5, 9, 13, 13, 15, 11, 4, 2, 0, −2, −4.
   Column (4) should read from top to bottom: −, 5, 7, 9, 10, 11, 11, 10, 9, 8, 7, 6.
   b. In Figure 5–1(a), the TP curve first rises and then falls. In Figure 5–1(b), the MP curve first rises and then falls, eventually to a point below the horizontal axis. The AP curve rises until it intersects the MP curve, then falls.
   c. (1) increasing, (2) decreasing, (3) at a maximum, (4) falling, (5) rising, (6) at a maximum.

3. The AP_L curve rises as labor inputs are increased from 0 to 7. At $L = 7$, AP_L achieves its maximum value of 10. At $L = 16$, AP_L has fallen to 5. For low values of L, the MP_L curve is rising and lies above the AP_L curve. At $L = 5$, MP_L achieves its maximum, and thereafter it falls; at $L = 7$, $MP_L = AP_L$, and for values of L greater than 7, the MP_L curve lies below the AP_L curve. At $L = 12$, $MP_L = 0$, and for L values greater than 12, MP_L is negative and falling.

5. (1) constant, (2) decreasing, (3) increasing, (4) constant, (5) increasing, (6) constant, (7) constant, (8) increasing.

7.* Write out the expressions for MP_L and AP_L. Next take the derivative of AP_L with respect to L, and set it equal to zero. From the resulting expression, it is obvious that, when AP_L achieves a maximum

$$\frac{f(L)}{L} = f'(L); \text{i.e., } AP_L = MP_L$$

CHAPTER 6

A. Definitions and Review

1. a. all of the different minimum input combinations that can be used to produce a given level of output, $\bar{q}$.
   b. higher. rise. ratio.

2. *a.* a ray from the origin. the isoquant turns a right angle.
  b. not change.   zero.

3. *a.* negative of the slope. marginal product of capital.

$$MRTS = MP_L/MP_K$$

  b. labor can be substituted for capital or vice versa. diminishes.
  c. the marginal product of one of the inputs would be negative and total output could be increased by cutting back on the use of that input.

4. *a.* the locus of all points or input bundles that cost the same amount.

$$\bar{c} = wL + rK$$

  b. $\bar{c}$; w; r; L; K.
  c. $\bar{c}/r$. how much capital the firm could buy (given $\bar{c}$ and r) if it bought no labor. $\bar{c}/w$. how much labor the firm could buy if it spent all its funds on labor.
  d. $-w/r$. with a fixed amount, $\bar{c}$, to spend, the firm can buy more labor only if it buys less capital and vice versa. it is the prices w and r that determine the terms on which the firm can trade capital for labor or vice versa while holding total expenditures at $\bar{c}$.
  e. increases. does not.

5. *a.* an isocost curve. any other point on the $\bar{q}$-isoquant would lie on a higher isocost curve and therefore represent a more expensive point of production.
  b. an isoquant. any other point on the $\bar{c}$-isocost line will lie on a lower isoquant and therefore yield less output for the amount $\bar{c}$ being spent on inputs.
  c. $MRTS = w/r$

6. steeper. capital. labor.

7. its isoquants and isocost lines. different levels of output. linearly homogeneous.

8. zero. negative. it could reduce costs and increase output simply by cutting back its use of the input whose marginal product was negative.

B. Multiple Choice   1. *b*; 2. *a*; 3. *b*; 4. *b*; 5. *c*; 6. *c*; 7. *c*; 8. *d*.

C. Problems

1. *a.*

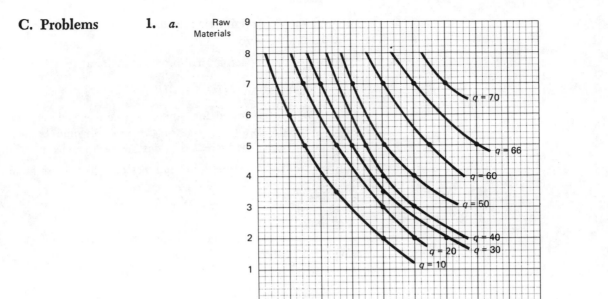

b. The production function is characterized by diminishing returns with respect to both L and R.

Table 6–2 should read from top to bottom:

Column 1: 0, 1.5, 2.5, 3, 3.5, 4, 5.5, 7

Column 2: 0, 10, 20, 30, 40, 50, 60, 66

Column 3: —, 6.7, 10, 20, 20, 20, 6.7, 4

Column 4: 0, 1.5, 2, 3, 4, 5, 6

Column 5: 0, 20, 30, 50, 60, 66, 70

Column 6: —, 13.3, 20, 20, 10, 6, 4

Column 7: 0, 2, 3, 3.5, 4, 5, 7

Column 8: 0, 10, 20, 30, 40, 50, 60

Column 9: —, 5, 10, 20, 20, 10, 5

All three *MP* curves first rise and then fall as the variable input is increased.

3. Here's a map that displays increasing returns to scale and diminishing returns to labor. Note if inputs are doubled from (1,1) to (2,2), output more than doubles. Also if capital inputs are held constant at 1 ($\overline{K} = 1$), and labor inputs are increased, MP_L diminishes

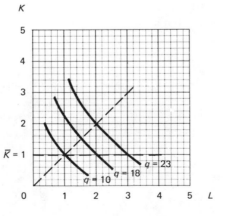

5. These curves would for example suffice:

a.

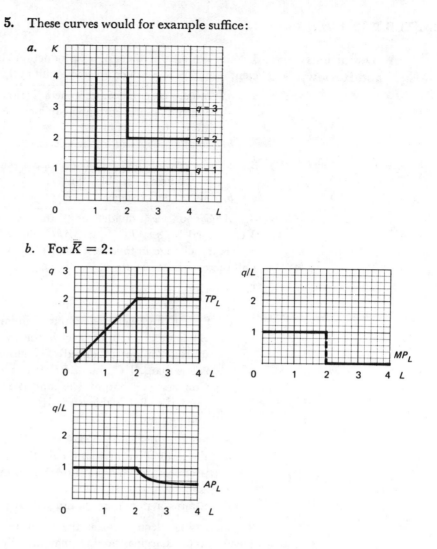

b. For $\bar{\bar{K}} = 2$:

7. *a.* (1) $2 = L + 2R$; (2) $6 = L + 2R$, (3) $10 = L + 2R$

Figure 6–8(a) should show three parallel, downward-sloping isocost curves where higher curves correspond to higher levels of expenditure on inputs.

upward. no.

b. (1) $10 = L + K$, (2) $10 = L + 2K$, (3) $10 = L + 5K$, (4) $10 = L + 10K$.

Figure 6–8(b) should show four isocost curves, all of which have different slopes, and all of which meet a single point, $L = 10$, on the horizontal axis.

no effect. decreases. lowers.

9. ———

11. *a.* The inputs x_1 and x_2 are perfect substitutes.
b. Constant. No. No.
c. The isocost lines will be flatter than the isoquants, leading to a "corner" solution along the x_2-axis.

CHAPTER 7

A. Definitions and Review

1. the number of units of q_2 production that must be forgone to free sufficient resources to produce one more unit of q_1.

2. *a.* money costs the entrepreneur incurs in purchasing inputs. the opportunity cost the entrepreneur incurs when he employs his own capital, labor, etc., in the firm.
   b. total explicit *and* implicit costs.

3. *a.* the cost of the firm's fixed inputs (e.g., plant and equipment). the cost of the firm's variable inputs.
   b. lower. not change.

4. *AFC* equals *FC* divided by q, the level of output produced. *AVC* equals *VC* divided by q. *ATC* equals *AFC* plus *AVC* (i.e., *TC* divided by q). *MC* equals the change in total cost (or *VC*) that would occur as a result of a one-unit increase in total output.

5. *a.* rise.
   b. slope. decreasing. increasing.
   c. first fall and then rise. attains a minimum.
   d. *AVC* at any output level is the average of the marginal costs of all units of output produced. Therefore, if output is expanded and *MC* is less than *AVC,* then *AVC* (the average of the *MC* values) must fall. Conversely, if output is expanded and *MC* is greater than *AVC, AVC* must rise. But if this is so, *MC* must equal *AVC* where the latter is at a minimum.

6. *a.* capital stock and perhaps other inputs are fixed. all inputs are variable.
   b. the level of output and the minimum average cost at which the firm can produce provided that it makes optimal adjustments in its capital stock.
   c. is tangent to. *LAC. SAC.*
   d. attains a minimum. is tangent to the *LAC* curve.

7. increasing. decreasing. as the quantity of the variable inputs used is increased, their marginal product may initially rise due to greater possibilities for division of labor, etc.; *but* eventually as more variable inputs are used, they will be subject to diminishing returns due to the presence of a fixed factor; i.e., their marginal product will fall.

8. input prices, the production function. technology, input prices. capital stock.

B. Multiple Choice

1. *d;* 2. *a;* 3. *c;* 4. *c;* 5. *d;* 6. *c;* 7. *c;* 8. *c;* 9. *b.*

C. Problems

1. *a.* VC.
   b. VC/q.
   c. FC/q.
   d. $AFC, VC/q, FC/q$.
   e. $\Delta q, \Delta VC/\Delta q$.
   f. TC, VC.

3. The columns in Table 7–2 should read from top to bottom:
   q: 0, 5, 10, 25, 40, 45, 45
   VC: 0, 10, 15, 20, 30, 40, 50
   FC: 20, 20, 20, 20, 20, 20, 20
   TC: 20, 30, 35, 40, 50, 60, 70

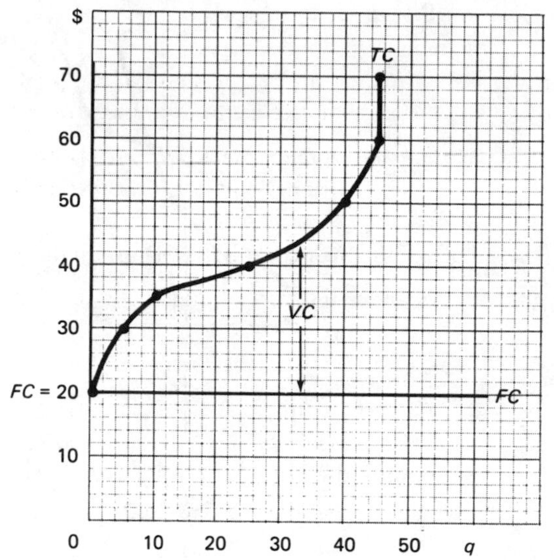
$
70
60
50
40
30
FC = 20
10
0
10
20
30
40
50
q
TC
VC
FC

5. *a.*

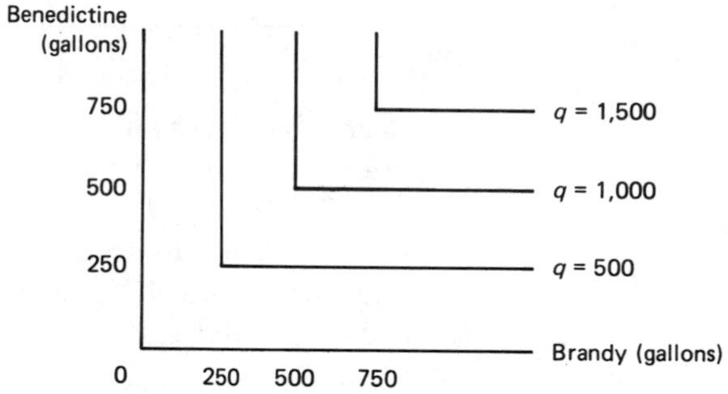
Benedictine (gallons)
750
500
250
0
250
500
750
q = 1,500
q = 1,000
q = 500
Brandy (gallons)

b. The figures in Table 7–4 should read from top to bottom:
FC: 20,000; 20,000; 20,000; 20,000
VC: 0, 7,500; 15,000; 22,500
TC: 20,000; 27,500; 35,000; 42,500
AVC: –, 15, 15, 15
ATC: –; 55, 35, 28
MC: 15, 15, 15

7. *a.* *L* equals approximately 4.2. *R* equals approximately 3.4. *TC* equals $76.
b. a little over 10 units.

9. *a.–d.*

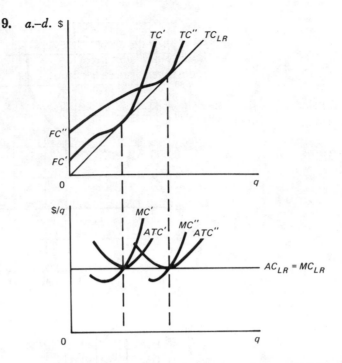

e. Decreasing returns to scale: As q increases, TC rises at an increasing rate; MC_{LR} and AC_{LR} are both positively sloped; and at any value of q, $MC_{LR} > AC_{LR}$.

f. Increasing returns to scale: As q increases, TC rises at a decreasing rate; MC_{LR} and AC_{LR} are both negatively sloped; and at any value of q, $MC_{LR} < AC_{LR}$.

CHAPTER 8

A. Definitions and Review

1. *a.* takers.
   b. takers.
   c. homogeneous.
   d. certain and perfect.

2. *a.* be less than. depress.
   b. exceed. raise.

3. *a.* the demand curves of all individual buyers in the market.
   b. because the demand curves of almost all if not all the individual buyers will slope downward, and because the lower price, the more buyers will enter the market.
   c. infinite. horizontal. the single seller supplies such a small segment of total market demand that he has an imperceptible effect on market price; i.e., demand for his output appears to him to be horizontal.

4. *a.* revenue. the price he gets for his output.
   b. more than. more than. fall.
   c. more than. more than. fall.

5. *a.* TC. slope. MC. MR.
   b. maximum loss. maximum profit.

6. *a.* MC. AVC.
   b. zero. vertical.
   c. AVC. VC. $-FC$.

7. p = short-run MC = long-run MC; i.e., $p = SMC = LMC$. equals.

8. *a.* bowl. upward. positively-sloped.

   b. horizontal. unlimited. the minimum LAC at which each firm in the industry can produce output.

B. Multiple Choice

1. *b*; 2. *d*; 3. *a*; 4. *a* and *c*; 5. *a, b,* and *d*; 6. *c*; 7. *d*; 8. *a* and *b*; 9. *a, b, c,* and *d*; 10. *d*; 11. *c*.

C. Problems

1. *a.* (1) 8,000 bu., \$10,000. (2) 7,000 bu., \$5,000. (3) 0 or 5,500 bu., − \$2,000. (4) 0, − \$2,000. (5) 0, − \$2,000.

   b. It lies along the vertical axis for values of price less than \$1.75, skips discontinuously over to 5,500 bu. at price equal to \$1.75, and lies along the MC curve for values of price greater than \$1.75.

   c. TR, minimum AVC.

   d. No effect.

   e. His supply curve would shift upward indicating a *decrease* in supply.

3. *a.* 4,000 units; downward; increasing; decreasing; greater than zero.

   b. 4,000 units; upward; decreasing; increasing; greater than zero.

   c. \$3; 0; 4,000.

5. *a.* (1) rise to \$4; (2) fall to \$2; (3) fall to 3,000; (4) rise by \$6,000.

   b. same as (*a*).

   c. does not; elasticity; elasticity.

7. *a.* 13,000 bu. They are equal. They are equal.
   $$\pi = (p - SAC)q = (\$5 - \$3.60)\,13,000 = \$18,200.$$

   b. 12,600 bushels. They would fall. 11,600 bushels. They would rise but not to the level he earned when price was at \$5/bu. The SAC curve would be tangent to the LAC curve at the output level of 11,600, and SMC would also equal LMC at this output level.

   c. \$2/bu. The SAC curve would be tangent to the LAC curve at the point where the latter achieves a minimum. The SMC and LMC curves would also both run through this point and intersect at it. Profits would be zero.

   d. no price. never. at such a point MR could equal MC only if the MR curve cut the MC curve from below indicating a point of *minimum*, not maximum, profit.

CHAPTER 9

A. Definitions and Review

1. there are many buyers but only a single seller. close.

2. (*a*) market. negative. below. (*b*) bowl. crosses the horizontal axis. 0.

3. (*a*) monopsony. monopsony. (*b*) exceed.

4. MC. positive. zero. negative.

5. $MR = MC_1 = MC_2$.

6. (*a*) increasing price and output. (*b*) increasing capital stock and adjusting price and output so that he operates at a point where marginal revenue equals long-run marginal cost. (*c*) rise. rise. fall. rise.

7. (a) $MC = MR_1 = MR_2$. (b) probably differ. price discrimination.

8. there is one buyer and one seller. taker. decreased. raised.

B. Multiple Choice

1. *a* and *d*; **2.** *c*; **3.** *c*; **4.** *a* and *d*; **5.** *b* and *d*; **6.** *a, c,* and *d*; **7.** *a*; **8.** *b*; **9.** *a*.

C. Problems

1. Smith is correct. You can easily place the demand curve facing a monopolist so that his *LMC* curve cuts his *MR* curve from below at an output level at which *LAC* is falling. However, it's impossible to do this for a perfect competitor since he faces a horizontal demand curve.

3. *a.* No. Demand elasticity less than one implies negative marginal revenue.
   b. No, unless he operates at zero marginal cost (e.g., operated a toll bridge with excess capacity).
   c. (1) (*a*) No. (*b*) No. A perfectly competitive *firm* always faces an infinitely elastic demand curve.
      (2) (*a*) Yes. (*b*) Yes.

5. *a.* 40 units. *b.* Approximately $4.40. *c.* 20 units. *d.* 20 units.

7. *a.* 50.
   b. $1.50.
   c. 30.
   d. $2.00.
   e. 20.
   f. $\pi = 30(\$1.50) + 20(\$2.00) - 50(\$1.50) = \$60$.
   The kinked joint *MR* curve runs through the following points: (0,3), (10,2), (50,1).

9.* *a.* 4 workers. $1.50. 4 units. $6.00. $13.00.
   The figures in Table 9–3 should read from top to bottom:
   TC_L column: 0, .50, 1.50, 3.00, 6.00, 10.00, 18.00
   MC_L column: –, 0.50, 1.00, 1.50, 3.00, 4.00, 8.00
   MP_L column: –, 1, 1, 1, 1, 1, 0
   MRP_L column: –, 9, 7, 5, 3, 1, 0
   b. Yes, at an output level of four, $LMC = MR$; but this output level should be produced with one unit less of capital ($L = 4$, $K = 4$).

CHAPTER 10

A. Definitions and Review

1. (*a*) *MC* and *AVC*. the tax. demand. the tax. identical. (*b*) vertically upward by the amount of the tax. a decrease. vertically upward by the amount of the tax. (*c*) rises. falls. falls. the amount of the tax times the new equilibrium level of industry output. (*d*) vertically downward by the amount of the tax. decrease. vertically downward by the amount of the tax. (*e*) net market demand curve. raise. lower. lower.

2. fixed percentage of the price of the commodity.

3. (*a*) a tax of some fixed amount, the amount being independent of any economic decision (price, output, input mix, etc.) the firm makes. (*b*) no effect. no effect. raise. no effect. no effect. no effect. lower by the amount of the tax. (*c*) no effect. no effect. lower by the amount of the taxes collected. (*d*) raise. no. (*e*) fall. rise. fall. rise.

4. fall. rise. zero.

5. the ceiling is not set below the level at which the MC and AR curves intersect. at a price below the level at which the MC and AR curves intersect.

6. decrease. increase. supply.

<table>
<tr><td style="text-align:right">B. Multiple
Choice</td><td>1. c and d; 2. d; 3. a and d; 4. a and b; 5. a, c, and d; 6. d; 7. c; 8. c.</td></tr>
</table>

C. Problems

1. *a.* $4/bu. 6 million bushels.
   b. The curve D' should pass through the points $(4,3)$ and $(6,2)$.
     (1) no change. falls to $2. no change.
     (2) rises to $5. falls to $3. falls to 4 million bushels.
     (3) rises to $6. returns to $4. falls to 2 million bushels.
   c. (1) $12 million. (2) $8 million. (3) $4 million.

3. *a.* (1) falls to $2; (2) rises to $4; (3) increase to 5,000 units; (4) rises by $10,000.
   b. same answers as for *a.*
   c. does not. elasticity. elasticity.

5. Under either program farmers will receive the same total revenue, $500,000 —part paid by consumers, part by the government. Under the subsidy program price would be lower to the consumer than under the price-floor, crop-purchase program. Therefore, if consumer demand were inelastic, as it frequently is in agricultural markets, consumers would spend more on corn the higher the price to them, and the price-floor, crop-purchase program would thus be cheaper to the government. The crucial factor is the elasticity of market demand. If it were greater than one, the subsidy program would be cheaper.

7. *a.* lower to 2,000. *b.* raise to $7. *c.* lower to $5. *d.* lower to $1,000. *e.* $4,000.

9.* *a.* 60 units. $360. $17,900.
   b. 100 units. $200. $9,900. No effect.
   c. 54 units. $384. $324. $14,480. $3,240.
   d. no effect.
   Proof:
   a. $TR = 600q - 4q^2.$ $MR = 600 - 8q.$ $MC = 2q.$
      At $MR = MC$, $q = 60.$
   b. $MR = 200.$ At $MR = MC$, $q = 100.$
   c. $MC = 2q + 60.$ At $MR = MC$, $q = 54.$

CHAPTER 11

A. Definitions and Review

1. there exists some basis on which buyers can distinguish among the outputs of rival sellers: design, packaging, advertising, location in retailing, etc.

2. buyers and sellers are both numerous and the product sold is differentiated.

3. negatively sloped. The perfect competitor sells a homogeneous output and, consequently, has to accept the going market price; the monopolistic competitor sells a differentiated product and, consequently, will lose to his rivals some, but not all, of his buyers if he raises price and will gain some, but not all, of his rivals' buyers if he lowers price.

4. *a.* marginal revenue. cost. revenue.

    b. design. packaging. advertising.

5. *a.* will not. will not. will not.

    b. greater. zero. perfect competition.

B. Multiple Choice

1. *d;* **2.** *b;* **3.** *c;* **4.** *b;* **5.** *c;* **6.** *b.*

C. Problems

1. *a.* $q = 1,000(10 - p)$; $q = 100[1,000(10 - p)] = 100,000(10 - p)$

    b. 1. 1.

    c. \$5. 5,000. 500,000. \$10,000.

    d. D' will run from the point $(0,10)$ on the vertical axis through the point $(3,1)$. 300 firms. 3,000 units. 900,000 units. \$1. \$0.

3. *a.*

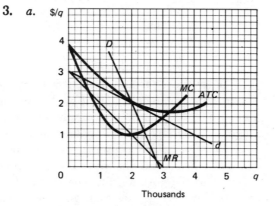

    b. The firm attains long-run equilibrium at a point where its d curve is tangent to its ATC curve, and this has to be at a point where ATC is falling because the slope of the d curve will always be negative in monopolistic competition.

CHAPTER 12

A. Definitions and Review

1. there are many buyers and a few (or a few dominant) sellers. homogeneous. differentiated.

2. *a.* there are two sellers. quantity. level of output. larger. smaller.

    b. price. price. unstable and indeterminate.

    c. mutual dependence. profits.

3. will not. sharply. will. by a small amount.

4.* *a.* the sum of the winnings of the players is the same regardless of its distribution among participants. completely inelastic. the winnings of one player are matched exactly by the losses of another.

    b. play the strategy that maximizes the minimum return he could earn under any strategy his opponent might play. under this strategy the minimum profits he will earn, depending on his rival's response, will be greater than they would be with any other strategy.

    c. he selects his strategy on a probabilistic basis. every.

5. *a.* limit competition. price, total output, the allocation of the production of this output among participating firms, limitations on nonprice competition, possibly a redistribution of profits.

   b. all producing firms have adjusted their output levels so that they have identical marginal costs.

6. *a.* price leadership does not guarantee that the cost of producing industry output will be minimized, does not preclude nonprice competition, and need not guarantee that the output level established will be the one that would maximize joint profits.

   b. takers. *MC.* less than.

   c. market price would rise, industry output would fall, output would be allocated among firms so that all firms had the same *MC*, nonprice competition would be eliminated, and industry profits would rise.

B. Multiple Choice

1. *d;* 2. *d;* 3. *a;* 4. *c;* 5.* *a, b,* and *d;* 6. *c;* 7. *d;* 8. *d.*

C. Problems

1. *a.* $5. 5,000. $25,000.
   The new demand curve is given by $q = 1,000(5 - p)$
   $2.50. 2,500. $6,250. Fall to $12,500.

   c. The new demand curve is given by $q = 1,000(7.5 - p)$
   $3.75. 3,750. $14,062.50. Rise to $9,375.

   d. The new demand curve is given by $q = 1,000(6.25 - p)$
   $3.13. 3,125. $9,781.25. Fall to $11,737.50.

   e. $q = 1,000(10 - p)$; i.e., $p = 10 - q/1,000$.
   3,333. $3.34. $11,132.22.

3.* *a.* $p = a - bQ = a - b(q_A + q_B)$ where q_A and q_B are the outputs of firms A and B respectively; therefore $\pi_A = [a - b(q_A + q_B)]q_A$ and $\pi_B = [a - b(q_A + q_B)] q_B$. The first-order conditions for profit maximization, obtained by setting $d\pi_A/dq_A$ and $d\pi_B/dq_B$ equal to zero are $a - b(2q_A + q_B) = 0$ and $a - b(q_A + 2q_B) = 0$. These conditions imply that in equilibrium $q_A = q_B$, $a - b(3Q/2) = 0$, and therefore that $Q = 2a/3b$.

   b. Same argument except now $\pi_A = [a - b(q_A + q_B)]q_A - c(q_A)$ and expression for π_B is similarly modified.

5.* *a.* A will adopt the strategy promising the maximum minimum-return; i.e., strategy *b.* B will adopt *b'.*

   b. It is indeterminate. *b. b'. c. d'. b.* Note A's period-5 choice brings the two players back to the same place they started, indicating that the process of strategy changing will continue indefinitely.

   c. The row minimum must equal the column maximum.

7. 2,000. 850. $27.50. 1,150. $37. 1,500. 500. 0. The joint *MR* curve starts at (0,50), runs to (1000,30) then flattens and runs on through point (3000,20).

CHAPTER 13

A. Definitions and Review

1. *a.* *MP*. the price at which output is sold. *MP*. marginal revenue.
   b. equals.
   c. MP_L will eventually decline due to diminishing returns.
   d. $w = MRP_L = VMP_L$.

2. *a.* *VMP*. negatively. negatively.
   b. the firm's production function, the firm's stock of fixed inputs, the prices of other variable inputs, demand for the firm's output. will not.

3. positive. negative. market demand equals market supply.

4. labor-leisure preferences. but not. more. more or less.

5. quasi-rent. the opportunity cost incurred by the firm in using the fixed inputs pure economic profit.

6.* equal. zero.

7.* *a.* the ratio of the induced percentage change in (K/L) to the percentage change in *MRTS*.

$$\sigma = \frac{\Delta(K/L) \ / \ (K/L)}{\Delta MRTS \ / \ MRTS}$$

   b. less than. greater than. equals.

8.* *a.* diminishes. more than. raises.
   b. increase.

B. Multiple Choice

1. *c;* 2. *b;* 3. *d;* 4. *b* and *c;* 5. *b;* 6.* *a* and *d;* 7.* *a* and *c;* 8.* *b;* 9.* *b.*

C. Problems

1. *a.* 6 workers. 13,010 units. $3,510.
   Table 13–1 should read from top to bottom as follows:
   Column (2) : 0; 1,000; 3,000; 6,000; 9,500; 11,500; 13,010; 13,510.
   Column (3) : −; 1,000; 2,000; 3,000; 3,500; 2,000; 1,510; 500.
   Column (4) : 1; 1; 1; 1; 1; 1; 1; 1.
   Column (5) : −; 1,000; 2,000; 3,000; 3,500; 2,000; 1,510; 500.
   Column (6) : 1,500; 1,500; 1,500; 1,500; 1,500; 1,500; 1,500.
   Column (7) : 0; 1,500; 3,000; 4,500; 6,000; 7,500; 9,000; 10,500.
   Column (8) : 500; 500; 500; 500; 500; 500; 500.
   Column (9) : 500; 2,000; 3,500; 5,000; 6,500; 8,000; 9,500; 11,000.
   Column (10) : 0; 1,000; 3,000; 6,000; 9,500; 11,500; 13,010; 13,510.
   Column (11) : − 500; − 1,000; − 500; 1,000; 3,000; 3,500; 3,510; 2,510.
   Column (12) : −; 1,000; 1,500; 2,000; 2,375; 2,300; 2,168; 1,930.
   b. Whenever $VMP_L > w_L$, an increase in *L* will increase *profits*. Whenever $VMP_L < w_L$, a cut in *L* will increase profits. Therefore, profits must be maximized where $VMP_L = w_L$.
   c. In this one-variable-input example, if $w_L > ARP_L$, then $VC > TR$ and it would pay the firm to shut down in the short run. The firm's demand curve for labor thus corresponds to the portion of the VMP_L curve for which $ARP_L > VMP_L$.

d. (1) no change. (2) no change. In the short run, the company will move along its existing demand curve for labor. (3)–(4) with each change, you get a new VMP_L curve. Thus D_L shifts. (5) VMP_L increases for all levels of L, and D_L shifts upward.

3. *a.* (1) $2.00. (2) 40,000. (3) $2.25. (4) $1.75. (5) 35,000.
   b. (1) $2.50. (2) 30,000. (3) $3.00. (4) $2.50. (5) 20,000.

5. *a.*

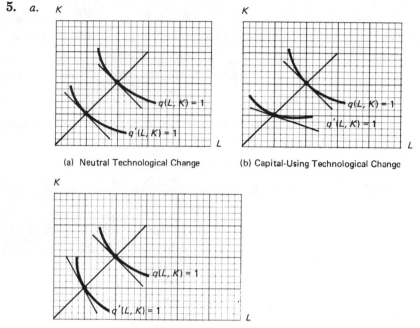

(a) Neutral Technological Change   (b) Capital-Using Technological Change

(c) Labor-Using Technological Change

b. remain unchanged; increase; decrease.

CHAPTER 14

A. Definitions and Review

1. *a.* $VMP = MP \cdot AR = MP \cdot p. \qquad MRP = MP \cdot MR.$
   b. exceeds.
   c. labor's marginal product will eventually decrease. more labor inputs means more output, and the greater output is, the lower marginal revenue will be.
   d. $w = MRP_L > VMP_L.$
   e. exceeds. equals.

2. *a.* $MRP.$ negatively. negatively.
   b. the production function, the firm's fixed inputs, the prices of other variable inputs, and demand for the firm's output. will not.

3. *a.* $VMP.$ does. does not. for the monopolist $MRP_L < VMP_L$, while for a perfect competitor $MRP_L = VMP_L$.
   b. little. little. force the firm to lower its output price.

4. *a.* there are many sellers but only a single buyer. there are many sellers but only a few buyers.
   b. the quantity of that input he employs and the average cost of the input to him. $AC < MC.$ the quantity of that input he employs and the marginal cost of the input to him.

c. input's MC. input's MRP. have to look at the input's AC or supply curve which shows the minimum wage that must be paid to elict the quantity of labor the monopsonist demands in equilibrium; i.e., the quantity indicated by the intersection of the MRP_L and MC_L curves.

d.
$$\frac{MP_L}{w} = \frac{MP_L}{MC_L} = \frac{MP_K}{MC_K} = \frac{MP_K}{r}$$

$$\frac{MP_L}{w} > \frac{MP_L}{MC_L} = \frac{MP_K}{MC_K} < \frac{MP_K}{r}$$

e. $w = MC_L = MRP_L < VMP_L$. $\quad w < VMP_L$.

f. $w < MC_L = MRP_L < VMP_L$. $\quad w < MRP_L < VMP_L$. $\qquad$ force the firm to pay a higher wage rate.

B. Multiple Choice

1. b; 2. a, b, c, and d; 3. d; 4. c; 5. a; 6. b, c, and d; 7. c; 8. a and d; 9. b.

C. Problems

1. a. (1) $MRP_L = MR \cdot MP_L$; $VMP_L = p \cdot MP_L$.

   (2) When an additional worker is hired, output increases. The dollars of revenue that the firm receives by selling this output equals VMP_L. In contrast, MRP_L equals the *change* in total revenue that occurs when the extra output is sold. If selling extra output forces the firm to lower price, MRP_L will be less than VMP_L. ARP_L equals average revenue per worker.

   (3) equals; equals, less than, less than.

   b. As labor inputs are increased, (1) MP_L eventually begins to fall due to diminishing returns and (2) the increased labor inputs raise output, which in turn forces the firm to cut price with a resultant fall in MR.

   c. Initially, as labor inputs are increased, MP_L may rise. If the rise in MP_L exceeds the fall in MR, the MRP_L curve will be positively sloped initially.

   d. Yes. The standard average-marginal-curve argument applies. At any level of labor inputs, ARP_L is the average of the MRP_L values. Consequently, ARP_L must be rising if MRP_L is greater than ARP_L, and it must be falling if MRP_L is less than ARP_L. Thus, $ARP_L = MRP_L$ where ARP_L is neither rising nor falling; i.e., at the point where it attains a maximum.

   e. 0; 0 or 50; 70; 80.

   f. $-\$3,000$. $-\$3,000$. $\$18,000$. $\$33,000$.
   Note that with labor the only variable input,
   $$\pi = (TR - VC) - FC = (ARP_L - w_L) L - FC$$

   g. The answers to (e) would not change. The answers to (f) would all be $\$3,000$ smaller. The level of FC does not influence a profit-maximizing firm's *short-run* price-output decision.

   h. The portion from $(50,750)$ to $(85,0)$. If $w_L > ARP_L$, then $VC > TR$ and the firm can reduce its losses by shutting down.

   i. For every firm, in the case at hand, it's a portion of the MRP_L curve that constitutes the firm's demand curve for labor. However, for a perfectly competitive firm, $MR = AR$ and, consequently, the VMP_L and MRP_L curves are identical.

3.* The price ceiling will have no effect on either MP_L or AP_L, but it will affect MR and AR for input lepels below L', the level of labor inputs required to produce sufficient output to satisfy full market demand at p_c. The effects of a price ceiling on MR and AR were described in problem 6 Chapter 10. From this description it follows that the ARP_L' and MRP_L' will have the general shapes indicated in the diagram. Also L' will be the new equilibrum employment of labor.

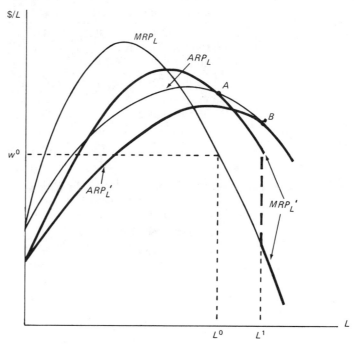

5. *a.* 5 workers. $100. $400. $200.

The missing figures Table 14–2 run from top to bottom:
Column (3) : 0; 5; 16; 36; 64; 100; 144; 196.
Column (4) : —; 5; 11; 20; 28; 36; 44; 52.
Column (5) : —; 50; 110; 110; 90; 40; 20; − 70.
Column (7) : 0; 50; 160; 270; 360; 400; 420; 350.
Column (8) : 100; 100; 100; 100; 100; 100; 100.
Column (9) : − 100; −55; 44; 134; 196; 200; 176; 54.

b. exceeds; is less than; was equal to.

7. No. To maximize profits Firm Y equates MC_L with MRP_L, which might well occur where $MRP_L > ARP_L$. Note, however, that Firm Y, like Firm X, would never operate at a point where $w > ARP_L$.

9.* $TR = p \cdot q = g(q) \cdot f(L,\overline{K})$; therefore, $MR = g'f + g$; also $MP_L = f_1$. Thus, $MRP_L = f_1(g'f + g)$.
Profit, π, can be written as a function of labor inputs as follows

$$\pi = p \cdot q = g(q) \cdot f(L,\overline{K}) - w_L L - FC$$
$$= g(f(L,\overline{K})) \cdot f(L,\overline{K}) - w_L L - FC$$

Taking the derivative of π with respect to L and setting this expression equal to zero, we get

$$g'f_1 f + gf_1 - w_L = 0;$$

that is, at the maximum-profit point

$$f_1(g'f + g) = w_L$$

or $MRP_L = w_L$

CHAPTER 15

A. Definitions and Review

1. all markets are simultaneously in equilibrium. must.

2.   *a.* the indifference curve of one consumer is tangent to that of the other. will. will not. will not. will.

    b. there exists no feasible reallocation of the available stock of goods that would increase the utility of one consumer without decreasing that of the other. the contract curve.

3.* the utility enjoyed by one consumer and the *maximum* that could be enjoyed by the other given the available stock of consumption goods. the contract curve. another point along the contract curve.

4. an isoquant from the production function of one good is tangent to an isoquant from the production function of the other good. will. there exists no feasible reallocation of inputs between production of the two goods that would permit an increase in the output of the one good without forcing a decrease in the output of the other good.

5.   *a.* the level of production of one good and the maximum amount of the other good that could be produced given technology and the economy's fixed stock of resources.

    b. on the contract curve.

    c. output levels. below.

6. general equilibrium.

B. Multiple Choice

1. *a, b, c,* and *d ;* 2. *c ;* 3.* *d ;* 4. *a, c,* and *d ;* 5. *a* and *b.*

C. Problems

1. *a.*

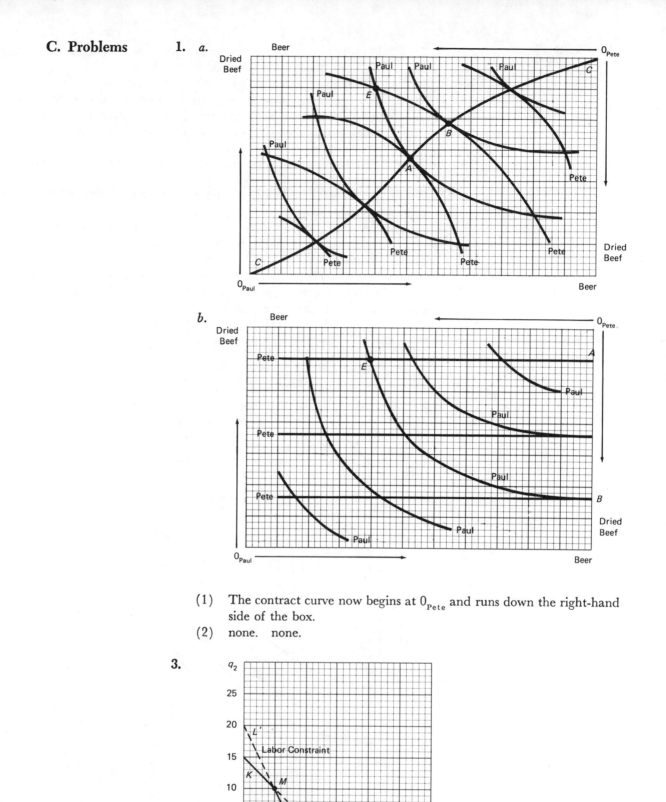

b.

(1) The contract curve now begins at 0_{Pete} and runs down the right-hand side of the box.

(2) none.   none.

3.

The kinked, unbroken line *KML* is Mazul's production possibility curve.

5. *a.* (1) Yes, Yes. The lump-sum tax does not interfere with efficiency in either consumption or production.

(2) Same answer as (1).

b. Yes. No. The difference in wage rates in the two areas means that producers in the country will not all have the same rates of factor substitution between labor and other inputs. Therefore, production cannot be efficient.

c. Yes. No. The price discrimination would interfere with efficiency in consumption.

d. Yes. No. The difference in wage rates would interfere with efficiency in production.

e. Yes. Yes. Consumption of apples and pears in the economy would be efficient if X and Y reached through their trading a point on their contract curve.

f. Yes. No. The tax would interfere with efficiency in consumption.

7.* The problem is to maximize the utility function subject to the budget constraint. Begin by forming the equation

$$V = U(Q_D, L_S) - \lambda\,(wL_S + R(w) - pQ_D)$$

where λ is the Lagrange multiplier. Differentiating V with respect to Q_D, L_S and λ we get

$$U_1 + \lambda p = 0 \qquad\qquad (1)$$
$$U_2 - \lambda w = 0 \qquad\qquad (2)$$
$$wL_S + R(w) - p(Q_D) = 0 \qquad\qquad (3)$$

Equation (3) tells us the consumer will attain equilibrium at a point on his budget line. Equations (1) and (2) tell us that this point will be the point where

$$\frac{\partial U/\partial Q_D}{\partial U/\partial L_S} = -\frac{p}{w};$$

i.e., a point where the slope of the budget line equals the slope of the indifference curve through that point.

In the diagram $U^1 < U^2 < U^3 < U^4$.

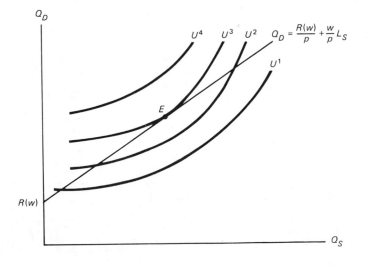

CHAPTER 16

A. Definitions and Review

1. a. the marginal rate of substitution in consumption between any pair of goods must be the same for all individuals who consume both goods.
   b. the marginal rate of technical substitution between any pair of inputs must be the same for all producers who use both inputs.
   c. for every pair of commodities, the marginal rate of substitution in consumption of every individual who consumes both goods must equal the marginal rate of transformation in production between these goods.

2. a. assuming that consumers are utility maximizers, every consumer will attain equilibrium by consuming at a point of tangency between his budget line and an indifference curve; and, consequently, in equilibrium all consumers' rates of commodity substitution between these goods will equal the ratio of their prices.
   b. assuming that firms are cost minimizers, every firm will attain equilibrium by producing at a point of tangency between an isoquant and an isocost line; and, consequently, in equilibrium all firms' rates of factor substitution between these inputs will equal the ratio of their prices.

3.* a. the level of utility enjoyed by one consumer and the maximum level of utility that could be enjoyed by the other consumer given available input supplies and technology.
   b. the marginal rate of substitution in consumption between the two goods equals the marginal rate of transformation between the two goods in production.
   c. Pareto optimal.

4.* a. social welfare. on the grand utility-possibility frontier that the social welfare function ranks highest.
   b. is. only one. is.

5. shift upward. is greater than. will not. exceed. social marginal cost.

B. Multiple Choice

1. *b;* 2. *a* and *b;* 3. *a, b,* and *c;* 4. *b;* 5. *b;* 6. *c.*

C. Problems

1. *a.* The production function determines the production possibility curve *PP,* which shows the relationship between the amount of leisure Sam enjoys and the maximum output he can produce. Because of diminishing returns to labor, the *PP* curve is concave to the origin. Sam's point of maximum satisfaction (which in the case at hand corresponds to the efficient point you are looking for) clearly corresponds to point *E.* At this point the slope of Sam's indifference curve equals the slope of the *PP* curve. The slope of the *PP* curve equals $\triangle q/\triangle F$ which (since $F = 24 - L$) equals $- \triangle q/\triangle L$; i.e., the slope of the *PP* curve equals $- MP_L$. The *negative* slope of the indifference curve through point *E* equals Sam's rate of commodity substitution (RCS_{qL}) between *q* and *F.* Thus he attains equilibrium at a point where

$$MP_L = RCS_{qL}$$

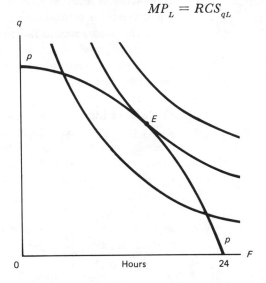

b.* (1) MP_L in production (which will be the same for all firms) must equal the rate of commodity substitution in consumption between *q* and *F* (which rate will be the same for all consumers).

(2) Yes. Since the market in which output is sold is perfectly competitive, every producer will adjust his labor inputs, and consequently MP_L, so that

$$p = w/MP_L$$

where *w* is the wage rate, *p* the output price.

Consumers, in deciding what combination of *q* and leisure to consume, will maximize their satisfaction when they operate at a point on their budget constraint where one of their indifference curves is tangent to (i.e., has the same slope) as their budget constraint. The latter in symbols is

$$w(24 - F) = p \cdot q$$

Substituting w/MP_L for *p* and rearranging terms, we get

$$q = MP_L (24 - F)$$

The slope of this line, $\triangle q/\triangle F$, equals $- MP_L$. Also, $RCS = - \triangle q/\triangle F$. Thus, every consumer attains equilibrium by operating at a point on his budget line where

$$RCS_{qL} = MP_L$$

and the condition for efficiency is fulfilled.

3. *a.* Yes. 1 is preferred to 3, which is preferred to 2.

   b. No. The majority's votes would indicate that people preferred 1 to 2, 2 to 3, and 3 to 1, which is inconsistent. The composition of the majority shifts from one vote to another.

5. *a.* (1) 200 units. $40. $2,000. His price would exceed his marginal cost.

   (2) yes. $35. 250 units. $1250. $p = MC$.

   (3) a lump-sum tax of $1,250.

   (4) approximately 240 units. (Note what the price ceiling does to the monopolist's MR curve.) Approximately $960. No. Price would equal MC, but since the monopolist would not be willing to satisfy full market demand, some consumers who wanted his product would not be able to purchase it, and consequently, satisfied and unsatisfied consumers would have different rates of commodity substitution between his output and other outputs. His profits would fall to zero. No. If he satisfied full market demand, the condition $p = MC$ would not be fulfilled.

   (5) a little less than 240 units. zero profits. no. Price would equal MC but there would be unsatisfied demand at that price.

   b. (1) $40. 200 units. $2,000. Yes. His price would exceed MC.

   (2) $15. $2,250.

   c.

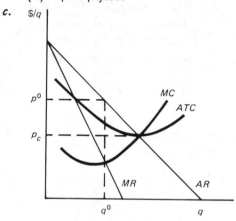

   d. (1) No. In the situation at hand, for resource allocation to be efficient, the wage paid by Tripp, would have to equal MRP_L.

   (2) A wage floor. $1.50. 600.

7. no. too little. Since expansion of the railroad system lowers the cost of other firms, the *social* marginal cost of railroad services is less than *private* marginal cost. To promote an efficient allocation of resources, the government should price railroad services at social marginal cost; since social marginal cost is less than private marginal cost, such a policy would lead to a lower price and greater output than pricing at private marginal cost would.

9.* *a.* To obtain conditions for maximizing U_1 subject to the constraint that $U_2 = U_2^0$, form the Lagrangean

$$V = U_1(q_{11}, q_{12}) + \lambda [U_2(q_1^0 - q_{11}, q_2^0 - q_{12}) - U_2^0]$$

Take the partial derivatives of this expression and set them equal to zero. This yields

$$\frac{\partial V}{\partial q_{11}} = \frac{\partial U_1}{\partial q_{11}} - \lambda \frac{\partial U_2}{\partial q_{11}} = 0 \tag{1}$$

$$\frac{\partial V}{\partial q_{12}} = \frac{\partial U_1}{\partial q_{12}} - \lambda \frac{\partial U_2}{\partial q_{12}} = 0 \tag{2}$$

$$\frac{\partial V}{\partial \lambda} = U_2(q_1^0 - q_{11}, q_2^0 - q_{12}) - U_2^0 = 0 \tag{3}$$

Conditions (1) and (2) imply that at the point of maximum U_1

$$\frac{\partial U_1/\partial q_{11}}{\partial U_1/\partial q_{12}} = \frac{\partial U_2/\partial q_{11}}{\partial U_2/\partial q_{12}};$$

i.e., that $RCS_1 = RCS_2$

b. Yes. To maximize satisfaction, each of the n consumers would adjust his consumption of q_1 and q_2 so that his rate of commodity substitution between the two goods equaled the ratio of their prices, p_1/p_2. But if $RCS_i = p_1/p_2$ for every consumer, $i = 1, \ldots n$, then all consumers must have the same rates of commodity substitution.